The Practice of Death

THE

PRACTICE

OF

DEATH

Eike-Henner W. Kluge

New Haven and London, Yale University Press,

1975

Designed by John O. C. McCrillis
and set in Times Roman type.
Printed in the United States of America by
The Colonial Press, Inc., Clinton, Massachusetts.

Published in Great Britain, Europe, and Africa by
Yale University Press, Ltd., London.
Distributed in Latin America by Kaiman & Polon,
Inc., New York City; in Australasia and Southeast
Asia by John Wiley & Sons Australasia Pty. Ltd.,
Sydney; in India by UBS Publishers' Distributors Pvt.,
Ltd., Delhi; in Japan by John Weatherhill, Inc., Tokyo.

FOR ELKE

Contents

Preface

We live in a time of profound moral crisis. Traditionally accepted moral tenets are no longer deemed immune from analytic questioning, and the doubts and vacillations in moral practice that invariably attend such a process have as yet not yielded to a coherent solution. If anything, current positions on morality are more confused—even contradictory—than at any other time in history.

Nor are the moral uncertainties confined to those areas traditionally covered by the term 'morality': sex, marriage, and related concerns. Quite the contrary: The spirit of the "new morality" manifests itself in every area of human interaction. And the challenge it poses is the more profound, as it goes to the very heart of moral theory itself: It questions the very legitimacy of moral judgments. It suggests that moral theories and tenets as traditionally understood are nothing more nor less than codifications of historically determined and culture-bound codes of behavior; that therefore these cannot lay claim to universal validity, but are mere expressions of pro and con attitudes; and that consequently those preeminently moral epithets, 'good' and 'bad', do no more than indicate purely personal evaluations relative to a given situation and point of view.

Such a challenge to morality itself could be borne with equanimity, were it confined to the sphere of theory alone. But such is not the case. This attitude on morality has begun to effect changes in current moral attitudes and practices. In the forefront stand changes in the attitudes and practices dealing with life and death. Abortion, suicide, euthanasia, infanticide, and senicide have seen the impact of these changed attitudes, and the shibboleth "Do your own thing!" has become the password even here.[1]

1. Cf. Germain G. Grisez, *Abortion: The Myths, the Realities, and the Arguments* (New York and Cleveland: Corpus Books, 1970), pp. 270 ff.,

Once more, this situation could be viewed without qualms, were the relevant practices and attitudes based on a reasoned understanding of the issues involved, were the fundamental assumptions on which this reasoning is based sound, and were the reasoning itself consistent. After all, the fact that a moral tenet is traditional makes it neither correct nor sacrosanct. Unfortunately, however, the conditions just mentioned are not met —sometimes not even in the slightest degree. In fact, if there is one thing that characterizes the current moral scene, it is the abandonment of deliberate reason in favor of unreasoned personal preference.

It is this lack of reasoned understanding that prompted the present investigation into the moral attitudes currently surrounding the issues of life and death. It is my opinion that because of this lack of reason, our society has failed to understand the moral nature and consequences of the actions variously advocated; and that as a result of this, it is presently embarked upon a course of action that is dangerous. Dangerous not merely in the practical sense that what is done touches the life of every individual within society; but dangerous also in a moral sense, in that what is condoned and advocated in the name of personal freedom and the new morality is frequently morally evil. And as philosophers, it is our duty to point this out.

With these last statements, I have of course betrayed my own fundamental position on the issues at hand: I am opposed to the course so frequently advocated by the proponents of the new morality. But I am not opposed to it on the grounds of tradition —on the grounds of established custom and hallowed philosophical belief. I am opposed to it on the basis of the reasoned conviction that there exists something of absolute and intrinsic value in the universe, namely, rational consciousness or awareness; and that human beings—although not human beings alone —are the centers of such awareness. I am convinced that it fol-

---

for a discussion of what she calls the "subjective view." See also Daniel Callahan, *Abortion: Law, Choice and Morality* (New York: Macmillan. 1970).

lows logically from such a premise that, all other things being
equal, the deliberate destruction of what has absolute value is
a morally reprehensible act. Consequently, I deem the destruction of human beings as centers of such awareness to be immoral
in all except the rarest of circumstances.

Having confessed to such a bias, let me hasten to add that
this book is not written with the purpose of urging upon the
reader this point of view. For, I must confess to an even more
fundamental bias, a bias going back to Socrates: The unexamined life is not worth living. The purpose of this book, therefore,
is analytical. I propose to present and examine critically the
more representative positions currently subsumed under the
heading of life and death: topics such as abortion, infanticide,
suicide, senicide, and so on. The aim of this analysis will be to
expose the structure of these various positions and, if need be,
to point up their incoherence. But this work itself would be
guilty of pragmatic inconsistency if it subjected only the various
variants of the new morality to such an analysis. I have therefore divided each chapter into four parts. In the first, the problem itself is stated; in the second, the traditional stance on the
problem is illustrated by representative arguments and is analyzed; in the third, the new morality is given its say, once more
by means of representative arguments, and is treated to a similar analysis. In the final section of each chapter, I attempt in
an explicit manner to disentangle and present coherently the
various aspects of the issue.

It goes almost without saying that I hope that in the end the
reader will come to share my own position. To this end—and it
would be dishonest to pretend otherwise—I have devoted the
last chapter to an explicit discussion of what I take to be some
of the more fundamental moral views involved and have given
what I myself take to be the correct answer. But I shall not
judge the success or failure of this investigation by the ratio of
conversions to my point of view. My major purpose will be
served if, because of having read these analyses, the reader will
have gained a deeper understanding of the implications of the
various positions currently held on this most fundamental question of all: Who shall live?

1

Abortion

Ours has been described as an "abortifacient" society. The reason for this is not entirely clear. Certainly, abortions have been performed prior to the present era—in fact, have been performed since antiquity and even prehistoric times.[1] Doubtlessly, also, they will continue to be performed in times to come. So, the mere fact that abortions are performed cannot be the reason for this epithet. Why, then, is our society called abortifacient?

The reason must be sought not in the mere fact of abortions. Instead, it is to be found in the relative ease with which abortions can presently be procured. And once again, not merely in this relative ease of procurement, but also—and perhaps mainly—in the relative lack of legal sanctions attaching to abortions[2] and the increasingly widespread disregard of the moral issues that are involved. Those who describe the present society as

---

I should like to thank my colleague, John Woods, for acting as a foil for many of the ideas and arguments expressed in this book. Without his constructive criticism, it would read much worse.

1. For a good but brief account of the history of abortion and the law, see Bernard M. Dickens, *Abortion and the Law* (London: MacGibbon and Kee, 1966), chap. 1.

2. Cf. U.S. Supreme Court decision on state abortion laws handed down on January 22, 1973, opinion in the Texas case *Roe* v. *Wade* and the Georgia case *Doe* v. *Bolton,* when that court declared unconstitutional the Texas and Georgia abortion laws. These laws ruled abortion permissible only when deemed necessary to save a woman's life, as in Texas, or when required by her health to prevent the birth of a deformed child or when the pregnancy resulted from rape, as in Georgia. This ruling implied that similarly restrictive abortion laws in other states are also unconstitutional.

abortifacient use the term in a pejorative sense: For them, it contains a value judgment, namely, that such a state of affairs is morally undesirable and therefore ought not to be condoned.

But our society has also been described as liberated. The reasons for this are somewhat more apparent. Current moral theory as well as practice is in the process of emancipating itself from what are sometimes called the shackles of tradition. Human egalitarianism has become the password of the avant-garde as well as of the broad masses. Nor is it merely an empty shibboleth; for the efforts to realize this ideal are all around us: in the area of interrace relations, in the domain of civil liberties, as well as—or especially—in the arena of women's rights. Here, too, the word 'abortifacient' has currency. But as used by those who are in the vanguard of women's liberation, it has a completely different meaning. Instead of being pejorative, it is considered laudatory: It describes the liberation of women from the state of being brood animals—of having as their primary function the bearing of children. Once more, the term connotes a value judgment—this time, however, of an opposite sense.

The battle lines are thus drawn: tradition versus the new morality.[3] The controversy that currently rages over the permissibility of abortions can be seen as a confrontation between these positions. To be sure, there are splinter groups on both sides; and equally as certainly, there are various middle positions. However, like almost any attempt to maintain a middle ground, the latter are essentially efforts at compromise, and as such trade on the arguments adduced by both sides. Therefore, they generally add nothing new to the controversy and in fact tend to obscure the real issue, for the heart of the matter is found in this opposition between the two extremes. The present

3. These distinctions will be refined in a moment. For an analogous division of positions, see Roger Wertheimer, "Understanding the Abortion Argument," *Philosophy and Public Affairs* 1, no. 1 (1971): 67–97, and Michael Tooley, "A Defense of Abortion and Infanticide," *Philosophy and Public Affairs* 2, no. 1 (1972): 37–65. However, neither Wertheimer nor Tooley share the particulars of the present analysis or its conclusions.

analysis will therefore be confined to these extreme sides of the controversy. Nor will it be possible to reproduce and analyze all the arguments that both sides adduce in support of their respective positions. But there are several key lines of reasoning that are characteristic of the one side or the other. These will be presented and analyzed in some detail.

However, prior to doing this, the term itself must be clarified. What, precisely, is an abortion? How are we to understand that term? Is an abortion any termination of a pregnancy prior to the birth of a child? Or does the term refer only to an artificial termination of a pregnancy prior to its natural termination in the natural course of events? If the latter, is an artificial termination an abortion irrespective of the intentions and aims of the people involved? After all, some artificially induced terminations are the result of accidents and, as such, are wholly unintentional. Further still, does it matter at what time the pregnancy is terminated? Say, the second, the third, or the fourth month of the gestation period? Or is this sort of consideration irrelevant? Also, what of the development of the fetus: Is this a relevant criterion? Is the termination of pregnancy an abortion only after a heartbeat has been heard? Or, after the "quickening in the womb"? and so on. Finally, there is the phrase 'spontaneous abortion': How does this fit into the whole picture? [4]

We are thus faced with a whole host of problems before we have even begun the discussion proper; and we might therefore be tempted to abandon the whole enterprise at the very outset: to leave it safely within the ambiguous and comfortingly impersonal domain of common practice. However, to do so is neither necessary nor morally defensible. Unexamined and unreflective acquiescence in current practice—whatever that practice may be—is fraught with moral danger. What is currently accepted may in fact be morally wrong. And as moral beings, we cannot afford that risk. For, if abortion in fact is murder, as some of

---

4. For a discussion similar to this one, see Grisez, *Abortion,* pp. 7 ff.

its opponents claim, then the mere fact that we acquiesce in common practice will not detract from the gravity of the moral charge.

Therefore we should press on. And here the phrase 'spontaneous abortion' suggests at least the beginnings of an operative definition around which the following discussion can be organized.

> DEFINITION 1. An abortion is the artificially and intentionally engendered termination of a pregnancy prior to its natural termination in the course of events.

It is important to realize that this definition does not presume, nor indeed does it imply, that all pregnancies would normally and naturally terminate with a birth at the end of roughly nine months. It is perfectly natural—that is, perfectly possible in the course of nature—that some pregnancies should not come to full term. These are what are called cases of spontaneous abortion. (They are spontaneous not in the sense that they have no cause, but in the sense that their cause is not to be sought in the intentional interference of man.)

This last consideration raises a further point vis-à-vis Definition 1: a point that is best brought out by considering the notion of a spontaneous abortion more closely. It is a common assumption that when we talk about an abortion's having taken place, that this abortion resulted in the death of the fetus. However, this need not be the case. As is apparent from the case of spontaneous abortions, some occur at such a late stage of the pregnancy that the fetus is viable and indeed, when given intensive care, does survive. To be sure, such cases we no longer call spontaneous abortions. We call them premature births. But this is a difference of terminology only and, consequently, can be disregarded.

The point, then, is that not all spontaneous abortions result in the death of a fetus. To make these considerations germane to the present discussion, we need only point out that the same thing holds true for abortions as they have just been defined above: Some of the beings that are thus aborted have the po-

tential for survival, especially in the last stages of pregnancy—
say, in the fifth month or later. If the entities that are aborted
at that stage were to be given intensive care, at least some of
them would survive; and in their case, certainly, we should
ordinarily not want to say that an abortion had been performed.[5]
In other words, it emerges from the foregoing deliberations that
the concept of an abortion seems to include as an essential and
indeed central constituent the concept of the death of whoever
or whatever is aborted. And this, in turn, suggests the following
emendation of the definition:

> DEFINITION 2. An abortion is an artificially engendered ter-
> mination of a pregnancy prior to its natural termination in
> the course of events, where this termination is effected with
> the express purpose of bringing about the death of the en-
> tity[6] that is aborted, and where this intention is actually
> realized.

With this as a working definition, we can once more address
the essential question: Is abortion murder? As stated in the
beginning, positions on this issue divide into two opposed
camps: into what I have called the traditional stance on the one
hand, and the position of the new morality on the other. The

5. On this point, see Judith Jarvis Thomson, "A Defense of Abortion,"
Philosophy and Public Affairs 1, no. 1 (1971): 47–66. This author maintains that establishing the moral permissibility of an abortion is one thing,
establishing the right to bring about the death of the entity aborted is another, and that the first does not entail the second. However, the author
differs from the view presented here in maintaining that cases where both
were not secured nevertheless are cases of abortion. Callahan, however, in
Abortion (p. 497), favors the present definition, going so far as to say that
"abortion is an act of killing, the violent, direct destruction of potential
human life already in the process of development." While I differ from
Callahan on the notion of potentiality, I agree with him on the issue of
intended death as essentially involved in abortion.

6. I employ this terminology so as to avoid prejudging the issue of
whether or not what is aborted is a human being. Cf. Norman St. John-
Stevas, *The Right to Life* (London: Hodder & Stoughton, 1963), p. 32
and passim. See also Callahan, *Abortion,* p. 377.

former holds, by and large, that abortions are murderous, whereas the latter maintain the contrary. Let us examine each position in turn.

THE NEGATIVE ARGUMENT

The traditional stance generally holds that to perform an abortion is to commit a murder;[7] that to request an abortion is to demand a murder; and, consequently, that to be involved with an abortion is to be an accessory to the fact. Nevertheless, this general agreement hides a disagreement of some importance. Not all traditionalists maintain that, no matter what, an abortion constitutes a murder. Some traditionalists maintain that the time at which the abortion is performed and, above all, the stage of fetal development are considerations of paramount importance.[8] Thus these—let us call them moderate traditionalists to distinguish them from the extreme traditionalists of the first sort— would maintain that only after the "child has quickened in the womb," "has acquired a soul," and so on can we speak of murder. Extreme traditionalists, of course, are more severe. Again, let us consider these positions in turn.

The Extreme Traditionalist

The argument underlying the extreme traditionalist's position is relatively simple and straightforward. It centers around the notion of the rights that accrue to a person and goes something like this:[9]

> The death of either ovum or sperm is not the death of a person. It is not even the death of a potential person, for

7. This emerges clearly from several traditional discussions. Cf. St. John-Stevas, *The Right to Life*, chaps. 1 and 2; Grisez, *Abortion*, esp. chap. 6.

8. Cf. Wertheimer, "Understanding the Abortion Argument," on what he calls the conservative view. See also Callahan, *Abortion*, esp. chap. 10, pp. 384–90.

9. Cf. Thomson, "A Defense of Abortion," for a similar presentation of the traditional position; see also Wertheimer, "Understanding the Abortion Argument," on what he calls the "extreme conservative" position.

neither ovum nor sperm is a potential person. Each lacks the requisite genetic information or makeup to develop into a person, even if conditions of development should prove to be optimal. Consequently, the death of such an entity, even if it should be brought about intentionally, cannot possibly be considered murderous.

However, matters stand otherwise in the case of a fertilized ovum. It does contain the necessary genetic information to develop into a human being, given only adequate time, nourishment, and barring accidents. Therefore, a fertilized ovum is a potential person. Consequently, the act of destroying such an entity with full intent and purpose, in full knowledge of what is being done—in short, the act of abortion as we have defined it—is an act of murder.

This argument rests on one fundamental assumption, namely, that potential persons have the same moral status as actual persons—that in a very clear and definite moral sense an entity which in the course of time would become a person has the same rights and privileges as someone who already is a person. From this assumption the argument deduces—quite correctly— that therefore acts dealing with potential persons receive the same moral evaluation as acts dealing with actual persons. In particular, it goes on to conclude that one particular kind of act —that of premeditated killing by means of an abortion—has the same moral nature as an act of killing an actual person "with malice aforethought." In short, that it constitutes an act of murder.

Undeniably, this train of argument has great emotional appeal; and, so it must be admitted, it is difficult to see at first glance how the cogency of its reasoning could be faulted. Nevertheless, closer consideration raises grave doubts as to its acceptability. For the acceptability of its conclusion—as indeed that of any other argument—depends not merely on the validity of the reasoning employed to reach it, but also on the truth of the premises from which the reasoning starts. In this particular case, however, more careful consideration of the argument reveals that the conclusion touted as the outcome of the reasoning is jeopardized on both counts. As to the truth of the premises, one of them is open to doubt: namely, that a potential human being has the same moral status as an actual person. That is, we may grant that, all other things being equal, a fetus is a potential human being. We may also grant that a fertilized ovum is a potential human being. We may even grant that the intentionally caused death of a fertilized ovum, no matter what its stage of development, is the death of a potential human being. However, we need not and indeed should not conclude from this that therefore the intentional killing of a fertilized ovum or of a fetus is an act of murder. That conclusion requires another premise, namely, that a potential human being has the same moral status as an actual person. Only if this assumption is granted, will the conclusion follow. But as stated a moment ago, that particular premise is certainly questionable.

As to the cogency of the reasoning itself, its shortcomings can be summed up quite simply: The transition from the first to the second step in the argument is logically unacceptable. A brief restatement of the relevant aspects of the argument will show how this is the case:

(1)   A fertilized ovum contains the necessary genetic information for developing into a human being, given only adequate time, nourishment, and barring accidents.

(2)   Therefore a fertilized ovum is a potential person.

It is this transition from being a fertilized ovum having a certain genetic structure to being a potential person that is logically questionable. That is to say, the transition from (1) to (2) involves the tacit assumption that "potential human being" and "potential person" mean one and the same thing; that to be a member of the species *homo sapiens* is the same thing as to be a person. As it stands, however, that is not at all clear. Indeed, it is one of the very things in doubt. Merely to assume it, as in this context, is to beg the question. The logical transition from (1) to (2), therefore, is guilty of a nonsequitur.[10]

This particular argument against abortion, therefore, is invalid and must be rejected. However, there are several subsidiary arguments that frequently are adduced to buttress the conclusion. Of these subsidiary arguments, the following three are encountered most frequently and seem to have the greatest intuitive appeal. They are what I shall call the argument from valuation, the argument from the principle of helplessness, and the argument from the principle of gradation.

The *argument from valuation* goes something like this:[11] It is a plain matter of fact that we value potential beings just as much —or at least almost as much—as we value actual beings. The instance of a pregnant cow is here a case in point. If someone willfully caused the cow to abort its calf, the owner of the cow could, with all the justification in the world, go to the courts to seek redress. And assuredly, he would be successful in his claim. The offender would be obliged to pay damages of an amount equal to the value of the calf had it been born. Nor is this an isolated case. In any situation involving living things, where what is destroyed is not yet an actual but a potential being, if someone destroys it, he will be held guilty of an act whose moral and legal gravamen is at least as great as that attaching to the act of destroying the fully actualized being. Nor is this sort of consideration confined solely to the context of animal husbandry. It extends even to the human sphere. As evidence of this, we may cite the recent public outcry and ultimate legal decisions dealing with the deformation of babies due to the fact

10. Grisez, *Abortion,* is guilty of a similar move, e.g. pp. 277, 306 ff., and passim. See also Callahan, *Abortion,* chap. 11, pp. 378–83, for a discussion of a similar genetic position. Callahan does not, however, agree with the present analysis.

11. Cf. Callahan, *Abortion,* pp. 458–60, for discussion of a similar argument. As Callahan notes, the moral framework of the argument is derived from R. B. Perry, *A General Theory of Value* (Cambridge: Harvard University Press, 1926).

that during part of their pregnancy, the mothers in question had taken a certain drug, thalidomide. Sentiment and judgment found in favor of the babies, because, so it was argued, they were seriously stunted and changed in their appearance due to the action of this drug on them during their development. This judgment would hardly have been made unless, as a matter of fact, the babies had been considered as having the same rights as actual persons during that stage of their development when the damage occurred. That is to say, finding in favor of the babies presupposes that they be considered to have at that fetal stage of development at which the damage occurred the same moral status as actual persons. For, if their status had not been the same, then what happened to them at that time could in no way constitute the basis for a later claim for damages. The damage, after all, was done then, not now; and if the fetus then and the baby now are on morally distinct planes, the latter could never possibly claim damages for what happened to the former, which simply was not on the appropriate plane to warrant such consideration. To decide otherwise would be to be guilty of an ex post facto argument. Actual practice, then, both in the human and animal sphere, seems to support the contention that potential persons enjoy the same moral privileges as actual ones. Consequently, so this argument concludes, it would be inconsistent to admit this on the one hand, yet to deny it on the other by permitting abortions.

The second subsidiary argument centers around the *principle of helplessness*.[12] This principle holds that the more helpless a being is, the more right it has to our care and consideration. Of course, this principle does not apply across the board. Thus, we do not think that helpless Japanese beetle grubs fall under this principle, any more than we think that mosquito larvae and such are covered by it. But we do apply it in the case of the higher baby animals, and more particularly, in the case of human babies. In fact, negligence and lack of care and consideration are considered morally reprehensible, even legally punish-

12. For a discussion of a similar point, cf. Callahan, *Abortion,* p. 345.

able. Why, then, should not the same thing apply to babies before they are born? After all, the only thing that has changed is their place of residence, from womb to crib, and their manner of acquiring nourishment, from internal to external dependence on the mother. Consequently, so this argument concludes, the very helplessness of the as yet unborn children not merely merits our solicitous concern; it also merits that in the interest of moral consistency we extend them at least that degree of care and consideration that we feel obliged to expend on actual, mature persons—at least with respect to their lives.

Finally, there is the third subsidiary argument, the argument from the *principle of gradation*. This argument is so called since it is based on the principle that the various morphological changes that a baby undergoes during its development are merely gradations in the realization of the potential inherent in it and are characteristic of the being in question, but that in no case do these gradations effect an alteration in the entity's fundamental nature as a being of a particular kind.

In the context of abortions, this principle finds employment in the following line of reasoning: Given a creature that naturally, in the course of its growth, goes through various stages of development, it is impossible to single out any point or stage of its development as being a change of an absolutely fundamental nature, marking a change of this being from one kind of thing to another kind of thing. To claim that there is such a point of distinction is to draw an artificial and unwarranted line of demarcation. Thus, if we consider the case of the larval development of an insect—surely as profound a change in the nature of a living thing as can be imagined—there is no doubt but that in essence we are always dealing with one and the same kind of thing. A mosquito, whether in the larval or the pupal stage, is just as surely a mosquito as when it is an adult. It may look, function, and even act differently, but it is still the same thing: a mosquito. If it were not, we should have to classify it as some other kind of animal and would have to consider its development from larval through pupal, to adult stages as involving changes in species. But, clearly, that is absurd. The genetic blueprint, after all, as well as the continuation of life, is one and the same.

Similarly, so the argument continues, with the case of human beings. They, too, are one and the same thing, as well as one and the same kind of thing, throughout the whole history of their development. The sole difference between their case and that of the mosquito is that the morphological changes which humans undergo are not quite so pronounced as are those of a mosquito,[13] and that what changes there are take place within the womb, inside the mother, rather than outside and independently of a parent organism. Therefore—so this line of reasoning continues—by parity of reasoning from all other cases, we must conclude that in a rather obvious sense an as yet unborn human being—a potential person—is fundamentally the same as an actually born person. To insist otherwise is to be inconsistent and to fly in the face of all usual practice. In other words, we must consider fertilized ova, fetuses, infants, and adults to be one and the same throughout the whole history of their development. And being thus the same, they have the same moral status—the same rights and privileges—throughout. To decide otherwise, to claim that there is a cutoff point in the development prior to which there is no personhood and there are no rights, is to impose arbitrarily and inconsistently a division in nature that cannot be defended. In other words, the principle of gradation to which we appeal in other contexts applies across the board, to fertilized ova as much as to insect larvae or piscene fry.[14]

13. In this context, however, the argument bids us consider the fact that in its development the human fetus does undergo something like the evolutionary line leading from unicellular organisms to vertebrates to *homo sapiens*.

14. It is obvious that, combined with the principle of helplessness, the principle of gradation will yield a further argument, something like this: By the principle of gradation, the fertilized ovum, fetus, etc. are essentially the same being as the baby that will be born. Consequently, they have at least the same moral rights as that baby. By that principle of helplessness, the baby has claim to special care and treatment. The fer-

So much by way of sketching the subsidiary, supporting argumentation. Whatever the differences among the lines of approach, and whatever the differences among their respective premises, all nevertheless have these two factors in common: All go on the assumption that potential beings have the same rights and privileges—the same moral status—as actual beings (of their kind); and all three assume that to be a human being —a member of the species *homo sapiens*—is to be a person. Therefore, all three agree further in proposing the same conclusion: that to destroy willfully and with express intent a potential, developing human being—in a word, to perform an act of abortion—is to kill, willfully and with intent, a person. And that, so the arguments conclude, is to commit a murder. Hence they assert, one and all, that to perform an abortion is to be guilty of a murder; to demand an abortion and to aid with it, either directly or indirectly, is to become guilty of inciting murder and of being an accessory to the fact.

Undeniably, a great deal of what is contained in the arguments just sketched is true: To kill a person, in the aforesaid manner, is to be guilty of murder. Furthermore, no matter how we look at it, unless we do wish to impose arbitrary cutoff points, a developing living organism *is* one and the same thing and *is* of one and the same species throughout the whole career of its life. Nevertheless the conclusion advanced by these arguments—that for these and associated reasons all abortions are murderous—does not follow. It does not follow, firstly, because the claim that potential persons, in virtue of being potential persons, have the same moral status as actual persons, is mistaken;[15] and, secondly, because these arguments assume an

tilized ovum, fetus, etc. are even more helpless. Consequently, by that very same principle, they should merit even more care. In other words, they have an even more privileged position than the baby.

15. Cf. Joel Feinberg, ed., *The Problem of Abortion* (Belmont, Calif.: Wadsworth, 1973), p. 4. For a somewhat different approach to the problem, based on the rights of persons as such, see Thomson, "A Defense of Abortion." For a different approach to and interpretation of the notion of potentiality, see Callahan, *Abortion,* pp. 364 ff.

illegitimate identification—that of potential humanity with potential personhood.

To see why the first claim is mistaken, we must start with the concept of a potential person itself. In a rather obvious and clear sense, a potential person—indeed any potential x, whatever x may be—is not yet an actual person or x; and this is so, no matter how near to or distant from realizing its potential the thing may be. The potential frog is an egg or tadpole; it is not a frog. When we kill such a potential frog, while we may be accused of killing a living being, even a tadpole, we cannot be accused of killing a frog. Similarly, with an acorn. An acorn may be a potential oak tree; but as it is, it is not an oak tree. If we were to feed it to the pigs, it would not merely be wrong, but downright silly to say that we had fed an oak tree to the pigs.

Potential x's, therefore, are not x's. They await the realization of their x-hood, so to speak. Thus, if any rights or privileges accrue to a potential x at all, they cannot accrue to it *as an x*. After all, an x it isn't! Therefore, if it has such rights, they must accrue to it in virtue of its present nature: an entity having a particular sort of physiology, makeup, and composition—say, being an acorn, a grub, or a fetus. The reason for this is simple: No moral prerogative can attach to an entity in virtue of a constitution that it does not have. Therefore, while the right to life and sundry other rights may very well attach to a potential person, if they do, they will do so in virtue of the constitution that it has here and now. And if it is assumed that a fertilized ovum, a fetus, or an as yet unborn child is a potential person, as the present line of argument purports, then the conclusion that follows from this is surely obvious: the same moral prerogatives do not belong to it as those that belong to an actual person. Or, if they do, they do not belong to it for the same reason. After all, they belong to the latter because it is a person—something that cannot be claimed for a merely potential person, such as a fertilized ovum.

Therefore the claim that potential persons have the same moral prerogatives as actual persons cannot be argued on the basis of their status as persons: They are not persons. Furthermore, it is difficult to see how the present constitution of a fertilized ovum or of a fetus considered in its constitution here and now can yield the basis for an argument that moral prerogatives accrue to it at all, let alone those weighty prerogatives accruing to a person. Consequently, the only way in which their claim to this privileged moral position can be made good is to appeal to their potential—to that which they could or would become. It is not because of their constitution here and now, but because of the potentiality inherent in them, that they could be said to have the same moral status and prerogatives.

However, if this train of reasoning is considered closely, it turns out to be quite unacceptable. To see why this is so, let us consider a particular case; and to vary the case a little, let us consider an ordinary physical object—say, a chair. The chair, as it exists, is of course an actual chair. It is also clear that the pieces of wood out of which the chair is constructed are not themselves an actual chair prior to their construction: They are a potential chair. But by parity of reasoning, the same thing holds true for the tree from which the wood came. It, too, is a potential chair. The only difference between its potentiality and that of the pieces of wood is that the potentiality of the tree is one step further removed from actualization than is the potentiality of the pieces of wood. Nor need we stop with the tree. Again, by parity of reasoning, the seed from which the tree grew, together with the various material nutrients that finally resulted in the tree, the pieces of wood, and ultimately the chair, are all together a potential chair. It is also clear that, unless the limits of potentiality are somewhat more narrowly circumscribed, the analysis need not rest even here: Claims to potential chairhood can be made on behalf of even more unlikely candidates. Thus, the material constituents of both tree and nutrients are ultimately the result of matter-conversion in stars from a primitive state of hydrogen; and the stars themselves are the results of gravitational processes operative on primeval hydrogen clouds. Are we then to call both star and primeval hydrogen cloud a potential chair? In a sense, that is certainly correct. But surely, only in a sense. For, by an analogous train of reasoning and with due alteration of detail, we should be required to call a primeval hydrogen cloud a potential person as well; for here, too, the ultimate beginning in the chain of potential beings is such a hydrogen cloud.[16] In other words, the limits of what constitutes a potential x—be it a potential tree, rock, or person—must be drawn more narrowly. Otherwise, if we insist on the principle that a potential person has the same moral prerogatives and privileges as an actual person, we should have to accord the same moral status to a primitive mass of hydrogen as to an actual person. And that, surely, would be silly.

What counts as a potential x must, therefore, be defined more circumspectly and closely. The following distinction immediately comes to mind: a distinction, namely, between being a potential x in the way in which a primitive mass of hydrogen is a potential tree, and being a potential x in the way in which a seed is a potential tree. In the first case, we are talking about what might be called a pure and unlimited potentiality. The mass of hydrogen could equally as correctly be described as a potential frog or even a potential person. For, given unlimited yet lawlike development of it in the course of nature, the material constitutive of such a cloud can become the constitutive matter of all sorts of things. In the second case, however, we are talking about potentiality in a more limited sense. The potentiality of a seed with respect to a tree is of quite a different sort; the plan of development that the seed must undergo in order to realize its potential as a tree is already inherent in it. There is no need for an outside agency to determine this particular course of development. In fact, no other course of development is open to it by its very nature. All other possibilities are foreclosed and in that sense are not possibilities at all.

Undeniably, the distinction between these two sorts of potentialities—between pure potentiality, on the one hand, and

16. For a similar analogy, albeit in a somewhat different context, see Marvin Kohl, "Abortion and the Argument from Innocence," *Inquiry* 14 (1971): 147–51.

potentiality properly speaking, on the other—goes some way toward alleviating the problem. For, clearly, we should reject as hyperbolical and downright mistaken any claim to the effect that what we mean by a potential person is a person in the sense of pure potentiality. Instead, what we have in mind is something that is potential in the second, more limited sense. And, in this sense, sperm and ovum by themselves will not, whereas fertilized ovum and fetus will—quite properly—count as potential persons.

However, this dichotomy by no means provides a solution to the problem. Even if we were to accept the second meaning of 'potential', it would still not follow that potential persons in this sense deserve the same moral consideration as actual persons. For, unless this is so by definition, the mere fact that something *will* happen to x does not as yet raise x to the level of a person. Not even if what will befall x is that it will become a person.

Happily enough, the dichotomy just discussed is not exhaustive. It can be expanded to a trichotomy. For, over and above the notion of pure potentiality and potentiality properly speaking, there is the notion of potentiality that we ascribe to a sleeping cat when we say that potentially it is awake. In other words, there is the notion of a potentiality where the realization of that potentiality does not involve a constitutive change in the relevant and defining aspects of the being in question: There is no essential, specific difference between a cat when asleep and a cat when awake.

It is this third notion of potentiality, and not the other two, that provides a clear reason for saying that a potential person has the same moral status as an actual person. For, in this sense of the term, a potential person has all the essential constitutional characteristics of a person. What it lacks is merely the final actualization. Since it has the essential constitutive characteristics of an actual person, it will also thereby have those rights and privileges that accrue to an actual person in virtue of that constitution. The claim that it has the same moral status as an actual person is now seen to be well-founded.

However, while sense can thus be made of the claim that potential persons have all the rights and privileges of actual persons, and whereas such a claim even seems to be well-founded, it does not follow that a fetus in all stages of its development will have such rights and privileges. For, according to this interpretation of the term *potential,* a fetus is not a potential person during all stages of its development. It will be a potential person only during those stages where no further constitutional change will be necessary in order for it to have all the essential characteristics of a person. Therefore, the only way in which it can be shown that potential persons have the same moral status as actual persons—without resorting to mere definition—indicates at the same time that it is not unconditionally true to say that *all* abortions are murderous. Only those abortions that result in the death of a potential person in the third and last sense discussed will be shown to be murderous. As for the rest, such acts are attended by a correspondingly less grave charge.[17]

So much for the first general shortcoming of this line of approach. Let us now turn briefly to the second general flaw mentioned earlier—the mistake inherent in identifying potential humanity with potential personhood. In the critique just concluded, this identification has not been an issue. Indeed, here and there we have even assumed that it is correct. Thus, when going from talking about persons to talking about fertilized ova and fetuses we have tacitly assumed this identity. Nevertheless, as pointed out once before, this identification is unwarranted. Unless we agree to define personhood in purely genetic terms, a fetus is not a person, as neither is a fertilized ovum. Nor is a fetus or a fertilized ovum a potential person—that is, once more, unless we identify being a person and being a genetically determined

17. For a somewhat different analysis of the notion of potentiality and its role in this context, see Tooley, "Defense of Abortion and Infanticide." For a still different analysis, see Grisez, *Abortion,* p. 284 and passim. Grisez argues that the it-is-not-yet-a-person attitude justifies infanticide with equal facility. However, the present argument escapes this implication due to the crucial differences between the definition of a *person* given here and that used by Grisez in her argument.

member of the species *homo sapiens*.[18] That identification may, in the end, turn out to be correct. But then it will have to be supported by cogent reasoning. In no case can it merely be assumed, as is here the case. And even if it should turn out that ultimately this identification is correct, there will still remain this sobering realization: Even from the (putative) fact that a fetus or a fertilized egg is a potential person, it does not follow that it has the same moral status as an actual person. In other words, a positive decision on the question of personhood still does not decide the issue of abortion in favor of the extreme traditionalist.

This, by and large, disposes of the arguments in support of the extreme traditionalist's position. However, the three subsidiary arguments remain. Sometimes they have been thought to have probative force in and by themselves. Therefore, it will not be inappropriate, over and above disposing of them in the general way just done, to consider their particularities in somewhat greater detail.

As to the first—the argument from valuation—its peculiarity lies in the fact that it goes from the premise that something is valued to the conclusion that therefore it has a particular moral status of its own accord, and that this attendant valuation of it is correct. Nothing, however, could be logically less acceptable. The fact that fetus, embryo, and so on are valued does not thereby show that such valuation is correct.[19] We could equally as easily appeal to the fact that they are aborted with impunity, in order to establish the opposite point. Appeals to facts of custom, therefore, are incapable of deciding this point of moral principle. Furthermore, we could point to a lessening of the moral gravamen traditionally attached to acts resulting in the deformation of fetuses, depending on how much of a burden to

18. For a similar point, see Tooley, "Defense of Abortion and Infanticide"; for an opposite point of view see Thomson, "A Defense of Abortion."

19. For a similar point, cf. Wertheimer, "Understanding the Abortion Argument."

society ultimately results from the action on the fetus. This seems to indicate that what is involved here is the welfare of society as a whole, not of the fetuses as potential powers. Finally, there is this further fact: If the fetus should be aborted as the result of the mother's taking certain drugs, or as a result of her being subjected to some other experience, suit may indeed be brought against the people responsible for this outcome. However, the suit will not be one of murder—or even of manslaughter—nor is it brought on behalf of a being that was thus killed. It is brought on behalf of the parents. However, if the being that thus died had enjoyed all the rights of a person, the suit would have been on its part, and the charge would have been at least one of manslaughter.[20] Therefore, the conclusion that this argument seeks to establish—that as a matter of fact, potential persons enjoy the same moral privileges as actual ones —does not follow.

As to the second supplementary argument—the argument from helplessness—it, too, does not establish what it is intended to prove. For, as it stands, the argument presupposes that fertilized ovum, fetus, and so on are potential persons in our sense of the term. It is on this assumption that the conclusion—that in virtue of their helplessness they are entitled to special consideration—is based. However, this premise is the very point at issue. If it should turn out that from the moment of conception fetuses are indeed potential persons in our sense of the term, then it would follow that they deserve special consideration. But the fact that this would be so does not establish that the premise is true. In other words, this supplementary argument simply begs the question.

Finally, there is the argument from gradation. This argument claimed that in the development of a fertilized ovum through

20. Here we have a peculiarity in the law in that the practice with respect to suits brought as a result of thalidomide deformation is inconsistent in principle with suits brought in the case of fetal deformation as a result of other accidents. In the latter cases where death to the fetus results, suit is brought by the parents on behalf of the parents, whereas in the former case suit is brought on behalf of the child.

various stages to fetus and ultimately child, we have an un-broken development of one and the same organism. Therefore, if it becomes a genuine person in the end, then, because of its identity as an organism through the stages of its development, it must be a potential person throughout. And, furthermore, since it is one and the same organism throughout, it must have the same moral status. This argument must be handled with care, for there is much in it that is correct. Indeed, the whole of its factual premises must be granted. Nevertheless, the con-clusion that it wishes to draw does not follow. There is one and the same organism throughout, but it is one and the same only in the sense that it is one continually growing aggregate of mat-ter that develops according to a genetically fixed plan. This con-tinuation, however, does not mean continued identity—any more than the continuation of protein molecules when ingested and assimilated by us entails that we have become the cow that we have eaten. The cells undergo a fundamental, organizational change. A nervous system of a highly specific and specialized sort develops—and that development makes all the difference. In other words, the argument is based on the assumption that the continued and lawlike development of a certain aggregate of matter entails that no matter what constitutional changes the aggregate undergoes throughout its history, the aggregate is identical with the final result. This principle, however, is not merely question-begging but is also blatantly false. It confuses the identity of a constitutional complex with the identity of the material aggregate that makes up the complex. To accept it is to confuse a gradual transition from one thing to another, with no transition at all. This argument, too, then, is a failure. There-fore the claim based on it, namely, that a fertilized ovum or fetus has the same moral status as a potential person in our sense of that term, and indeed as a person as such, is unaccept-able.

It would therefore seem that the position of the extreme tra-ditionalist lacks all logical support. However, to conclude this would be somewhat hasty. There is another argument that is sometimes adduced in support of it—an argument that is much more radical in its basic premise than any we have discussed so far. It is the so-called argument from the sanctity of life.[21] This argument takes its cue from the premise that all taking of life—all intentional killing—is a moral crime. Therefore, necessarily, abortion falls into that category.

The trouble with this argument is not its logic—that is impeccable—but rather its basic premise. For the argument to have any force at all, this premise must be true. But is it? It is said to be intuitively obvious that all life is sacred. However, as is the case with most things that are said to be intuitively obvious, what is obvious to the one is not obvious to the other, and one person's intuition is another's prejudice. It will not do merely to assert this premise. It must be supported in some way. And, in the present context, it is difficult to see how such support can be forthcoming without at the same time involving the whole position that the principle itself is intended to support.

Furthermore, when carried to its consistent conclusion, the argument goes further than almost anyone is prepared to go—including the proponents of the argument itself. For, by this principle, which supposedly makes abortions at any stage morally reprehensible, it would follow that any premeditated killing of any entity whatever is murderous. After all, the principle involved is the principle of the sacredness of life—all life. But, a principle that makes the very act of breathing, of walking, or of brushing one's teeth a murderous activity in the moral sense of that term surely goes too far. If it were correct, we should be hard put to escape the charge of murder in any of our activities.

The only way to escape this consequence is to alter the fundamental assumption of the argument qualitatively—to limit the principle of the sanctity of all life in some way. Nor is this difficult. We just have to say that not all life is sacred, but only that life which belongs to a being of a certain sort—to be precise, only the life of a person or potential person. Only when thus

21. This is the position expressed by Albert Schweitzer and lies at the basis of various Buddhistic critiques of abortion. It is also discussed briefly by Callahan, *Abortion*, chap. 9. See also Grisez, *Abortion*, chap. 4.

modified can the principle be consistently and acceptably applied in practice. But when modified in this way, the argument that results is merely another version of the argument from the moral status of potential persons, as we have discussed it above in various forms. As such, it is subject to the same shortcomings that we have already pointed out.[22]

However, there is a variation on the argument from the sacredness of life that remains untouched by what has been said so far. It is a variation that is religious in its tenor and basis, and it goes like this:

> God is the creator of the universe. As such, all things are dependent on him, not only with respect to *how* they are— with respect to their natures—but also with respect to *that* they are: for the fact that they exist. Human beings, whether developed to their full potential or merely in the incipient stages of their development, constitute no exception. Their natures, as well as their very existences, are free and gratuitous gifts from God. As such, we do not have the right to take away this gift. That is to say, we do not have the right to deprive a human being, whatever its stage of development, of its God-given gift of life. To do so would be to interfere in the work of God, to go against his wishes. And that, on peril of our souls, we cannot and must not do.[23]

This argument is fairly traditional in contemporary religious circles, in particular, in those of the Christian persuasion;[24] and,

22. Thomson, "A Defense of Abortion," points out another consideration: that from the fact that something is accorded the status of a person, it does not follow that it ought not to be killed. Therefore, from the assertion of personhood as such, the denial of abortion does not follow.

23. This seems to be the standard Christian position. For a more detailed discussion, see Karl Barth, *Church Dogmatics*, vol. 3, *The Doctrine of Creation* (Edinburgh: T. and T. Clark, 1961), pp. 415 ff. See also Grisez, *Abortion*, p. 321 and passim; Callahan, *Abortion*, pp. 309–33 and 410 ff.; St. John-Stevas, *The Right to Life*, p. 12 and passim.

24. It finds its classic statement in Thomas Aquinas *Summa Theologiae* II, Q. 65, A. 3. It is based on Deut. 32, 39.

undeniably, there is something very persuasive about it. We are
inclined to say that if we believe in a God whose gift is life,
then surely it does follow that we cannot take such a gift away
from someone except at our eternal peril. But at the same time,
whether traditional in religious circles or not, and whatever the
persuasiveness of the position, the argument is beset by grave
problems. First of all, the acceptability of its conclusion depends on the acceptability of the premise that all life—human
life included—is a gift from God. And that premise, in turn,
depends on the acceptance of the premise that such a deity
exists. As believer and unbeliever alike are aware, both of these
premises have been doubted. Second, this argument assumes
that man has free will, for only on that assumption could the
act of aborting a fetus be construed as an action contrary to the
will of God. However, as religious believers and speculators are
only too well aware, that issue is far from being solved. That is
to say, how the following—(a) God's supposed omniscience,
(b) his eternal plan for the whole universe, and (c) his creation
—can be reconciled with the simultaneous claim of freedom for
man is not at all clear. To be sure, Church dogmatics flatly assert all of these at the same time—but no less a person than
Augustine, as well as Thomas Aquinas, has found it necessary
to try to establish the reasonableness of these religious assumptions; and as the history of philosophical and religious thought
shows, it is not at all clear that such attempts have succeeded.
Therefore, the fact of dogma notwithstanding, the thesis that
man could do anything contrary to the will of God can be
doubted. In which case, abortion cannot be condemned for this
reason. Finally, there is this consideration: As the beliver himself tells us, God's actions are inscrutable—certainly to man.
We do not understand his plan. Nor, to continue in religious terminology, can we claim to know his counsel. What, then, are
we to do if someone claims that an abortion is commended by
God? Refuse to believe it on the basis of what someone else has
said? For certainly, we do not know God's will since he has not
revealed it to us beyond all possibility of doubt. Furthermore,
with respect to the particular case in question, how can we
claim to know that God does not want this particular life to be

taken? Are there specific injunctions given by him and indubitable in nature that cover this particular instance? The general pronouncements of a biblical nature, after all, are admitted to be metaphorical and in need of interpretation. And here, as the history of religious dogma as well as papal pronouncements have shown, man is capable of error.

Counterarguments along the lines suggested could be multiplied. In fact, however, the whole train of reasoning with which we have been concerned comes to this: (1) We must accept, and accept on faith alone, the corpus of religious beliefs of which the premises of the argument are part and parcel. (2) We must accept the internal consistency of the religious position. (3) We must assume that we have understood perfectly the commands and metaphorical pronouncements of an admittedly incomprehensible being. And (4), we must assume that man has free will. Only if all four are granted, will the argument get off the ground. And surely—so the logically inclined may argue —until the acceptability of these points has been established, the argument itself as an argument against abortion must at best be deemed inconclusive.

The Moderate Traditionalist

The discussion so far has amply substantiated the claim that the extreme traditionalist's position on abortion either, at best, is incoherent or, at worst, results in conclusions that even the extreme traditionalist himself would not want to accept. We may therefore regard it as without probative force. Not so, however, with the position of the mitigated traditionalist. That position, you may recall, was to the effect that not all abortions are murderous, only those that are performed after the fetus has passed a certain point of development. This point has been variously identified as the time at which the fetus quickens in the womb,[25]

25. Cf. Aristotle *Politics* 8; this view is mentioned by St. John-Stevas, *The Right to Life,* p. 36, as part of the position of Blackstone in his *Commentaries*; Wertheimer, "Understanding the Abortion Argument," mentions it as part of the conservative tradition; as does Tooley, "Defense of Abortion and Infanticide." It was finally repudiated by Pius IX in 1869. Cf. Grisez, *Abortion,* p. 387.

acquires a soul,[26] assumes a more or less human form,[27] becomes independently viable,[28] and so on.

Several, sometimes distinct, arguments are adduced in favor of designating abortions murderous after this critical point. As to the first criterion—that of quickening—it is said that only at that point is the entity properly a person—indeed, only then is it properly alive; whereas previously it had been no more than a lower sort of entity, perhaps even merely a cancerous growth (a "clot of blood," as the Islamic tradition puts it).[29] The argument from the acquisition of a human form is similar—with the added assertion that only what looks like a human being can properly be a person. From the religious side, the argument is that the presence of a soul, and only the presence of a soul, changes a material object from a mere biological organism of no special moral status or significance into a person.[30] That is to

26. This view seems to be involved in Canon 747 of the Roman Catholic church. However, as is generally agreed in religious circles, this point is difficult if not impossible to pinpoint, and therefore the concept itself is almost useless. Cf. Wertheimer, "Understanding the Abortion Argument"; J. F. Donceel, S.J., "Abortion: Mediate and Immediate Animation," *Continuum* 5 (1967): 167–71; Grisez, *Abortion,* pp. 147, 151–53, 167, and passim.

27. See Tooley, "Defense of Abortion and Infanticide." See also Philo Judaeus, *Commentary on Exodus* 21:22–23; Callahan, *Abortion,* pp. 411 ff.

28. This is currently the most popular position. For diverse discussions, see John T. Noonan, "An Almost Absolute Value in History," in John T. Noonan, ed., *The Morality of Abortion: Legal and Historical Perspectives* (Cambridge: Harvard University Press, 1970), pp. 51–59, who rejects it; Wertheimer, "Understanding the Abortion Argument." The U.S. Supreme Court decision in *Roe* v. *Wade,* January 22, 1973, defined viability as occurring between twenty-four and twenty-eight weeks. See also Callahan, *Abortion,* p. 391 and passim; Grisez, *Abortion,* pp. 276 ff. and passim.

29. Wertheimer, "Understanding the Abortion Argument," mentions the phrase "an amorphous speck of apparently coagulated protoplasm" as descriptive of a fetus or an unborn child. Cf. Grisez, *Abortion,* p. 275, for similar expressions.

30. Clearly, this argument is related to the argument discussed previously, that human life is a gift from God. However, it differs from it in according the relevant moral value not to the gift of life as such, but to the gift of life to a soul.

say, when the fetus has a soul, then it is a person. Consequently, the act of ensuring its unnatural death with full knowledge and intent is, by that very token, an act of murder. Finally, there is the argument from viability.[31] This argument holds that a fetus has attained the level of a person as soon as it is capable of surviving on its own once born. For the greater part of its development, a fetus is incapable of surviving in this way: it requires the womb. Consequently, for that period, it is not a person and can be killed without the act of killing at the same time being one of murder. However, for a considerable amount of time, it is capable of survival. Therefore, for that time, it is a person and to abort it would be to commit murder.

QUICKENING IN THE WOMB   The first argument, centering on the quickening in the womb, is fairly traditional. And, if matters were to be decided on the basis of tradition, this argument would surely carry the day. However, the fact that a custom or belief is hallowed by tradition does not thereby make it morally acceptable or true: It was tradition that women were bound to bed and kitchen, considered incapable of other things; it was tradition that slavery was right—yet both traditions have been seen to be morally unacceptable, just as the tradition that the earth is flat was found to be false. Furthermore, the present argument hinges on the assumption that movement within the uterus is a valid criterion for the fetus's having become a person. But this is patently false. As has been shown in the case of radically deformed offspring born to mothers who have survived Hiroshima and Nagasaki, some fetuses that move in the uterus turn out, when born, not to be persons at all: They have exceedingly rudimentary nervous systems and brains and die soon after birth. Furthermore, in a great many cases, they do not even look like persons, nor do they have anything like a human physiology. Yet they did move in the womb! Therefore, if we went by the criterion of quickening in the womb, we should be forced to call them persons. Nor is this the only shortcoming of the criterion. In some cases of pregnancy there is no ordinarily perceptible

31. Cf. Grisez, *Abortion*, pp. 32–33, 276 ff., and passim.

movement—no perceptible quickening. Nevertheless, normal children are born. Are they, then, *not* persons? The criterion would seem to entail this. Finally, the criterion of quickening within the womb is intended to determine when someone or something becomes a person. However, what possible connection could there be between these two? The fact that something outside of the uterus is moving does not thereby qualify it as a person. Why should the fact that something is moving within the uterus be any different? Furthermore, animal fetuses also quicken: Are they therefore persons? This last consideration really brings out what lies at the bottom of the quickening criterion: the fact that the womb is human and that the fetus is of human parentage. Thus understood, what the criterion really amounts to is the claim that the genetic offspring of a human being has realized its personhood—has begun to be a person in its own right—as soon as it begins to move. And this occurs rather early: approximately four months after conception. Since at that time it is still in the womb, quickening is the only criterion available.

The argument as it stands, however, is still faulty. It runs head-on into the fact that some fetuses, when they are born, simply turn out not to be persons—they are radical mutations. Such cases are rare, to be sure, but they do occur. Yet, in such cases quickening frequently does occur. Furthermore, the argument still leaves unanswered the fundamental question indicated above: What possible connection is there between moving and being a person—even within a human womb? This is not meant to deny that any connection obtains, but merely to point out that, at best, the quickening criterion must provide a complete explanation of this supposed interrelationship before the argument on which it is based can be accepted.

THE RELIGIOUS ARGUMENT   The religious argument, centering around the acquisition of a soul, also employs a traditional criterion: To be a person is to have a soul. That, after all, is how animals, vegetables, and inanimate things are said to differ from people. However, at its best, the criterion is useless in the pres-

ent context, and the argument centering around it lacks probative force. For, even if there are such things as souls—and no
one has as yet either perceived them or proved their existence
—how are we to determine when a fetus has acquired a soul? [32]
Since we can neither hear, see, feel, taste, smell, or otherwise
experience a soul, this criterion would appear to be useless from
the very start. The only way in which this situation could be
remedied would be by arguing that some other physically ob-
servable behavior or phenomenon serves as an indicator that
the fetus has acquired a soul.[33] Thus, we could say that the
quickening of the fetus in the womb, in fact, is no more and no
less than the indication of the acquisition of a soul and thereby
is an indication that the fetus has become a person. Such a move
would not merely strengthen the present argument, but would
also reinforce the cogency of the previous argument at least on
the criterion of the quickening within the womb. And, in fact,
traditionally these two have often been connected.

However, all this goes no way toward solving an even more
fundamental difficulty that besets the present suggestion, namely,
the acceptability of the underlying premise. How and when has
it ever been established that to be a person entails having a
soul [34]—that to be a person and to have a soul amount to one
and the same thing? Experience and experimentation certainly
have not proved this point; neither have purely rational speculation. Only intuition and revelation seem to be left. But, unfortunately, both are extremely unreliable guides, to say the least;
unreliable, that is, unless somehow supported or proved in some
other way. And, here, there is nothing else forthcoming.

Furthermore, whatever else we may think about souls, the
notion of a soul plays no role whatsoever in our ordinary judgments to the effect that something is a person. For instance,
when we are being introduced to someone, we neither look for

32. See note 26.
33. For a similar argument in connection with viability, see Noonan,
"Absolute Value." See also Grisez, *Abortion*.
34. Ibid.

nor indeed inquire after the soul of the putative person in question. Nor do we simply presume that the person has a soul. The plain fact of the matter is that the question as to whether or not this being has a soul is never even raised. We judge personhood on completely different grounds. But if this is the case, then why, in the case of a fetus, is the criterion of the possession of a soul at all relevant? Surely, aside from all else, to use it in this context would constitute a gross inconsistency in practice. Finally, and within the religious parameters of the argument itself, surely these considerations are relevant: It is the soul, not the compound of body and soul, that is the essential person. And the true destiny of a person is without this physical body, which is thus bestowed. Furthermore, death is said to be but a separation of soul and body, where the soul goes on to live eternally. If that is so—that is to say, if these religious premises are accepted, as by the argument itself they must be—then surely death is nothing horrible. On the contrary: it is devoutly to be wished, particularly before the child-to-be has had the chance to sin.[35] Therefore, the logic of the argument itself brands its conclusion as unacceptable.

The upshot of these deliberations is clear: The mitigated traditional position as encapsulated in the argument from a soul is either incoherent or appeals to principles and criteria that in practice are either not adhered to consistently or are incapable of application. Of course, by itself, this does not entail that the mitigated traditionalist's position is wrong. But it does mean that if it is correct, it must be correct for reasons other than those cited above. However, until such reasons are presented and are shown to be immune from attacks similar to those above, the position retains the status of a personal conviction, on a par with all others.

ARGUMENT FROM VIABILITY   The argument from viability is even less acceptable than the religious argument, for this argument is premised on the principle that the only fetuses that are

35. Its original sin would be taken care of by baptism.

persons are those that are viable—that is, able to survive on their own. But what, precisely, is it to survive on one's own? Surely, if the term is understood in its ordinary sense, a new-born baby cannot do so any more than can a fetus that is as yet unborn.[36] Yet the argument has it that such beings are persons. And what of the aged, infirm, and the seriously ill of all ages? Are they, too, not persons?

Of course, so we are told immediately, the premise of the argument ought not to be construed so widely. Its point is that a fetus requires a uterus in order to survive. It is in this sense that a fetus is said to be nonviable on its own and therefore not a person. Understood in this sense, the argument draws an explicit and clear distinction between fetuses on the one hand and all other persons on the other hand. However, even this will not do as a reply because the factual premise is simply mistaken. It is not true that a fetus requires a womb at all stages of its development.[37] All of us are familiar with the practice of incubating premature babies. Such babies are every bit as viable or nonviable as those that are not born prematurely but instead are still in the womb. The sole difference between them is the type of surroundings in which they find themselves and the machinery that supplies their needs. In the one case, the machinery is mechanical; in the other, organic. The viability in both cases is the same. In fact, the baby in the incubator may be even less viable than the one in the womb. Therefore, if the viability criterion were applied strictly and consistently, the as yet unborn child would be more of a person than the born one.

Furthermore, what counts as viability is a relative matter. It all depends on what we are willing and/or able to do for the

36. This is essentially the position of Tooley, "Defense of Abortion and Infanticide." For a critique of this, see S. I. Benn, "Abortion, Infanticide, and Respect for Persons," in Feinberg, *The Problem of Abortion,* pp. 92–104, although, like Tooley, he too accepts infanticide (p. 101). See also Grisez, *Abortion,* pp. 3–33 and passim; Wertheimer, "Understanding the Abortion Argument."

37. See G. Chamberlain, "An Artificial Placenta," *American Journal of Obstetrics and Gynecology* 100 (March 1968): 615–26.

fetus or the baby in question. As the frontiers of medical science are pushed back further and further, the realm of the viable is correspondingly extended.[38] Thus, if we were to employ all the medical techniques at our disposal, we could keep alive and growing a fetus or a baby which, if these techniques were not to be used, would certainly be hopelessly nonviable and could not survive. On the other hand, projecting into the future, we can say with reasonable certitude that in a few decades even the barely fertilized ovum will be considered fully viable in the sense of not being dependent on a (human) womb.[39] For even today we can keep such an ovum alive and growing for several weeks. Therefore, once again, what counts as being viable is a relative matter, depending on what techniques we are able and/or willing to employ. Yet in none of these diverse circumstances, where in one situation a fetus or baby counts as viable and in another as not, did any change occur in the constitution of the fetus or the baby in question. That remained the same. Therefore, if viability in the aforesaid sense is the criterion for being a person, then being a person has nothing really to do with what you are, but instead depends on the medical techniques that the society in which you live is willing and/or able to employ. In other words, personhood is seen as a function of medical technology. And this, surely, is absurd.

ARGUMENT FROM HUMAN FORM   As to the argument from human morphology—from human form—it is a two-edged sword at best. To be sure, if accepted it would provide a cutoff point prior to which a fetus would not count as a person. However, the following considerations must always be kept in mind: Consistent application of the criterion would entail that we should exclude as nonpersons all those fetuses that do not have a human form. But surely, the point at which deformity becomes a deciding factor is a matter of degree. Those suffering from the effects of hard radiation or chemotherapy or from drugs like thalido-

---

38. For a similar position, cf. Wertheimer, "Understanding the Abortion Argument."

39. See Chamberlain, "An Artificial Placenta."

mide come to mind. In what sense are such deformed individuals *never* persons? While one might, with a fair degree of confidence, exclude those extremely deformed and morphologically deviant entities that are the results of Hiroshima and Nagasaki, one would feel not nearly so confident in the cases just mentioned. Here, behavioral and psychological criteria—in short, nonmorphological criteria—seem to be operative. In other words, the morphological criterion is inconsistently applied, and when it seems to offer difficulties, it is quietly abandoned.

Furthermore, the morphological criterion, as such, is not inherently confined to fetuses and fertilized ova. In fact, it can apply in such cases only if it is a general criterion of personhood. In which case it will apply with equal force to the gravely wounded and injured and to those accidentally deformed in various ways. And while this may just possibly be acceptable to the mitigated traditionalist, the following point still remains to be considered: What connection, if any, is there between human morphology and personhood? Unless it is a matter of definition that only what has a human morphology can be a person, the criterion itself is very much in need of reasoned support. And that, traditionally, has not been forthcoming. Nor is it easy to see how it could be. In the absence of such reasoned support, however, the criterion itself is unacceptable, and the conclusion based on it does not follow.

Thus even the four arguments designed to support the mitigated traditionalist's position fail in their objective. Nevertheless, they are not completely worthless, for they all share a common theme, namely, that persons, insofar as they are persons, do not appear fully grown upon the scene like Minerva out of the head of Zeus. Instead, they evolve and develop with the bodies that we ordinarily associate with persons. This is a point well worth keeping in mind. We shall return to it in considering the positive argument later in this chapter.

For now, the untenable nature of the various traditional arguments designed to prove that abortions are murderous has been demonstrated. All such arguments have been shown to break down for want of logic, because of question-begging premises, or simply because the premises professed are not in fact premises with which we operate in ordinary life, where to implement them consistently would be unacceptable to the very people who propose them. This state of affairs suggests that in fact nothing is wrong with abortion; that is to say, that the contemporary stance of the new morality is correct. We shall therefore now consider this position in greater detail, in order to see whether this impression is actually correct.

THE POSITIVE ARGUMENT

The contemporary stance—the position of the new morality—is characterized by the basic contention that to abort is not to commit a murder, ever; that abortions are morally acceptable and sometimes even highly desirable. However, once this basic theme of the new morality has been stated, the position disintegrates into a welter of divergent stances, none of which have any particular and central line of argumentation. In fact, if we consider closely the plethora of arguments adduced by the proponents of the new morality, it becomes obvious that this morality is not really a unified position but rather a series of positions grouped around this one central theme. In fact, it also becomes apparent that the new morality, far from being the finished product of various trains of reasoning, is more of a series of ad hoc responses relevant to particular situations and developed to meet particular challenges. This, of course, makes presentation and evaluation of the contemporary stance on abortions very difficult. Nevertheless, there are certain lines of argument that are typically present in various contexts. It is on these that we shall concentrate. To be sure, none of them by itself claims to be representative of the new morality as a whole; but taken together, they will provide an insight into what the contemporary stance on abortion is all about.

The Social Argument

The social argument centers around what, at least to some of us, is an obvious fact: We do not live in a utopia. Many people live in such penury that they barely exist at a subsistence level.

In such a situation, an additional mouth to feed, body to clothe, and person to take care of would tax the resources beyond any reasonable or even possible point. That is to say, the birth of a baby would spell catastrophe to those already on the scene.[40] Nevertheless, especially in such a deprived environment, contraceptive techniques and/or devices are frequently unavailable or unknown. Consequently, pregnancies do occur. However, since an unborn child, a fetus, is not yet really a human being, to abort it would not be to commit a murder. It may be on a level with killing an unwanted cat or dog, but murder— No! Therefore, since in the interest of the persons already on the scene it would be better that such a child not be born, and since from a moral point of view the fetus is not really a person, it would be better if the pregnancy were not brought to term. That is to say, it would be better if the pregnancy were aborted. As an additional consideration along analogous lines, it is also frequently pointed out that it would be unfair for a child to be born into such an environment, where its life would be utterly miserable from its very beginning. In other words, added to the consideration dealing with the quality of life of those persons that already exist, there is an analogous consideration centering around the quality of life of the person-to-be.[41]

Undeniably, this sort of argument has an air of extreme reasonableness about it. What could be more obvious than the fact that some people live in utter misery? And, what could be clearer than that everyone born into such a situation would also be miserable, as well as increase the already existing misery? But, despite its air of reasonableness, the argument is far from being logically cogent. Its purpose, let us recall, is to show that it is *morally acceptable* to perform abortions in situations of extreme or even merely great misery such as we have described.

40. For a somewhat different discussion, see Callahan, *Abortion,* pp. 370 ff.

41. See Edward Pohlman, *How to Kill Population* (Philadelphia: Westminster Press, 1971), for a presentation of this position; see also Grisez, *Abortion,* chap. 2; and St. John-Stevas, *The Right to Life,* pp. 27 ff., who are opposed to this reasoning and agree with mine.

However, as it stands, all that it shows is—at best—that in such cases abortions would be practically *useful*. But then, so would murder. That is to say, in the ordinary sense it would also be useful to achieve the desired effect of not increasing the misery if, instead of the as yet unborn child, one of the people already on the scene were to be killed. If usefulness and reduction—or at least, nonaggravation—of misery is the aim, then the one will do as well as the other: From that point of view, murder has as much to recommend it as abortion.

However, as we said, practicality is no guide to the moral nature of the case, neither in the case of abortion nor in that of patent murder. For, once again, to be morally acceptable and to be practically useful need not be the same thing. That in such situations abortions would be morally acceptable would follow if and only if the following further premise were added to the argument:

> An abortion is morally acceptable if it leads to a state of affairs that is practically preferable to the state that would obtain were the abortion not performed.

But, once more, it is not at all clear that this principle is morally acceptable. To be sure, it makes good practical sense.[42] But then, so does ritual murder in cannibalistic societies and the burning of warlocks and witches in societies that believe in magic. In neither case, however, is practicality—or even convenience—a guide to truth. As to the special circumstances that might be pleaded in the present case, there is always this consideration: If the principle just enunciated were to be accepted, why should we not also accept an analogous justification for murder? For example, that a murder is morally acceptable if it leads to a state of affairs that, from a practical point of view, is preferable to the state that would otherwise obtain. To be sure, there may be some who would accept this extension of the principle. But they are neither very numerous nor, generally, are they consistent. They would balk at being murdered for a prag-

---

42. Cf. Grisez, *Abortion,* pp. 289–94 ff.

matic reason and having that murder lauded beforehand as morally acceptable—indeed, as praiseworthy.

In point of fact, all attempts to establish the principle just enunciated ultimately revert to an even more fundamental premise, namely,

> All and only those acts are morally good which promote— or are likely to promote—the greatest amount of good for the greatest number of people.

This principle has sometimes been called the principle of utility; and our principle governing abortion is seen as a special instance of it. When put in this way, our principle permitting abortion is not devoid of rational support. However, this support is not at all one-sided in favor of abortion. One could—perhaps just barely, but nevertheless one could—make a case for saying that according to the principle of utility some abortions are not morally acceptable, that in some cases it would be better for the mother to die—for instance, in cases where the mother is an extreme social misfit and causes all sorts of problems for the society. However, we cannot analyze this problem in as great detail as would be necessary for the issue to be fully developed. It suffices to note that the auxiliary principle mentioned above depends for its validity on the principle of utility; and that the latter principle does *not* imply that (*a*) abortions should be performed on demand, or (*b*) that the utility or preferable state of affairs should accrue to the mother. We should also note that we have not presented the principle of utility as an ultimate truth. It is not. And if it is false—as may well be the case—then the whole position built around it collapses. However, to pursue the matter further is to go beyond the present scope; it belongs properly into the realm of ethics, or the philosophy of morals.

But to return to the argument proper. Over and above the assumptions already indicated, the argument depends on a further premise: that the entity which is killed—the fetus—is not a person prior to its birth. For, if it were a person, then the act of aborting certainly would have moral consequences. In fact, it would be an act of murder. However, we cannot be asked to assume that a fetus is not a person: It must be shown that this is the case. The matter is much too serious in its moral implications for us to make blind, unargued assumptions. But how could such an assumption be argued? Certainly, the position stated is of no help at all. In fact, within the context of the present argument it is difficult to see how the premise could be established—except, of course, by definition. And that would beg the question.

The preceding considerations all have one factor in common: They all deal with only one aspect of the situation, namely, the quality of life of the people who are already on the scene; and they take this to be of overriding importance. However, there is a second principle underlying the social argument: namely, that even from the point of view of the potential person, nonexistence would be preferable to existence in such a social context.

However, once again, this argument looks much more cogent than it really is. For, consider what it really says: It says, that if miserable conditions await a child upon its birth, it is in the best interest of the child that it not be born but be killed instead—preferably as early as possible. But—and surely this question cannot be overlooked by anyone who seriously considers the argument—precisely how is it established that its being killed prior to its being born is in fact preferable to being born, even when the circumstances are as we have just indicated? Certainly, no studies have been performed to establish that this assumption is correct.[43] Nor, barring a miracle, will it ever be possible to conduct such a study. Consequently, lacking an empirical basis for this contention, the proponents of the argument must base their thesis on some other ground. Only three possibilities come to mind: (a) what children who live in such an environment say and how they act, (b) what adults who have grown up in such an environment say, and (c) what we think we should prefer, given our empathetic feelings for those

43. This lies in the nature of the case: We would have to be able to observe both possibilities in order to arrive at a logically tight conclusion. As to the likelihood of the hypothesis being true, what studies there are, are inconclusive. Cf. Callahan, *Abortion*, chap. 3.

trapped in such an environment. Once again, however, it is not
at all clear that (a), (b) and (c) provide a sound basis.
Grounds (a) and (b) run afoul of the fact that no studies have
been done to show that they are true. In fact, if there is anything at all to the psychologists' claim that the drive for survival
is an almost insuperable drive in human beings, we should expect that if such a study were conducted, the evidence would
point the other way. Certainly, given what little data we do have
—and, admittedly, it is only of a sketchy and largely psychological nature—it would be more reasonable to assume the opposite of this contention. That leaves only (c)—the fact, or apparent fact, of empathy. However, empathy is a very unreliable
foundation on which to base a theory prescribing who shall live
and who shall die. First of all, these are *our* feelings. Second,
there is no guarantee whatever that they are shared. After all,
the child is not yet born, and those who are already on the
scene, by and large, would probably not share our feelings, as
we just saw. To be sure, this does not mean that they are not
miserable. It only means that misery does not go hand in hand
with a death wish.[44]

However, even if somehow it should be established that the
persons involved—or more correctly, that the potential persons
involved—would prefer to be dead rather than born, the conclusion would still not follow. For the consideration of the
wishes, desires, and preferences of the people and potential
people involved is really a red herring. The issue is not what
they would prefer, but whether or not they would be better off
dead rather than miserable. In other words, the issue is a moral
one, not a psychological one of preference.[45] And from a moral
point of view, there are only two ways of establishing this conclusion: (a) by proving that an as yet unborn child is not a
person or (b) by espousing the following principle:

44. Cf. St. John-Stevas, *The Right to Life,* p. 20.
45. Cf. Tooley, "Defense of Abortion and Infanticide," for a similar
evaluation; see also Wertheimer, "Understanding the Abortion Argument."

It is morally better to kill someone rather than let that person live, just so long as by killing that person we save it from a life of misery, disease, and so on.

As to (a), we shall postpone consideration of it until a later time. Suffice it to say that if it could be shown that an unborn child (at any stage of development) is not a person, the problem would solve itself. In fact, there would be no problem. That leaves (b). However, as it stands, this principle is quite unacceptable to most people, simply because when treated consistently, it applies to all persons. Thus, it would license not merely abortions, but also infanticide, suicide, senicide, and the killing of all those who face a bleak future. In other words, it would permit—indeed, *enjoin*—us to "put out of their misery" all those whose misery will continue to be great. After all, the principle says that it would be better to kill under these circumstances. However, we venture to say that very few of those advocating abortion for this reason would be willing to accept a principle having such implications. Nor would it do to plead special circumstances in the case of abortion; for example, that the degree of misery would be uniquely great, or that the entity to be killed is not a person. For, if the second were the case, then the principle would simply not apply. And as to the first, lacking any means of accurately predicting the future, any such claim would amount to pure guesswork.

Finally, we come to a third principle which seems to underlie the social argument: the principle that considerations dealing with the quality of life of an individual are relevant when considering the purely moral question of whether or not someone should be killed. That is to say, the argument depends in no small degree on the assumption that if a state of life is of a particularly low and excessively unpleasant nature, such that the properly human potential of the person living it is stunted, killing the person who is about to lead such a life is the less reprehensible the lower and more unpleasant and degrading that sort of life is.

Again, most proponents of the social argument for abortion

would not accept this thesis if it were to be applied to all persons. In other words, they would not be willing to accept this as a general principle. But if not, some justification must be given as to why the principle should hold good only in the case of abortions. Usually, such justification takes the form of an argument to the effect that a fetus or an unborn child is not a person, and that therefore it is only natural that the principle should hold good only in the case of abortions. In all other cases, we should be dealing with *persons*—and to these the principle does not apply. To this line of argument the only reply possible is to point out that by simply assuming that fetuses and unborn children are not persons, the proponents of the social argument beg the very point at issue. If it is simply assumed that they are not persons, the question of whether or not abortions are murderous is rendered nugatory. The question has force if and only if it is not clear beforehand whether or not they are persons. And it is only on the assumption that they are, that there is any need for an argument in favor of abortion such as this social argument is intended to provide.

We should also note a line of reasoning that is diametrically opposed to this third principle underlying the social argument. It is essentially Judeo-Christian in nature, most particularly Christian. This line of reasoning has it that rather than legitimizing killings, the prospect of future misery for the child to be born enjoins the opposite. For, such a life will afford the individual the unique opportunity to acquire and develop those virtues that spell ultimate salvation. No other context will afford such an opportunity. To be sure, this line of reasoning may not find much favor in the eyes of contemporary society. Nevertheless, if the religious premises on which it is based are accepted, the argument is very powerful indeed. (A similar argument can be constructed for the Buddhistic faiths.)

However, despite its probable lack of popular appeal, this religious counterargument does touch on a very important point, even if only indirectly—the point that it is not at all clear that the quality of life has anything to do with whether or not a person about to live it should be killed. What is clear, and what is admitted on all sides, is that such a life is not worth living. But instead of implying that therefore the person who is about to live it should not live at all, this seems to imply that the person should be permitted to live another sort of life. Of course, given the context of the present considerations, the implementation of this suggestion would require a restructuring of the social order that makes for the miserable life in the first place. In other words, considered from this moral point of view, the upshot of the premises of the social argument seems to be that society must be restructured, not that individuals who are about to enter that society should be killed.

The Psychological Argument

What we shall call the psychological argument is, in at least one respect, quite similar to the social argument for abortion. Like the latter, it is concerned with the quality of life of the individual. And once more, like the latter argument, it argues that if the likelihood is great that either mother or child will live an utterly miserable existence in virtue of the child's being born, it would be better if the pregnancy were aborted. However, unlike the social argument, the psychological argument does not define a miserable life in material terms. Instead, it deals only with the psychological aspects of the situation. This distinction, however, makes for an even more profound difference: Whereas the social argument would license abortions in all and only those cases where the physical circumstances are as we have described, the psychological argument, being essentially independent of these circumstances, would license abortions even in those cases where the physical situation may be deemed ideal. It all depends on what the mental climate in the relevant circumstances is like.[46]

Like the social argument, the psychological argument has two sides: One, considering the point of view of the person-to-be,

46. For a discussion of this sort of position, see St. John-Stevas, *The Right to Life*, pp. 21 ff. For a discussion on the available data, see Callahan, *Abortion*, chap. 3; Grisez, *Abortion*, pp. 77–87.

deems this potential person to be all-important; the other, dealing with the psyche of the mother-to-be, considers the latter to
be the paramount factor. In both cases, however, the underlying
principle is the same: In the interest of the psychological welfare of the persons or individuals involved, the pregnancy
should not be brought to term but be aborted. Let us consider
these two versions separately.

It is a recognized, well-known fact that some people do not
get along well with children, that others are too self-centered
to be able to share the marriage or union partner with other
claimants on their attention, and that still others are emotionally
too unstable and immature to be able to handle the responsibility of having children. It is also a recognized and well-known
fact that children are psychologically and physically very vul-
nerable, that they can be marred and warped for life, not merely
physically but also psychologically. All it takes is an environment where they are unwanted and unloved.[47]

The psychological argument in its first version trades on these
facts. Starting with the preceding statements as premises, it continues something like this:

> Nevertheless, sometimes it does happen that a pregnancy
> occurs in a situation where some or perhaps even all of the
> negative factors mentioned above obtain. The parents-
> to-be are self-centered, irascible, emotionally immature
> people of an extremely possessive sort who are not ready
> to take on the responsibility of having a child. If a child
> were to be born into such a situation, it would grow up to
> be psychologically extremely maladjusted, stunted, and
> warped. It is better that a child should not grow up in such
> an atmosphere. Therefore, it is better for a child that it not
> be born; that is, that the pregnancy should be terminated
> prior to its natural termination in the course of events and
> the child should be killed.

47. Cf. Callahan, *Abortion*, pp. 451–60.

There is even a variant on this argument based on the fact that emotionally unstable people frequently are violent toward their children. In many cases, they do them grievous bodily harm. The battered child syndrome is only too well known to pediatricians and social workers. Once again, the conclusion is the same: Better for the child that it not be born than to endure such a life.

Like so many of the arguments which we have considered, this argument, in both its versions, has definite and immediate appeal. It sounds so eminently reasonable. After all, who would advocate that a child be born into such surroundings? And, who would take the responsibility for the psychological state—indeed, the physical state—of such a child? But underneath this air of reasonableness there lurks an assumption that does not seem quite so reasonable. It can best be expressed in the form of the following principle:

> If the psychological situation to be faced by someone is likely to be unbearable, it is better to kill that individual than to let him endure it.

A more cynical way of putting this principle is encapsulated in the statement "I shall kill you for your own good!" [48]

The principle which we have just elicited as underlying the psychological argument in its first version is no stranger to us. We have encountered it before, in a somewhat different version, when we considered the social argument. And here, as there, the principle cannot merely be adduced as self-evident. In fact, it is so far removed from our ordinary understanding of the matter that when considered as it stands it seems wholly preposterous. For—to rehearse but one part of our previous reasoning—the principle is far too broad in its implications. If applied consistently to all people, it would license all sorts of killings. And to

48. This sentiment seems to have been a component of Madame S. van de Put's reasoning, as stated at her trial in Liège, November 5, 1962 (as quoted by St. John-Stevas, *The Right to Life,* p. 7).

claim that it is restricted only to fetuses would require that special circumstances be shown why it should be applicable only here. Nor—as we saw—will it do to rest the case on the claim that fetuses are not yet persons. For, if they are not, the whole argument will be pointless; and if they are persons, then this contention is simply mistaken. In fact, of course, the situation could be shown to be even more contradictory and confused: What, after all, is the point of the whole argument? The answer, surely, is that some action—that of killing the fetus—would produce a better state of affairs than another course of action. But better for whom? The fetus? [49] It would no longer be around to enjoy it. But even that is irrelevant to the present context. The point is, Why should we be concerned to bring about a better state of affairs for the fetus? Surely, because we value it; or, more correctly, because a fetus is a being that has its own intrinsic value. In other words, we wish to produce a favorable state of affairs for the fetus because of the value attaching to it. A value, be it noted, that is not of the computable variety, but instead is a value in the sense that philosophers sometimes use when they talk about a human being as having intrinsic value. However, if a fetus does have intrinsic value, then surely so does a person who is already born and on the scene. (If we were inclined to deny that a fetus is a person, we would say that a person has even greater intrinsic value.) Nor can this value be of a different kind; as, for example, that difference which obtains between the intrinsic value of a dog and that of a piece of chewing gum. For, the reason given by the argument for wanting to produce an absence of psychological misery is that the psychological welfare of the person-to-be is at stake. And the argument can have this welfare at heart only if it sees a fetus as having an intrinsic value very much like that of a person already born.

But to return to our argument. The upshot of it is this: Since

49. Recently acquired data on prenatal awareness make this question less bizarre than it would otherwise seem.

we have the welfare of fetuses at heart, and since we also have the welfare of persons at heart, then—unless we see persons as having less value than fetuses—persons already on the scene should be accorded the same benefits as fetuses. Consequently, if the principle in question holds at all, it must hold for fetuses and persons alike. Therefore, it follows that unless we are to place greater value on a fetus than on a born person, we should also kill the latter if life threatens to become psychologically unbearable for them. Note well: We should kill them, not that they should commit suicide. For not all persons would in fact commit suicide, just as neither would all fetuses be party to their own demise. The principle in question requires that they be killed even against their will, for their own good, that is, for their own psychological welfare.

To many, the conclusion at which we have just arrived would seem ridiculous. However, short of rejecting the principle of killing someone for his own good, the train of reasoning cannot be faulted. Of course, there is always the alternative of rejecting the principle itself. For, like its sociological counterpart, the principle is really rather limited. It assumes that the only alternative to leading a miserable life is to be dead. But there is another alternative: to live another life. To be sure, in the case of our fetus that will be impossible unless the situation in which it will find itself once born, were changed. That is to say, it would require that to all intents and purposes, the child-to-be acquire different parents. That, however, is neither unheard of nor a difficulty. Adoption has been a recognized social practice for quite some time; and nowadays children given up for adoption are very difficult to find.

To conclude, then, we can say that the psychological argument as centered around the psychological welfare of the child-to-be must be adjudged a failure. For, not only is it based on a principle that does not admit of consistent implementation, but the principle itself is too limited in not recognizing that there is an alternative to abortion: adoption.

The second part of the psychological argument—the part

considering the matter from the point of view of the mother-to-be—can be stated in the following way:[50]

> It is generally recognized that when people are subjected to great psychological strain or are put into what are called situations of severe psychological stress, their state of mind might become unbalanced. And even if this should not occur, still, the quality of their life is frequently affected so adversely and so severely that they find life itself almost unbearable and not worth living. In such a situation, people quite seriously utter—and mean—such remarks as "I wish I were dead!" or "This life is not worth living." [51] Sometimes they even act upon this sort of conviction. In any case, whether they do or do not, it is generally held that the situation leading to a state of mind such as that underlying such remarks is extremely undesirable. Almost any way, any remedy for preventing its occurrence, is deemed acceptable. In other words, it is generally assumed that people have a fundamental and inalienable right to happiness; and that anything which interferes with the realization of this right is prima facie bad.
>
> Under such circumstances, the birth of a child would engender an unbearable state of affairs. That is to say, its birth would constitute a very real threat to the happiness and mental stability of the mother-to-be to such a degree that she might well become emotionally and/or mentally unbalanced. Still differently, a child would materially infringe upon the mother-to-be's right to happiness. Therefore, for the sake of her stability and happiness, the birth must never be allowed to occur. Since contraception is too late, abortion is the only means whereby it can be prevented. Consequently, the pregnancy must be aborted.

50. For a consideration of some of the issues discussed here, see Grisez, *Abortion*, pp. 77–86 and passim, and Callahan, *Abortion*, chap. 3.

51. There are passages to this effect in the Bible, particularly Job 3:5, Jeremiah 20:14 (cf. 1:5); see Matthew 26:24 for a Christian parallel.

This, in outline, is the psychological argument for abortion from the point of view of the people already on the scene; more precisely, from the point of view of the mother-to-be. However, contrary to initial appearance, this train of reasoning is not one but two closely intertwined but nevertheless quite distinct arguments. One deals with the happiness of the mother-to-be; the other, with her mental stability. As it stands, the argument considers them the same and shifts from one to the other at will. However, the two are quite distinct and carry very different weight. Certainly, for the sake of conceptual clarity, they ought not to be confused. Let us therefore disentangle them and evaluate them separately.

Let us call the first argument, which centers around the happiness of the mother-to-be, the argument from happiness. Quite clearly, it is based on the premise that everyone has the inalienable right to happiness. Separated from the other line of reasoning, the argument then runs something like this:

> Everyone has an inalienable right to happiness. In some cases, that right would be infringed upon and its exercise made impossible if a baby were to be born. Since the cause of this infringement is a mere fetus and not another person, it can be dealt with in a way in which we could not normally deal with persons: We can kill it by means of an abortion. It is not that we enjoy doing so. It is just that there is no other way. Consequently, under these circumstances, an abortion is morally justified.

As but a moment's sober reflection will show, logically speaking this argument does not hold water. This is not to say that it does not have emotional appeal—it does. But emotional appeal has nothing to do with the validity or invalidity of an argument. What counts is whether or not the conclusion follows from the premises in a non–question-begging manner. And this is not presently the case: The argument begs the very question at issue. Let us recall once again what the question was: Is it an act of murder to perform an abortion? By definition, murder is an act of killing with premeditation and malice aforethought another person. The last phrase is crucial: Murder can only be committed on a person. However, the argument from happiness as we have just sketched it merely *asserts* that a fetus is not a person. From this statement it goes on to conclude that therefore abortion is not murder. The logic of this reasoning is circular. For, to assume that a fetus is not a person is to beg the question of whether or not the premeditated killing of a fetus is murder. As we have already said, the whole position thus turns out to be circular and devoid of external logical support—it begs the whole issue.

However, this is not the only point on which the argument fails. There are two further assumptions, both of which are crucial to the validity of the argument, yet both of which may well be questioned. The first assumption is that everyone has an inalienable right to happiness. It is not at all clear that this is true. Some moral theorists have argued that although happiness indubitably is a good, nevertheless it is not a right.[52] In fact, they have argued that from a purely moral point of view the question of whether or not an act produces happiness is irrelevant. What counts is whether it is morally right. To be sure, this point of view needs arguing. But in that respect it is on a par with the blatant assumption that happiness is a right. The mere fact that we do have these opposing viewpoints therefore makes argument absolutely necessary. Furthermore, even if it should be granted that everyone has an inalienable right to happiness, it may also be that the happiness of the majority counts for more than the happiness of the minority. If this is true, then it would mean that, at least in some cases, the mother-to-be may be forced to sacrifice her happiness for that of her relatives or of the children that she bears.

The second controversial assumption underlying this argument is that fetuses, not being persons, have no overridingly moral status. Let us ignore the question-begging nature of this

---

52. Cf., for instance, Immanuel Kant's *Foundations of the Metaphysics of Morals,* sec. 1. Utilitarianism, particularly of the egocentric or subjective varieties, of course, disagrees.

assumption, since we have already dealt with it, and consider instead what this contention implies: that nonpersons have no moral status—no rights—or that if they do, their rights must yield to the rights of persons should any conflict arise. But once again, this is a brute assumption; and it is not even clear that it is true. For one thing, we can argue with a fair show of cogency that nonpersons do have rights. If they did not, all formal recognition of rights attributed to them, as in legislation involving cruelty to animals and the like, would be merely a farce. Therefore the contention that nonpersons have no rights whatsoever is on shaky ground. That leaves the assumption that when the rights of a person conflict with those of a nonperson, the nonperson is the loser—at least if the happiness of the person is at stake. But once again, that assumption, both in its general and in its particular form, is contradicted by actual practice. On several occasions, particularly those that involve properties left to animals in wills, the rights of these animals have been upheld in the courts, despite the fact that in upholding these rights, the happiness of certain persons contending these wills is definitely infringed upon. Furthermore, although these considerations are not enshrined in legal statutes, nevertheless it is generally admitted on all hands that to kill an animal merely for the sake of personal convenience or gratification is to perform an immoral act.[53] Therefore both by law and by common sentiment it is admitted that animals—nonpersons—do have rights and that in a situation of conflict, the rights of the person do not automatically take precedence.

In conclusion, let me emphasize once more the point made in the beginning: that in a very definite sense, all of these considerations are so much idle speculation. The important issue is whether a fetus is a person, and that question is begged by the argument.

The second argument—the argument from mental stability—is different in nature from the argument from happiness. Briefly, it goes something like this:

53. Antivivisection legislation is generally premised on this assumption.

Mental stability is one of the most important factors in our life because, in a very real sense, to become mentally unstable is to undergo a personality change: to become someone else. This fact is recognized even in ordinary locutions, such as "She (he) has become a completely different person" or "He (she) is not the same person any more." And however metaphorical such locutions may be, they still do have their point. But to undergo a personality change is not the only thing that can happen: The person in question may become mentally unstable in the sense of ceasing to be a properly functioning rational being. In a word, he or she may cease to be a person. The state of affairs involved may be, and generally is, quite unpleasant for whoever is undergoing this experience. However, quite aside from any unpleasantness that may obtain, there is also this further consideration: A person is an entity having intrinsic, absolute value. As such, anything that diminishes the personhood of an individual strikes at the very core of its being as an entity of intrinsic value. From a purely moral point of view, therefore, and leaving all questions of agony and pleasure aside, anything that has this effect ought to be rejected. This point could also be put by saying that the following is a fundamental principle: Everyone has an inherent and inalienable right to his own personality. Anything destructive of the latter is prima facie evil and ought to be stopped. Further—so the argument continues—even if this principle is not accepted, there is still the following: A state of mental instability is vastly inferior to a state of mental stability.

And with either of these as premises, the argument then concludes as follows:[54]

Sometimes the only way of preventing such a state of affairs from occurring is to abort the pregnancy. For, carrying the

54. Cf. Grisez, *Abortion,* for a discussion of a similar issue; see also Callahan, *Abortion.*

child to term would in fact result in such a disruption of
the life-style of the woman that the instability mentioned
above would in fact obtain. Therefore, once more, abortion is the only solution.

As is obvious at first glance, whatever probative force this argument has depends on the two premises: that everyone has an
inalienable right to his own personality, and that a state of
mental instability is less good than a state of mental stability.
Nor ought we even to consider denying them. They are true.
However, the conclusion alleged does not follow from them.
If it is not the birth itself but the resultant change in life-style
that would engender this instability, there is an expedient not
even mentioned in the argument: that of adoption. That is to
say, the argument paints a picture where the only way out of a
morally unacceptable situation is by means of what might be a
morally somewhat less than ideal expedient. However, there is
another way out which is not attended by the moral difficulty
of this expedient: adoption. By putting the baby up for adoption directly after birth, the life-style of the mother will not be
affected. Consequently, all things being equal, this is the correct
expedient to follow. In fact, this solution can be faulted only
if it can be shown that the mental instability will not be a result
of the baby's being born but of the pregnancy itself.

Nevertheless, the argument itself calls for further analysis,
and it would be well to begin with the premises on which the
argument rests. For one, the argument merely assumes that the
life to be destroyed is not the life of a person. By now, this is a
familiar assumption that requires no further comment. The
other assumption is that a state of mental instability, on the part
of the mother-to-be in particular, is much less desirable than the
killing of an entity which, all other things being equal, would
grow into a human being. Such an assumption requires rigorous
defense—especially in face of the contention that even though
not yet a person, a fetus nevertheless is a potential person and
as such is not without conflicting rights. Therefore, even if we
did grant that mental instability was an undesirable, it would

still not follow directly that a mother-to-be's rights take such precedence over the rights of a person-to-be, that the fetus's right to life is simply overruled.[55] At the very least, it would require careful argumentation to show why this should be the case.

Furthermore—in the interest of consistency—there is this, perhaps merely tangential, consideration: Those who propound the right of a mother-to-be to maintain her happiness and mental stability generally do not consider that the same course of reasoning, mutatis mutandis, would hold for the father-to-be. That is to say, they generally deny the father-to-be the right to request an abortion on the grounds that his mental stability and/or happiness would be adversely affected by the birth of the child. (There are cases of this sort of thing on record, so the hypothesis is not an idle one.) Only the mother-to-be is deemed to have such a right. But the obvious question to ask at this juncture is why that should be the case. And the perhaps equally obvious reply that is generally forthcoming is that after all, she is the *mother*: the single life-supporting unit directly responsible for the very continuation of existence of the fetus. The situation concerns her more closely, since it is her body and her pregnancy.[56] Her case, therefore, is said to be special.

However, in one rather clear-cut way, this sort of considera-

55. On the topic of conflict of rights in general, see Callahan, *Abortion*, sec. 3 passim; Tooley, "Defense of Abortion and Infanticide"; Thomson, "A Defense of Abortion," to mention but a few authors. Tooley's argument is interesting, in that it suggests that whereas later compensation is possible for the mother, this is impossible for the aborted fetus. Thomson expands the parameters of the discussion to include other rights (see also p. 48, note 1).

56. A variant of this is the I-have-a-right-to-my-body argument. Cf. Callahan, *Abortion*, chap. 13, pp. 460 ff.; Lawrence Lader, *Abortion II: Making the Revolution* (Boston: Beacon Press, 1973), pp. 13, 18. It is also an argument much in the forefront of women's liberation campaigns for more "liberal" abortion laws. Cf. Marya Mannes, "A Woman's View of Abortion," in A. F. Guttmacher, ed., *The Case for Legalized Abortion Now* (Berkeley, Calif.: Diablo Press, 1967), p. 59; Garrett Hardin, "Abortion and Human Dignity," in Guttmacher, *Legalized Abortion*, p. 82, to mention but a few contemporary authors.

tion is quite unacceptable. To be sure, it is the pregnancy of the mother-to-be, and it is her body. But it is her pregnancy not in any sense of peculiarly nontransferable ownership, but in the sense that her body happens to nourish and sustain the fetus. Things might have been otherwise; and, given continued advances in modern medicine, one day they very well might be. Still, let us grant that at present, there is this difference between the mother-to-be and the father-to-be: that the former is the continuing source of sustenance for the fetus, whereas the latter is not. However, in itself this does not establish the point at issue: namely, that therefore the mental stability and/or happiness of the mother-to-be holds a special position vis-à-vis that of the father-to-be. A separate argument will have to show why this should be the case. Nor will it be easy to give. For, the underlying principle of such an argument would have to be something to the effect that whoever directly sustains a life has a right to decide over its very existence, whereas whoever does not directly sustain it has no such right. Neither will it do here to appeal to the obvious correctness of such an assumption. As was said before, obviousness is a psychological consideration dealing with what people find convincing. It carries no logical force whatever. Furthermore, we could claim with equal justification that the very opposite of this contention is the case. That is to say, we could claim with a fair show of plausibility that in fact the sustainer of a life does not have the right to decide over the existence of that life but that, on the contrary, in virtue of being its sustainer has incurred certain very special obligations and duties. What is at stake, therefore, is this premise: that a sustainer of life has the right to decide over the existence of that life—and no one else. Both parts of that premise are very much open to question.

By way of concluding these considerations, let us consider briefly a subsidiary form of the argument for mental stability. It involves the fact that in some cases the pregnant woman is already mentally disturbed prior to the inception of the pregnancy; and the further fact that in such a case the pregnancy, when carried to term, would not merely worsen the existing situation considerably, but would also place the child-to-be into an intolerable situation. In such cases, so the argument concludes, it would be in the best interest of all parties concerned if the pregnancy were aborted.

Once again, this sort of argument has a great deal of initial plausibility. We feel moved by the prospective plight of the young woman, abhor what awaits the child, and therefore feel compelled to acquiesce in the solution. But again, if the conclusion is based solely—or even mainly—on what is contained in the argument, the whole will be a non sequitur. Impending mental aberration cannot be cited as a deciding factor: It already obtains. The best that could be argued is that this condition of aberration will become permanent and irrevocable by this birth. In the present state of the psychological art, this cannot be shown to be true.[57] At best, what could be shown is that this would be highly likely. However, as the law recognizes in various other instances, "highly likely" is not good enough. It must be shown beyond all reasonable shadow of a doubt.

Furthermore, considerations similar to those raised a few paragraphs ago are also relevant in this context: Why is this putative right to the termination of the pregnancy confined to the case of the mother-to-be? Surely a case could be made for all persons who are in any way closely connected with the pregnancy. Second—and much more important from a philosophical point of view—when was it ever established that the danger of permanent insanity takes precedence over the life of a potential person? In fact, much more generally, when was it shown that the danger of any disability to be sustained by anyone licenses the killing of an as yet unborn child?

Finally, there is this to be considered: The argument has it that the abortion would be in the best interest of all parties concerned. But in what way would the termination of the pregnancy be in the best interest of the child-to-be? (We forego any consideration of the claim that the child-to-be of an insane mother would itself be insane. [a] That is not necessarily true. In fact,

57. Cf. Grisez, *Abortion*, and Callahan, *Abortion*.

in almost all cases it is false. [*b*] If the principle underlying this train of reasoning were to be implemented consistently, it would result in the killing of all sorts of potential people.)

The upshot of these considerations is that the proponents of abortion must, at least in this instance, chalk up a "not proven" for their cause. But there is a series of considerations not yet touched upon that have not been affected by the analyses we have proffered so far. It is the series that goes under the heading of biological argument.

The Biological Argument

The biological argument—or, more correctly, the series of arguments that go under this name—are united by what purports to be a scientific outlook centering around the biological aspects of the situation. The biological considerations are taken to be decisive on the issue of whether or not to abort. They fall into two groups: those dealing mainly with the mother-to-be and those dealing with the fetus. Let us begin with those considerations that center around the mother-to-be.

Birth, so we are told in some quarters, is a painful, difficult and physically taxing process.[58] In some cases, the physiological condition of the mother-to-be is just not up to it, and any actual, normal birth would strain her physical resources beyond the breaking point. There is a very real danger that the mother would die in labor. Therefore—so this argument has it—in such cases the pregnancy should not be allowed to come to term. Instead, in the interest of the survival of the mother-to-be, the pregnancy should be aborted and the fetus killed. However, as is apparent upon even the most cursory of reflections, as it stands this argument does not carry much weight. It forgets— or simply ignores—the possibility of a Cesarean. To be sure, hundreds of years ago—indeed, even as short a time ago as a

58. Though by no means universally. There is a growing realization that by far and away the greatest part of pain in labor is psychosomatic and culturally induced. Natural childbirth clinics have shown this to be true in a great many cases.

few decades—Cesareans were dangerous and had a high mortality rate. Today, however, given modern surgical techniques, that danger no longer obtains. That is to say, it no longer exists unless the mother-to-be is physiologically in a very debilitated state. But if that is the assumption on which we are to proceed, then several things should be borne in mind: First, such cases are exceedingly rare. Second, in such cases an abortion during the later stages of the pregnancy would impose as great a strain on the mother-to-be as either Cesarean or actual labor. Furthermore, such extreme debilitation generally does not occur overnight, but is the result of a chronic or otherwise lengthy and protracted condition. Consequently, and almost invariably, the fact that such extreme danger would exist would have been known —or at least knowable—prior to the occurrence of the pregnancy itself. Therefore, such an individual would have no right to get pregnant in the first place.

But still—so it might be argued—pregnancies might occur in such cases. And given the parameters of the argument as outlined, the conclusion suggested would follow: that the fetus should be killed. More specifically, it could be argued that it should be killed as soon as possible. In this way, so the argument would continue, the objection raised a moment ago would be met, and abortion would be justified on purely biological— that is, physiological—grounds.

However, to argue this is to make a mistake. To see why this is so, we shall have to take a closer look at the notion of an action. There are two general ways in which we can approach an act: We can consider it from the point of view of its physical, spatiotemporal characteristics, and we can consider it from the point of view of its desirability. As to the former, all it will yield is a *description* of the act: as detailed as is deemed prudent or necessary. The second approach, however, yields what the first does not: a value judgment as to whether the act ought or ought not to be performed. No amount of description could possibly yield such a result, simply because all the premises of such an analysis are factual. Only an evaluative approach can give an appropriate answer, precisely because some of its premises are prescriptive in nature. They tell us not whether or not something is the case, but whether or not something ought to be.

Nor is that the end of the matter. Prescriptive analyses may again be divided into two sorts: those whose prescriptive premises are ethical in nature and those whose prescriptive premises are not. Thus, consider the following judgments: "To drill a hole, it is better to use an auger than your thumb." "Murder is sometimes a very messy business," and "Murder is morally reprehensible." The first two do make evaluative judgments, and they do prescribe or proscribe a certain course of action—but on what we might call purely pragmatic grounds. The third alone has a moral underpinning and is prescriptive in a moral sense.

The point of all these considerations in the present context is the following: The question of whether or not to abort is not merely a pragmatic issue. It is a moral one. In fact, without this ethical parameter, there would not even be an issue, for the situation would be solved automatically by the prevailing pragmatics. The difficulties are of an ethical nature. Is it morally all right to abort—the efficacy of the procedures available notwithstanding? In the present context, this question can be posed thus: Even if it should turn out to be safer for the mother to have an abortion than to carry the fetus to term, is it morally right to have an abortion? And here, as will be obvious immediately, no amount of information about the facts of the matter —about its physical nature and its pragmatic feasibility and/or desirability—could hope to settle the issue. In fact, such details would be simply irrelevant. What is at issue is whether or not an abortion is morally right in such a situation. And here, the biological and other pragmatics of the situation notwithstanding, we are really faced with the problem of deciding (*a*) whether or not a fetus is a person, and (*b*) if it is, whether its right to life takes precedence over that of the mother-to-be.[59] If there

59. On the issue of conflict of rights, see note 55. See also Grisez, *Abortion,* chap. 6 passim. In an opposing vein, see Benn, "Abortion, Infanticide, and Respect for Persons," pp. 93 ff.

were some clear-cut way in which (*a*) could be decided, the issue would be relatively clear-cut and easily answered. In the absence of such a criterion, however, the situation is somewhat up in the air.

As to (*b*), nothing adduced so far has shown that the life of the mother-to-be takes precedence over the life of the fetus. In point of fact, the following train of reasoning is here quite apropos and would seem to indicate the opposite: A moral agent is responsible for the results of his or her acts if these results were either intended by the agent, were in the sphere of knowldge had by the agent at the time of the act, or could reasonably have been expected to have been known by the agent at the time of the act. (This last may be called the condition of culpable ignorance.) In the present context, the act is intercourse; the result, pregnancy. Therefore, all things being equal and the act of intercourse not being one of rape nor the parent-to-be excused by reason of excusable ignorance, the individuals who engaged in the act of intercourse are responsible for the resulting pregnancy even if that pregnancy itself was neither expected nor wanted. In other words, in those cases that do not fall under excusing conditions, the unexpected or unwanted nature of the pregnancy is simply irrelevant, since the pregnancy itself would constitute the effect of an act involving culpable negligence: the negligence of those involved to take the necessary precautions that would have prevented the occurrence of the pregnancy itself.[60] (We can, for the moment, ignore the problem of the failure of preventive measures when employed in good faith with sufficient care.) The result of this negligence is the existence of another living being. That living being, simply in virtue of being a living being, has certain rights—or at least so it can be argued. (Otherwise, all legislation dealing with the prevention of cruelty to animals and so on is fraudulent.) Not only that: It can be argued that as a potential person, it has very special rights. In particular, the right to life. And the strength of these rights increases the further along in its development this

60. Cf. Thomson, "A Defense of Abortion."

potential person is. The perpetrators of the act resulting in the pregnancy, by engaging in that act without any of the excusing conditions mentioned above being operative, have thereby yielded their prerogatives to the precedence of the person-to-be which they have thus engendered; perhaps not consciously so, but certainly from a moral point of view. This is merely the particular application of the general principle stated above, that agents are responsible for the results of their acts. That being the case, the plea of danger to the biological survival of the mother-to-be can no longer count as an extenuating circumstance from a moral point of view. It ceased to be operative the moment intercourse was voluntarily engaged in. Just as the person who while driving a car kills a passerby is responsible for that killing, so the person who engages in intercourse in the indicated manner is responsible for the pregnancy that results. And just as in the case of the car accident the moral situation that results has prior claim over the moral rights of the individual responsible for the accident, so in the case of the pregnancy the moral situation that results in terms of the pregnancy itself has prior call on our moral consideration to those considerations involving the welfare of the persons who committed the act. In other words, once a life has been engendered, the welfare of the parents-to-be is a secondary consideration. Consequently, abortion for the sake of the mother-to-be is simply not a moral alternative. In this respect, the situation can be fruitfully compared with the de facto bringing into being of a contract: We may not like the results—in fact, they may be detrimental to us—but that does not alter the fact that the results of that contract entered into by us take precedence over our welfare except in very unusual circumstances.

This notion of a tacit contract, of a moral commitment and parameter inherent in the very act of intercourse leading to conception, has ramifications far beyond the limited context of the biological argument as we have so far discussed it. In itself, considered on a purely ethical level, the notion is of course nothing other than the notion that every voluntary act carries with it responsibility for the state of affairs resulting from it if that state of affairs lies within the range of what we normally could expect individuals to be aware of under the circumstances. At a more particular level, however, and more closely related to the present context, what this means is that to plead ignorance as to the outcome of the act of intercourse, and to request an abortion on those grounds alone, cannot be accepted. Further still, this train of considerations will brand as unacceptable that series of biological arguments which seize on the fact that in some instances, the very fact of pregnancy presents a physiological danger to the woman who is pregnant and, where, in order to save her life, the pregnancy ought to be discontinued.

That is to say, these arguments profess to deal with precisely those exceptional circumstances mentioned a moment ago: threats to the life of the mother-to-be. It is not that she will not survive the birth of her child, but that she will not survive being pregnant. Situations like that of ectopic pregnancy, of progressive heart and/or kidney failure, or of cancer of the cervix are deemed cases in point.[61] In all of these cases, so the general argument runs—and in other, similar cases as well—the mother will die unless the appropriate surgical techniques are employed: techniques which, either directly and intentionally, or indirectly and only as an unavoidable result, involve the death of the fetus. However, so the argument continues, in all such cases the termination of the pregnancy is not the actual aim of the operation. The primary aim is the preservation of the life of the woman. Furthermore, so the argument continues, it is only by means of such drastic techniques that the life of the woman can be preserved. Consequently, so the argument concludes, in these cases, and in these cases alone, surgical intervention having abortive effects is morally justified.

As stated previously, the moral considerations that we adduced in discussing the biological argument in its first version are relevant also in this context. To begin with, let us note that such cases as we have just mentioned are extremely rare. But

61. Cf. Grisez, *Abortion*, pp. 32 ff., for a fuller discussion of these and other cases.

that aside—it is not a morally relevant consideration—there is the fact that as voluntary agents we have the duty to be informed about the relevant parameters of our actions. If a woman is going to engage in intercourse possibly leading to conception, it is her duty to be aware of her state of health, and of her ability—or inability—to bring a pregnancy to term. Engaging in the act is the acceptance of responsibility for the outcome[62] —in this case, for the existence of a human life. The plea of ignorance about her condition will therefore have no extenuating force. On the contrary: It can only brand her as irresponsible. As to the possibility that the physiological condition developed during the pregnancy itself: First, with the exception of ectopic pregnancy itself, it is extremely unlikely that this should be the case. Second, and this is morally much more important, even if that eventuality should obtain, it is morally irrelevant as a consideration. To engage in an act leading to pregnancy is to engage in an act having moral implications. These implications depend on the act, not on the intention. If a fetus is a person, then it is morally just as wicked to engender a fetus on the condition that it pose no danger to our lives, as it is wicked to adopt a child on the condition that we can kill it should our own life be threatened. As to the case of ectopic pregnancy, that does not really constitute a problem. Since the fetus is doomed to death if it develops where it is—in a cavity other than the uterus—an attempt must be made to save its life, a genuine attempt—to the best of our ability. Therefore, what is indicated is an attempt at implantation in the uterine wall. This attempt may fail—in fact, it is highly likely that it will fail. However, the attempt must be made as early as possible and with the interests of the fetus at the focus of our attention, not those of the mother-to-be.[63]

62. The man has a similar responsibility, but that is not at issue here. In any case, the argument is similar.

63. For a different view, see Grisez, *Abortion,* p. 340. Grisez views the condition as pathological and therefore condones removal. That, however, is tantamount to saying that pathology justifies killing—a conclusion which is not affected by Grisez's acceptance of the doctrine of double effect.

Nevertheless, in spite of the considerations we have just proposed, the threat to the life of the mother is sometimes considered to be an excusing condition for abortion in virtue of something that has been called the doctrine of double effect. This doctrine is premised on the fact that some acts have two consequences, both of which are inevitable outcomes of the act itself: a good consequence on the one hand and a bad one on the other. The doctrine itself then has it that nevertheless such acts are morally acceptable and that the bad outcome is morally excusable if the following conditions are met:

(1) the act, considered as such and in itself, is not morally bad;

(2) the agent's intention in performing the act is directed toward the good effect only;

(3) the bad effect is not a necessary and temporally prior means to the good result; and

(4) there are grave reasons for considering the act in the first place: reasons of a gravity proportionate to the badness of one of the effects.[64]

Clearly, the argument continues, the case of a pregnancy involving a threat to the life of the mother permits of abortion. For, the act of saving the mother, whatever its medical nature may be, meets condition (1). It also meets condition (2), since only the good effect is intended. It meets condition (3), since there will be no causal chain leading to the good result of saving the mother and involving the death of the fetus as one of its necessary, antecedent links. Instead, the two—good effect and bad effect—are contemporaneous and materially identical. And finally, condition (4) is also met: the life of the mother—of a person—is at stake.

If the assumptions of this argument are granted, then the conclusion does seem to follow: Abortion would be justified in such

64. For a further discussion, see J. T. Mangan, S.J., "An Historical Analysis of the Principle of Double Effect," *Theological Studies* 10 (1949): 40–61. See also Grisez, *Abortion,* pp. 329 ff.; Callahan, *Abortion,* pp. 422–26 passim.

cases as we have mentioned. However, as we have noted so
many times before, the acceptability of a conclusion depends
not merely on the logic of its argument, but also on the acceptability of its premises. In this particular case, at least two of these
may be doubted [65]—premise (2) and premise (4), to be precise.
What does premise (2) really amount to? Stripped of its particular formulation, it amounts to this: that if we ignore the bad
effects of our acts, then the fact that we only intend the good
makes the act morally acceptable. And premise (4) adds the
condition that this will be the case if and only if the alternative
to the act is something at least as bad as the bad effect. In other
words, premise (4) adds the provisions for a calculus when
premise (2) goes into effect. In somewhat more formal terminology, this particular aspect of the argument could be repre-
sented as follows: If we have a particular situation S which
would obtain if an act A were not performed, and if R_G and R_B
are the concomitant good and bad results of act A respectively,
then it is morally acceptable to perform act A so long as (1)
we can do A by intending only R_G (and possibly by ignoring
R_B), and (2) the badness of S is at least as great or greater
than that of R_B. Since R_B and R_G are concomitant, and R_G is
the intended outcome of A, R_G and R_B must also stand in proportion to each other. In fact, since R_G is the intended outcome,
it must be the opposite of S. In which case, the value of R_G must
be greater than or equal to that of R_B. From this it emerges very
clearly that in employing the doctrine of double effect, we are
really engaging in a covert application of a utilitarian calculus.
Not only is that entirely unacceptable to many proponents of
the very doctrine,[66] it also requires that we previously establish
utilitarianism as a defensible and indeed correct moral theory.
And on that score, there can be grave doubts.[67] Nor are these
the only replies that can be made to the argument from double
effect. As a further consideration, the following question ought

65. For a different analysis, see Grisez, *Abortion*.
66. For example, to Grisez.
67. Cf. chap. 6 of this book.

to be borne in mind: If the two consequences of the act are as closely interconnected as premise (3) says they must be, how can condition (2) be fulfilled except by an act of deliberate self-deception—of what the existentialists would call an act of "bad faith"? In which case, is not the willing of the good intention also a willing of the bad consequent—except that we decide to ignore it? On all of these counts, surely, the doctrine of double effect must fail. In which case, it cannot come to the moral defense of a biological solution to the problem of abortion.

The preceding exhausts, in the main and in a general way, the biological argument for abortion from the mother-to-be's point of view. There are variations which can be run on it. For instance, instead of dealing with cases that involve the death of the prospective mother as highly likely—or even certain—the argument could consider cases where, carrying the fetus to term would "merely" result in her being physically disabled in a permanent manner. But, as we said, these are merely variations on the more dramatic theme of death, discussed above. The deciding issue always is whether or not the fetus is a person or has the moral status of a person. Further crucial factors here are whether the condition is the result of a voluntary act or the result of rape, excusable ignorance, or the like. In none of these situations is the threat to the mother-to-be, in and by itself, the ultimate factor. To put it in a nutshell, facts of biology and physiology simply are incompetent to decide an issue in ethics.

Or are they? There are three sorts of cases in which the biological facts of the matter frequently have been thought to be deciding: (a) situations involving eugenic considerations; (b) cases where we know with certainty that the child to be born will be grossly deformed physically or mentally retarded; and (c) incidents of incest. Here, so popular argument would have it, abortions are demanded by the very biological facts of the respective cases.

Let us begin with (a) situations involving eugenic considerations. The argument here, briefly, is this. There are various diseases and conditions of a debilitating nature which are passed on from parents to children by means of the genetic makeup which the latter inherit. Huntington's chorea, PKU (phenylketo-nuria), Tay-Sachs disease, and hemophilia immediately come to mind.[68] If not immediately debilitating to the child when born, such conditions ultimately prove to be exceedingly debilitating or even fatal. In any case, they are conditions which, to say the least, are deviations from any normally understood human genetic norm and are exceedingly undesirable. In the interest of maintaining or creating a "better" human stock, we ought to remove the genes that are responsible for these conditions from the gene pool. One way—indeed, the easiest way—to cull them is to abort all those pregnancies where such genetic defects manifest themselves. Nor is this at all a chance sort of operation involving guesswork and a crystal ball. Amniocentesis can tell us in some of those cases with absolute certainty whether the condition in question is present. In others, the mere fact that one of the parents (or both) is a known carrier of the gene gives sufficient likelihood to the hypothesis that the fetus itself is either a carrier of the defective gene, suffers from the disease, or both. In either case, in the interest of removing the undesir-able trait and of making absolutely sure that no such trait is passed on, abortion is called for. In other words, abortions are sanctioned by eugenic biological considerations.

This argument from eugenics is by no means new. It has had various and respectable proponents. Not the least of these was Plato who, in his *Republic*,[69] advocated both eugenic abortions and infanticide, should the child in question prove to be of what he considered an inferior or otherwise unacceptable nature. However, when considering abortion from this point of view, several factors should be borne in mind. The first of these is that, contrary to initial appearances, the argument is not purely biological in nature. It contains a series of value judgments hav-ing to do with the moral acceptability of the thesis of eugenics as applied to human beings and with the question of what pre-

68. Cf. Grisez, *Abortion,* pp. 29 ff., 93 and passim; Callahan, *Abor-tion,* pp. 254–55 and passim.

69. Cf. chap. 16. Infanticide is the real substance of Plato's discussion, but abortion also falls under its purview.

cisely counts as a "better" human being. Let us consider these in turn. As to the thesis of eugenics itself, neither biology—that is, genetics—nor any other science can tell us that it is morally acceptable. At best, biology can tell us what is likely to be biologically possible, what is genetically feasible, and what the predicted outcome of an accumulation of certain genes in the gene pool of humanity may be. It might even—just barely—be able to tell us what would be biologically and genetically advantageous for humanity from a pragmatic point of view. But it cannot tell us whether eugenic interference in the gene pool is as such morally justified. Certainly, those of a Judeo-Christian or Islamic religious bent would object to such interference in the manner proposed as sacrilegious, striking at the very heart of the thesis that man is created in the image of God. But even without an appeal to such convictions, the question of the morality of such interference is still open. From the fact that it is possible, it does not follow that it should be done. Biology and genetics are descriptive, not normative, disciplines. Consequently they are incompetent to decide the issue.

As to the question of what constitutes a "better" human being, it is closely related to what has been said: What counts as a better human being may be defined in biological or genetic terms, but it does not follow that it *ought* to be defined in that manner. In point of fact, there is no overwhelming reason why it should. For, consider: 'Better' is an evaluative term and as such carries with it an essential element of comparison. The state of affairs or thing labeled 'better' requires something else with which it is to be compared in order for the label 'better' to have any justification. However, what is taken as the basis of the comparison, what is to count as the other member of this opposition, is a matter of choice: It is relative to the particular purpose in question and to the particular state of affairs. If our aim is to produce a kind of human being that can easily adjust to certain urban conditions or that fits easily into a certain social context, then what counts as better is not dictated by biological factors but by sociological considerations. If our aim is to produce an emotionally well-adjusted being with particular intellec-

tual and emotional characteristics, then psychological criteria
predominate; and so on. In other words, what would count biologically as a better individual—physically fit and well adapted
for survival—might, from the point of view of sociology, psychology, and so on be deemed extremely undesirable and not at
all better. And, of course, we might employ other criteria entirely: criteria dictated by religious, aesthetic, or even philosophical considerations. The point is that the selection of a
standard of comparison—for what is to count as better—lies
outside the competence of biology. Nonbiological considerations are what determine which of these various possible mean-
ings of 'better' is to be accepted. Biological means may be
brought in to ensure the implementation of the program decided
upon by the selection of a so-called better state of affairs, but
that is the whole extent of the matter.[70]

The second general fact that we should note about this argument is that considered as a whole it is a non sequitur: its conclusion does not follow from its premises. The basic assumption
here is that the gene pool of *homo sapiens* should be filtered of
undesirable, physically and mentally deleterious genes, so that
ultimately a better human race will result. Even if that assumption were to be accepted, and even if the issue of what is to
count as a better human being had somehow been decided, the
conclusion that abortions are morally acceptable would still not
follow. That is to say, all else aside, from the assumption that
the gene pool ought to be filtered it does not follow that the
genetically defective or eugenically undesirable genes ought to
be removed by means of aborting future carriers of such genes.
Infanticide, even judicial execution on genetic grounds, would
be equally as licensed by the premise. Further still, not even
these other drastic measures really follow from the assumption.
All that follows from the latter is that the relevant genes should
be deleted from or somehow be made unavailable to the gene
pool of the remainder. To this effect, various other, morally less

70. The preceding is merely an instance of the general principle that
value judgments have no place in a science but either precede or follow
the construction of the science itself.

questionable methods are available: compulsory sexual absti-
nence, contraception, strictly enforced breeding laws, or even
sterilization immediately come to mind. All of these would
achieve the desired result, yet none of these would raise the
same moral problems. Therefore, so far as the principle of eugenics is concerned, the license to kill in general, and the license
to abort in particular, need not be granted. (As an aside from
a purely practical point of view, frequently it would be easier
to sterilize than to abort.)

Finally, there is this third consideration: To be sure, in a
great many cases, such as with Tay-Sachs disease, we can tell
without risk of error whether the fetus is genetically deviant in
the relevant sense or not. In many other instances, however, this
is not the case. While we can say that there is likelihood that genetic abnormalities and associated functional disorders obtain,
we lack certitude. Huntington's chorea is a case in point. And in
some cases, the degree of genetic malformation—something
which, as in the case of Down's syndrome, frequently is so important—cannot as yet be determined in utero. If we abort in
these cases for eugenic reasons, we should be aborting on the
basis of guesswork. Educated guesswork, to be sure, but guesswork nevertheless. To be certain, infanticide and not abortion
would have to be the answer. That is to say, even if the principle
underlying this whole argument were to be granted, and even
if we did agree that killing is the only way to ensure the deletion
of the undesirable genes from the gene pool, it would not follow
that abortion is the properly justified means of doing so. What
would follow is that we should kill as soon as we are certain of
the extent of the genetic damage, and even of the fact of genetic
damage itself. In some cases, as we have said, this cannot easily
be determined prior to birth. In such cases, a wait-and-see pol-
icy is the only justified solution. Infanticide—sometimes even
homicide, if the defect shows itself late, as in the case of Huntington's chorea—are entailed by the premises. And that, by and
large, is deemed to be out of the question.

This brings us to (b) situations where we know with certainty, or as near certitude as can be expected, that the entity to

be born will have serious mental and/or physical defects. There
are various diseases which, when contracted prior to conception
either by the mother or by the father, have such effects on the
fetus. Some of the venereal diseases come to mind. There are
also diseases which, when contracted by the mother alone, during certain stages of the pregnancy, make it extremely likely
that the child-to-be will be deformed. Similarly with drugs.
Rubella and thalidomide are two well-known instances.[71] Likewise, there are genetic and morphological abnormalities and defects in a fetus attributable to various factors, the age of the
mother being one among them—Down's syndrome comes to
mind. All of these cases, more or less definitely detectable during pregnancy, result in deformations and handicaps. These are
medical facts. And given these facts, the argument then goes on
something like this:

> The child who will be born in such cases may not be able
> to live in any other way than as a basket-case, confined to
> a wheelchair or otherwise restricted to an institution for the
> rest of his life. If the child were aware of his situation, it
> would spell a life of horror for him. In any case, it means
> a senseless drain on the resources of the community were
> the child to live. But aside from all this, and more impor-
> tantly from a biological point of view, according to which
> the survival of the fittest is the all-important consideration,
> such a child is unfit to live and ought not to be born. Abor-
> tion, therefore, is required.

Undeniably, there is a point to this argument. And the point
will be the more apparent, the more we are familiar with children born of syphilitic parents, of mothers who have contracted
rubella or who have taken drugs like thalidomide during the

71. On rubella, cf. Callahan, *Abortion,* pp. 93–114, and Grisez, *Abortion,* p. 29 and passim. Callahan reviews various research done on the
effects of rubella and concludes that deformation is not inevitable, nor
need the degree of deformation be serious. On thalidomide, see St. John-
Stevas, *The Right to Life,* chap. 1; Grisez, *Abortion;* Callahan, *Abortion,*
pp. 92 and 93.

crucial stages of their pregnancies. There is little doubt that the
children of such pregnancies have a good chance of being deformed; just as there is little doubt that pregnancies where the
fetus gives indications of Down's syndrome will result in a
severely retarded mongoloid child.[72] However—and here we
proceed to the analysis of the argument—there is equally as
little doubt that the degree of deformation as well as its severity
do vary, and that there is no way to determine its extent prior
to the actual birth. Therefore, if the biological considerations
are overriding, there will be no way to tell beforehand precisely which pregnancies should be aborted and which not. After
all, the biological criteria with which we are to operate must
allow for some variations and some deviations from the norm.
The affected fetuses just could fall within the range permitted
by the criterion. Thus, in some cases the ensuing deformation
could be very slight: only a minor visual impairment or some
such. But at the present time it is difficult if not impossible to
tell, prior to the termination of the pregnancy, whether a deformation actually does obtain, and if it does, to what degree.
Once more, infanticide would seem to be the answer. But even
if, somehow, certainty should obtain in all such cases, there is
still this ever-present factor of which we must not lose sight:
Are biological criteria the only relevant determinants of personhood? In fact, are they determinants at all? Are gross physical
abnormalities, be they of a morphological or a neurological nature, sufficient to exclude someone from the category of being
a person? If not, then the biological criteria will simply be incompetent in this domain, and no amount of physiological abnormality will be relevant.

As to (c) the argument from incest, this can easily be shown
to be based on mistaken data. It used to be a fairly common
assumption—and, indeed, it still is—that the children of an incestuous union are insane, physically deformed, or otherwise
subnormal. Further, it used to be common doctrine that such
deformation or other deviation from the norm was inevitably

72. Amniocentesis, once again, will provide us with data on that score.

the case should an incestuous union occur. The plain fact of the matter is that no such thing is true. To be sure, incestuous unions are more likely to result in the emergence of deleterious genes should these genes be recessive in those engaged in that union. However, as any husbandman or breeder of cattle is able to tell us, incestuous breeding—inbreeding, as it is sometimes called—has its own very definite advantages. Not only does it bring out deleterious genes and undesirable characteristics, should such be present; it has the advantage of bringing out precisely those recessive genes that we want to see established in the particular species. Therefore, from a purely biological point of view, the claim that incestuous unions inevitably result in biologically unsuitable individuals is without basis.[73] Furthermore, over and above this, there is the following question: Ought an otherwise probably perfectly normal fetus be killed merely because its progenitors stand in a certain relationship to each other? A relationship, furthermore, which, except in the case of monozygotic twins, is largely of social, not biological significance? To be sure, there is the biblical passage that the sins of the parents shall be visited on the children until the third and fourth generation. But if we accept that as a valid point at all—if we are moving within the Judeo-Christian Islamic framework—then we must also accept that "vengeance is mine! saith the Lord" and must accept the further point that the sins will be visited by God, not us. Of course, we need not accept the basic premise. In which case the whole argument disappears, and we are back to the facts of genetics.

Finally, in concluding the argument from incest—or indeed in considering any biological argument—we must not lose sight of the one particular point that we have made time and again: Biological considerations pure and simple are incapable of providing us with an answer to an essentially moral problem. They cannot tell us whether we ought to proceed eugenically, whether we ought to abort defective or deviant fetuses, and the like. In short, they are incompetent to tell us what is and what is not,

73. Cf. Grisez, *Abortion,* pp. 343 ff., for a similar discussion.

morally speaking, the case. The whole issue can also be considered from a slightly different angle: from the point of view of the distinction between the various qualities of life possible for a being of human parentage. The biological argument, in its various forms, tells us that if the quality of the life to be expected is not human—is not biologically within the human norm —then we ought to kill whatever or whomever would otherwise lead that life. In arguing thus, the biological position assumes not merely that it knows what it is to be human, it also assumes that to fall within the human norm *and within it alone,* is to be a person. In other words, it assumes that to be a person has something to do with having human biological characteristics —be these of a morphological or a neurological or a genetic sort. Admittedly, that assumption may be true. But it is of such overwhelming importance that it cannot merely be assumed. It has to be shown. Only when it has been shown that to be a person—a moral agent and the recipient of moral privileges—is to be an entity with a particular (human) biological makeup, only then will biological considerations in their various shapes and forms be relevant to the argument. However—and this is an ironic twist to the whole enterprise—they will not be relevant, let alone decisive, with respect to who (or what) should live and who (or what) should not. They will only be relevant in determining who is a person. Separate *moral* premises must still be introduced to settle the issue of whether it is moral to kill something that is not a person merely because it is not a person, because it is biologically defective, because it is convenient to do so, or whatever.[74]

A final note on this aspect of the biological argument. If, somehow, we were to decide that abortions are permissible in cases of extreme deviation from the norm, the result would be simply staggering. Not so much in the number of abortions that

74. Even from the putative fact that a living being such as the fetus is not a person in the biologically determinate sense, it does not follow that we are at liberty to kill it if we please. To be sure, if we did kill it, the extreme gravamen of murder would not attach to our act. That does not, however, mean that it would be without moral consequences.

would have to be performed—although this would indeed be great—but in the repercussions of this practice, once its underlying principle is applied consistently. The principle, let us recall, is that all biologically unfit or unsuitable beings born of human parentage should be killed. Consistency of application is a sine qua non of moral principles. Therefore, if this principle were to be applied consistently, it would require that we should kill all hopeless and congenitally deformed, all mentally abnormal by birth, and all otherwise congenitally deviant human beings. This was in fact done, at least in part, by the Nazis in Germany prior to and during World War II. This practice, as well as the principle underlying it, was later condemned by the Allies at Nuremberg, and most people would condemn them today. However, if the convictions expressed at Nuremberg are taken at all seriously, then those who advocate abortion on the biological and eugenic grounds just mentioned find themselves in a logical bind. For, it would be flatly contradictory to maintain such a moral stance on the actions of the Nazis and at the same time to advocate abortion on the very grounds on which the actions of the Nazis were condemned. That is to say, this inconsistency would obtain if a fetus is a person or has a moral status essentially equivalent to that of a person. And with this, we are back at our persistently recurring problem: Who counts as a person? But before we address ourselves to this issue, we shall have to consider several other arguments in favor of abortion.

The Ecological Argument

"This spaceship Earth!" The phrase has gained currency of late, and its implications are being appreciated more and more widely. It bespeaks the growing realization that the ecology of our planet constitutes a closed system, where any drastic change in one of its components will have catastrophic results for the remainder. It is in this spirit that the current antipollution groups are active, and it is for this reason that legislation is finally beginning to be drafted on that very score. However, this sentiment also lies at the heart of an argument—indeed, of a series of arguments—for abortion. In fact, a good case could be made from saying that the abortion angle is the oldest aspect of ecological concern—older, even, than considerations of pollution and the availability of natural resources.

The argument has two sides: one dealing with the fate of persons who are already alive and on the scene, and another dealing with the situation of those who are about to be aborted. In its generic form, the argument goes something like this:

> The earth, like any closed and finite ecological system, has only a fixed amount of resources and therefore has only a limited ability to retain a viable ecological balance. This balance becomes more and more upset—less and less viable—the more demands are made upon it for sustenance and the more it is polluted. If human population continues to grow, not only will the available resources themselves become exhausted, but the very environmental balance will become such that the manufacturing processes which gave rise to the situation in the first place—processes necessary to the survival of the expanded population group—will become impossible. To put the point crudely, both biologically and economically, the earth will become so polluted as to become totally unfit for human habitation. All people would die. Obviously, this would be an extremely undesirable state of affairs. Therefore, in order that those already on the scene may survive—and perhaps survive in a manner worth surviving—abortion should be employed as a means of controlling population growth. Furthermore, in the interest of generations still to come, abortion would ensure that the population would grow at such a minimal level, or even remain stable, that the possibility of *their* survival would thereby be ensured.[75]

75. For a discussion of abortion as a means of population control, albeit in a different context, cf. Grisez, *Abortion,* pp. 159 ff., 261–66, 293–94, and passim.

This argument may be varied, depending on whose point of view we take. As it stands, it represents the situation largely from the point of view of those already on the scene. If we were to take the side of the fetus or person-to-be, we could argue that it would be in the best interest of such an entity that it not be born into an ecologically disastrous situation where it would die from breathing the air, drinking the water, or eating the food.

There is no question but that the facts alluded to in this argument are just that: facts. The earth *is* a closed ecological system in a delicate homeostatic balance. The whole can take only so much strain before it collapses. It is also true that an unchecked population growth will require such a degree of interference in this balance, merely in order to keep the population alive, that sooner or later this balance will become irredeemably upset so that none of us will survive in the end.

These are facts, and there are figures and controlled scientific data to establish them beyond doubt. But from these facts as premises, the desired conclusion does not follow. It neither follows that abortions are necessary as a means of controlling population growth, nor does it follow that they are morally acceptable. What does follow—without a doubt—is that population growth should not proceed unchecked. But there are various ways in which such a check could be effected without resorting to abortions. Contraceptive techniques preventive of fertilization (conception) are one example; compulsory sterilization after having engendered a certain number of children (two, to achieve zero population growth) is another; and so on. None of these methods involve the moral problem presented by abortion, since none of them involve the killing of a (potential) human being. Therefore, there is no contradiction involved in subscribing to a Malthusian sentiment out of ecological concern, on the one hand, and rejecting abortion, on the other. Once again, therefore, the thesis that abortions are necessary has not been proven.

But for the moment, let us suppose that in the preceding considerations the case for abortion has been made, and has been made on the Malthusian and ecological grounds alleged. We could then ask ourselves what the general principle was that underlay this train of reasoning. And here the answer would be the following principle:

> If an individual or a group of individuals threaten the survival of a larger group by the mere fact of their existence —by their being alive—and the requirements that go along with their existence threaten the survival of the rest, then that individual or group of individuals ought to be killed.

This principle may or may not be correct. A separate and extended investigation into the ethics of the matter would have to be conducted to find this out. But if accepted, the principle ought to be applied consistently. That is to say, it ought to be applied not merely to fetuses and potential persons but to every member of the society. If applied in that way, it would mean that all those individuals who are in the care of society or even are mere members of it but without fulfilling an essential function—idiomatically, all those who are mere "mouths to feed"—ought to be killed. This would affect quite a number of people: the incurably ill, the aged, and the like. Even those not demonstrably necessary for the survival of society could be deleted. It is not always clear that our consistency would go this far. But if it does not, what happens to the morality of this position on abortion?

Let me put the point somewhat differently. If the ecological argument has any point at all, it is that the survival of *homo sapiens* as a species is a good and that his disappearance would be an undesirable state of affairs. It is to this end that population growth is to be checked. But not checked in a way that will seriously threaten survival of the whole, for that would be a self-defeating exercise. Checked, rather, by the killing of those who are not essential to the survival of the community and whose existence would in fact threaten it; namely, fetuses, children, the aged and unproductive, those in the care of society without providing any return, and the like. The eco-

logical argument has it that abortion is the correct solution to
the problem; that is to say, that of the various candidates just
mentioned, only fetuses ought to be killed. But the question is,
why the choice of death candidates should be thus limited. If
the criterion is the one advanced by the principle stated above,
then infanticide, senicide, and indeed any killing of anyone not
within the socially necessary bracket would be just as correct
as abortion. To argue otherwise would be inconsistent. Hence
consistent implementation of the principle underlying this argument would force us to conclude that all those who are not of
demonstrable use to the society or who are not needed for its
survival, ought to be deleted. Death candidates ought to come
from every such category.[76]

The ecological argument, therefore, fails on two counts: It
does not establish that abortion is the only means of effecting
population control, and it does not establish that as such a
means, it is morally defensible. Since that was the intended
thrust of the argument, it is only fair to conclude that the ecological argument fails.

So far, we have been concerned with arguments and positions that have considered abortion from the point of view of
its consequences; and we have considered both negative and
positive points of view. In our discussion we have been concerned to show that the logic of the various positions is defective—or, at least, is based on principles of such a sweeping
nature that, if consistently applied, the upshot would be morally
unacceptable even to those who advocate them in the first place.
In our discussion we have also seen how frequently the moral
is confused with the factual, the normative with the descriptive.
Part of that confusion undoubtedly is due to simple misunderstanding; but no small part of it is due to the fact that the various standpoints—whether religious, biological, ecological, or
what have you—are not explicitly ethical in nature. That is to

76. I forego all consideration of life-style in this particular context.
The argument would be essentially the same, complicated only by con-
siderations as to what counts as an ecologically acceptable environment.
"Man does not live by bread alone."

say, the difficulties we have encountered result largely from the fact that the considerations adduced by the proponents of the respective arguments do not proceed on the plane in which the problem of abortion arose: the moral plane.

However, leaving that aside, there is the other factor we mentioned above, namely, that all have been concerned with consequences. That is to say, they were all intended to show that abortion would materially benefit the mother-to-be, the society in which she finds herself, or even, paradoxically enough, the fetus or child-to-be itself. In other words, all the arguments considered so far purported to have a very real, tangible reason for advocating abortion; and they have attempted to make good this claim by somehow establishing that unless abortions were permitted, the goods that they envision would be lost.

But there is another sort of argument that has common currency: one that has no tangible benefit to offer mankind in return for an abortion—no physical, physiological, psychological, or ecological plum. Its only reason for advocating abortion is unreservedly personal and idiosyncratic in nature. To put it bluntly, the sort of argument I have in mind has it that abortion is wholly a matter of personal convenience and/or preference. Let us call it the personal argument.

The Personal Argument

This sort of argument is really a more or less coherently formulated or tightly interconnected series of contentions and considerations. It is based on the premise that a woman is a person, and that as such she has certain basic and inalienable rights. In particular, she has a right to her body, to her life-style, and to happiness. From these premises the argument continues as follows:

> In many cases the birth of a child and the subsequent duties and cares attendant on this—indeed, the very pregnancy itself and all the discomforts and inconveniences it involves—substantially interfere with these rights. In a word, they interfere with the woman's rights as a person: her liberty and her pursuit of happiness. Therefore, given

that she is a person and given that these are her rights; given, furthermore, that it is her body which is so intimately involved in the affair, it is her right to terminate the pregnancy or to have it terminated should she so decide. Furthermore, she is the *only* person who has the right to decide whether or not the pregnancy is to be terminated. It is her body, her physical and mental well-being that are involved—but, above all, it is her body. Over what is hers, indeed over what is thus she herself, she has a complete right of self-determination. If she and she alone were to decide to have an abortion, that would be her right, just as it would be her right to have an appendectomy, a tonsillectomy, or to have a cancerous growth removed. The fetus, in its early stages of development, is nothing but an undifferentiated lump of cells. As such, no rights accrue to it; and even if they did, the rights of the woman are prior and take precedence. Consequently, if she decides to have an abortion, then it is her right to do so and to have her decision carried out, irrespective of how anyone else might think about the matter.[77]

This sort of argument, in one form or another, is frequently put forward by those who agitate for women's rights. In fact, the case of abortion has become a central plank in the platform of the movement commonly called women's liberation. The right to abortion on demand is here presented as nothing less than a woman's right to be a person.[78]

But if we consider the matter rationally and dispassionately, several things become obvious at the very outset: The right to be a person cannot mean the right to an abortion on demand.

77. For a discussion of similar points, see Callahan, *Abortion,* chap. 13, pp. 448 and passim; Lawrence Lader, *Abortion* (Indianapolis: Bobbs-Merrill Co., 1966); Thomas Szasz, "The Ethics of Abortion," *Humanist* 26 (September–October 1966): 148. See also the various articles in Guttmacher, *Legalized Abortion.*

78. Cf. Guttmacher, *Legalized Abortion.*

It cannot mean that, unless at least one of two things is granted: (a) that a fetus is not a person, does not have the status of a person, and in fact is nothing more nor less than a part of the woman's body, much like a cancerous growth; (b) that even if a fetus had the status of a person, its rights are superseded by the rights of the woman who bears it. If (a) were granted, then a fetus would be considered a nonautonomous part of a woman's body. In which case, since a person has a right to decide what should or should not be done to his body, the woman would have the right to have that part of, or growth in, her body removed, even if only because of a personal and momentary whim. The fact that what would thus be removed from her died could be seen as confirmation of the contention that it was part of her body all along, and that this death should not be taken seriously. No more seriously, that is, than the death of, say, a liver once it is removed from a body. As to (b), if it were granted, it would thereby be admitted that a fetus is not a part of a woman's body. But the clause about the ranking of moral rights would ensure that abortions would not be morally reprehensible, since the rights of the woman will always outrank those of the fetus.

Should either of these assumptions be granted? Or, put differently, are either (a) or (b) reasonable assumptions under the circumstances? Let us begin with (a) the assumption that a fetus is a nonautonomous part of a woman's body, no more and no less than a growth in her body, on a par with all other growths. This assumption must be rejected because it is factually mistaken on at least two counts. First, it is a characteristic of growths within a body that, whether they are malignant or benign, they essentially have the same genetic structure and makeup as the remainder of the cells constitutive of that body within which they grow. This is not the case with a fetus. The genetic structure and makeup of a fetus differs by half from the woman within whose body it is. Nor is that surprising. After all, the genetic information that its cells contain is the result of the fusion of two cells, both of which come from respectively different bodies and both of which contribute one-half of the genetic information necessary for the growth and development of the fetus. From this it therefore follows that a fetus cannot simply be classified either as a part of the woman's body in any ordinary sense, or as a cancerlike growth.

Second, it is characteristic of growths that their development does not involve histological specialization into distinct organ groups, where the ultimate outcome of its natural development is an independently existing unit. Growths never specialize in this way and always retain a dependence on their parent body. Therefore, once again, the comparison of a fetus to a growth within a body will not bear scrutiny. It is equally obvious that the same refutation holds, mutatis mutandis, for the contention that a fetus is a part of a woman's body.

Nor, to vary the approach in keeping with contemporary discussion, is it correct to say that although indeed not a cancerlike growth, a fetus is essentially like a parasite and that the host of a parasite always has the right to rid itself of the latter, even at the expense of the parasite's life. The reason is that a fetus is not a parasite. A parasite, by definition, is a noxious being destructive of its host which has invaded the host without the host's consent.[79] Whereas it might just barely be said that the life-style of a fetus in its various stages of development approximates that of a parasite, still it is not correct that it fits the description of such an invader. As our discussion concerning the moral dimensions of intercourse and conception has amply brought out, the fetus cannot be an invader but is at best an unintentionally invited guest. Since to ask this guest to leave would be to kill it, the situation takes on the dimensions of murder that we discussed.

Furthermore, in what sense is the fetus parasitic? Surely, only in that it depends for its nourishment on the woman who bears it. But if that is true, then, by parity of reasoning, anyone who

79. The argument of the fetus as a pursuer, found in Jewish literature, is essentially covered by this—the intentional act of pursuit excepted. For a discussion of this approach, see Baruch Brody, "Abortion and the Sanctity of Human Life," *American Philosophical Quarterly* 10, no. 2 (1973): 133–40, where references to wider literature are given.

is solely responsible for the nourishment of a human being—
or, more accurately, anyone who is solely and directly responsible for its physical survival—has the right to decide whether
or not the latter should die. This, however, is not generally accepted as correct. We generally deny that a mother—or a father—has the right to decide on the life or death of her (his)
completely dependent infantile children. The fact of sole and
immediate support is not taken as an exceptive circumstance.

But, so it might be said, the circumstances surrounding
pregnancy are extenuating themselves. In fact, not merely are
they extenuating, they are special and unusual to such a degree
that comparison with any other situation would be inappropriate. No one else could support the life of the fetus except the
mother, whereas in all other cases the particular life in question could be maintained by someone else.

However, the plain fact of the matter is that the premises on
which this reasoning rests are not true. Not merely are ovary
transplants possible, it is also possible to transplant the fetus
from one woman's uterus into that of another—or even to put
it into a completely new sort of environment, an environment
that is not only not alive, but also mechanical, like a complex
assemblage of biological apparati. In other words, there is
nothing magical or unique in a particular woman for a particular fetus, any more than there is something magical or
unique about a particular mother for a particular child. What
is essential is that the needs of the fetus be met. But there are
a myriad of other people who could meet them—just as there
are a myriad of other people who could raise a particular child.
Furthermore, the age of the artificial womb is upon us.[80] Fetuses
have lived in artificial environments such a length of time that
they were killed only because of fear of legal complications
should they be permitted to develop further. Consequently, the
plea of special circumstances around which the argument centers, lapses. Of course, in and by itself this does not imply that
a woman does not have the right to an abortion. What it does

---

80. Cf. Chamberlain, "An Artificial Placenta."

imply, however, is that if she does have that right, then she must have it for some other reason. The fact that she is the sole supporter of the fetus is a mere biological accident and not a necessary feature. Furthermore, as such it is without any moral implications—at least, without implications of the sort suggested.

This leaves an assumption that we have discussed before, but that might just as well be considered from a new angle: the assumption that the rights of the woman take precedence over those of the fetus. Two reasons are generally adduced in favor of this assumption: that the rights of the mother have temporal priority and hence carry greater weight; and that since she is the major agent involved in the process, and above all a person, her rights should precede.

As to the first, if it were admitted by us, then we should also be bound to accept the further contention that the rights of older people in general take precedence over those of their progeny and of younger people. For instance, the rights of the grandmother would take precedence over those of the mother, and those, in turn, over the rights of the daughter. Consequently, by parity of reasoning, it would follow that if one of the progenitors desired the death of his or her progeny, he or she would have the right to bring about that death. Clearly, we admit no such thing. Therefore, by the same token, this premise of the present argument cannot be granted. Unless, that is, we are at the same time willing to implement far-reaching and profound changes in the whole of our ethical concerns. We *may* want to do this—but then, we should do this consistently. As to the second assumption, it goes to the very heart of the issue of abortion: to the question, namely, whether or not a fetus is a person. If a fetus is not a person nor has the moral status of a person, then the assumption is undebatable. Nor would it require a far-reaching and fundamental restructuring of our moral concepts. If a fetus is a person, however, then we would have a serious and genuine conflict of a moral sort, and the only way to resolve it would be by considering other aspects of

the case. Among other things, what we have said about intercourse as a de facto contract might just be relevant here.

Various other ethical considerations, as indeed the whole
problem of whether or not it is possible to rank moral rights
—and if it is possible, of how to do so—will have to enter our
deliberations. In fact, solution of this problem would involve
us in a thoroughgoing examination of the moral theory of rights
and obligations, an enterprise that transcends by far the parameters of our present deliberations. Nevertheless, even without
the result of such investigation, one point emerges clearly:
namely, that the issue of the conflict of the rights of mother
and fetus cannot be settled by mere statement, as the various
proponents of this sort of argument would have it. It may be
that in the end their contentions prove justified with respect to
the ranking. But in any area where a life is at stake, and where
one of the alternatives is the possibility of murder, "may be" is
not enough. It has to be shown.

EVALUATION

So far, we have considered arguments for and against abortion.
It has been my aim to show that the various arguments commonly presented on both sides of the issue are anything but
conclusive, and that in the majority of cases they are downright invalid. In the course of the preceding discussion, I have
on occasion asserted that this is right, that that is wrong, and
that certain moral facts do obtain. In making such statements,
I have expressed what in effect is my own conviction. This
conviction is not, however, suspended in logical space. It is
based on certain factual and moral premises, as well as on certain arguments having these as their basis. Since these premises
and arguments were formulated largely in response to many of
the issues discussed so far, a statement of my position could
well serve as a closing point of this chapter. Accordingly, it is
to a presentation and defense of my own views that I now
proceed.

To recapture what I have said in the beginning, the core of

the controversy concerning abortion can be stated simply in
the form of two questions: (1) In aborting a human pregnancy
prior to its natural termination in the course of events, are we
guilty of murder, or are we guilty of a lesser moral crime? Indeed, (2) are we guilty of a moral crime at all?

In what follows, I shall suggest that abortions performed
within a certain, more or less clearly defined period of fetal
development are murderous, whereas those performed prior
to this period are not. I shall also argue that this does not mean
that no moral gravamen attaches to the latter sort of action,
but that instead the moral seriousness of the act is reduced to
a degree commensurate with the stage of development of the
fetus. My argument for these conclusions will fall into three
parts. I shall begin by sketching a schematic analysis of acts in
terms of their objects. The purpose of this sketch will be to
delimit the sphere of the moral from that of the nonmoral. I
shall then present and argue for a particular definition of the
concept of a person, where the relevant criteria will be essentially neurological in nature. I shall conclude by arguing that,
given the preceding two factors, the solution to the problem
of abortion is as I have indicated above.

Moral vs. Nonmoral Actions

As traditionally understood, acts can be divided into two kinds:
those that are directed toward some object and those that are
not. Hitting a ball would be a good instance of the former;
doodling on a piece of paper, of the latter. Acts that are directed toward objects can once more be divided into those
that are directed toward persons and those that are directed
toward nonpersons. Examples of the former are giving a child
a sandwich or paying one's bill at the gas station; examples of
the latter are kicking a stone or bird-watching. Acts directed
toward persons are once again analyzable in a diversity of
ways: into those that are done with, and those that are done
without the consent of the particular person in question is but
one example. For our purposes, however, we need not pursue
these classifications any further. To delimit the sphere of the

moral from that of the nonmoral, particularly in the present context, what we have already said suffices. Thus, a schematic representation of our analysis so far would look something like this:

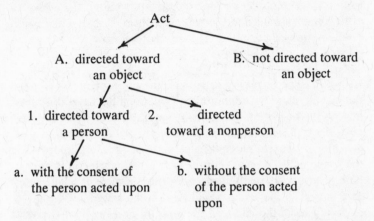

Act

A. directed toward
an object

B. not directed toward
an object

1. directed toward
a person

2. directed
toward a nonperson

a. with the consent of
the person acted upon

b. without the consent
of the person acted
upon

The analysis of acts up to this point is sufficient to permit us to indicate with some precision the domain of the moral: Acts of kind (1) have traditionally formed the core of moral inquiry, whereas acts of kind (2) have been deemed devoid of moral import.[81] In what follows we shall abide by this tradition. And having accepted it, we are obviously committed to the further thesis that only an act of killing visited upon a person can be an act of murder. Consequently, in order to show that abortions after a certain period of fetal development are murderous, we shall have to show that at the conclusion of the temporally preceding period of fetal development, a fetus has indeed become a person. That, however, will merely establish that an act of killing visited upon a fetus after that critical period of development *may* be murderous. It does not yet suffice to establish the conclusion that it is. Consequently, our final and concluding argumentation on the subject will be to

81. This is not to say that they may not be thought to have some other qualities, e.g., one of an aesthetic nature, etc.

that effect. It will show not merely that the possibility of murder obtains, but also that the possibility is in fact realized. All of this, of course, presupposes that we know what a person is, or, more correctly, it presupposes that we have criteria for the ascription of personhood and that after the so-called critical time, a fetus (normally) meets them. It is to a discussion of the notion of personhood, then, that we now turn.

The Concept of a Person

Although superficially perspicuous, the concept of a person is not at all easy to adumbrate. Traditionally, several criteria have been proposed which, both severally and together, have been deemed decisive. Chief of these have been morphology,[82] genealogy,[83] genetics,[84] and behavior.[85] As to morphology: Are the shape and the possession as well as arrangement of various limbs and organs really decisive in the question of what counts as a person? If so, criteria will have to be stated so vaguely as to permit us in the end to draw no hard and fast boundaries at all. For, clearly, the possession and arrangement of particular external limbs cannot be decisive: Moralist, lawyer, and layman alike agree in considering grossly deformed and congenitally crippled individuals as persons. Similarly with the possession—or lack of possession—and arrangement of various internal organs. In fact, at least one part of current thinking has it that so long as the ancestry of the entity in question is human, such anomalies must be discounted and the being considered a person.

The morphological criterion would therefore seem to yield to the genealogical one: To be a person is to be an offspring of a human being. But even here, practice is not consistent. For, by that token we ourselves, strictly speaking, could not

82. Cf. Grisez, *Abortion,* p. 131 and passim; Tooley, "Defense of Abortion and Infanticide," for this position.

83. Cf. Noonan, *The Morality of Abortion,* pp. 51–59 and passim; idem, "Abortion and the Catholic Church: A Summary History," *Natural Law Forum* 12 (1967): 126.

84. Noonan, "Abortion and the Catholic Church," pp. 128–29.

85. Cf. Callahan, *Abortion,* pp. 365 ff.

count as persons, since (a) the criterion makes personhood an inherited characteristic dependent upon the human status of one's progenitors, and (b) our ultimate progenitors certainly were not human. Furthermore, while restrictive in this sense, in another the criterion is too inclusive. For, by a process of reasoning similar to the one just indicated it would follow, mutatis mutandis, that our progeny, no matter what their characteristics and natures might be, would count as persons just as long as we ourselves do. In the light of our present knowledge of genetics, mutations, and evolutionary change, this cannot be accepted.

However, these last considerations suggest a refinement of the genealogical criterion: All and only those entities are persons which have a more or less human genetic makeup. In other words, a genetic criterion is substituted for a merely genealogical one. Once more, however, success evades us, for once again the criterion is not applied consistently. And that for good reasons: For the religiously inclined, it would entail that God and other immaterial entities could not be persons —an unwelcome consequence to say the least. And for those not of a religious bent, there remain two further issues: precisely where to draw the line with genetic changes—and for what reason. Even at the present time such radical genetic changes as the doubling of chromosomes do occur in beings that we account as unquestionably persons. Furthermore, all of the objections raised above against the morphological and genealogical criteria can be raised, mutatis mutandis, against the genetic one. After all, these criteria do find their essential biological base in genetic phenomena. Finally—to turn to a still more contemporary consideration—what are we to do with language-using animals like dolphins? Are we to accord them rationality without a vestige of personhood?

The considerations just advanced are nothing new. We have urged them at various times throughout the preceding discussion. But they also serve a useful purpose. They not only illustrate the difficulty in attempting to define 'person'; they also strain the traditional parameters of the discussion—in particular, the last series of considerations, involving as they do the notion of language-using and hence rational, but by any biological standard certainly nonhuman, beings. If we are really serious in countenancing the possibility—perhaps even the actuality—of these as rational beings, then we are faced with a threefold choice: *either* to admit them as persons in virtue of their rationality; or to admit them as persons in virtue of a characteristic had by them and us, but which so far we have not mentioned; or, finally, to deny that they are persons altogether.

Here, everything hinges on the concept of a rational being. So far, we have said relatively little about it, and it is now time to go into the concept in some detail. To begin with, let us note that the concept is tied not to actual behavior, but to inherent and constitutive potential. Thus, someone may be a rational being—have a certain nature—and yet not behave rationally. Such a lapse from rationality, even if it should be consistent, would not count against the claim that we have here a rational being, unless that deviation from rationality were a result of internal constitution. After all, we may choose—and choose consistently—to be irrational. Furthermore, we may be prevented from the exercise of our potential as rational beings either by internal malfunctioning, or by external chaotic situations or states of affairs. The second point to note is more definitive than the preceding: To be a rational being is to be capable of symbolic awareness of reality, that is to say, of responding to external reality by means of symbolic categorization processes that permit whatever it is that has this sort of awareness to apprehend the world as subsumed under certain more or less conventional categories of classification. Still differently, it is the ability to form judgments. Third, to count as a rational being, something must also have the capability for self-awareness. Fourth—and in a sense this overlaps with the last two criteria—the entity in question must be capable of internalizing and using a language.[86]

86. On the relationship between language and awareness, cf. Adam Schaff, *Language and Cognition,* R. S. Cohen, ed., Olgierd Wojtasiewicz, trans. (New York: McGraw-Hill, 1973), esp. part 3, which also has a

In my view, then, this is what it is to be a rational being. It will immediately be obvious that my definition does not include any reference to capabilities for emotions, for aesthetic appreciation, and the like. Nor does it involve anything like an appeal to the subconscious and similar Freudian and post-Freudian constructs. The reason for these omissions is very simple: We do not require them as necessary conditions for the ascription of the predicate 'rational being' to our paradigm examples of rational beings: to people. They may have them, and we shall consider them all the more "human" if they do; but if they do not, we do not cease to call them rational beings. One further thing stands out about this definition: It divorces the concept of being a rational being from any specific physical or biological constitution. And given this, we have our transition to a "species-free" definition of a person:

> A person is an entity that is a rational being; that is to say, it is an entity that has the present capabilities of symbolic awareness in the manner characteristic of rational beings as defined above. A person is an entity—any entity, irrespective of the precise nature of its constitution—that is either presently aware in a manner characteristic of rational beings, or can become thus aware without any change in the constitutive nature of its composition.

The advantages of this definition are immediately obvious: Personhood will be independent of precisely those elements that previously were seen to lead to difficulties. Personhood will depend solely on rational awareness. Nor need this awareness be actually present: the mere potential for it, as a constitutive potential, will suffice. In this way an individual, whether awake, asleep, or in a coma, will count as a person just as long as his constitutive nature is such as to permit rational awareness.

---

good though dated bibliography in the back. See also Noam Chomsky, *Cartesian Linguistics* (New York: Harper and Row, 1960). D. C. Dennett, *Content and Consciousness* (London: Routledge & Kegan Paul, 1969), proposes a slightly different analysis in terms of intentionality; however, Dennett retains the symbolic parameter of this definition.

Again, for a similar reason, mutatis mutandis, insanity will not prevent us from calling such a being a person. Likewise, this definition will enable us to countenance with equanimity the suggestion that animals not of the species *homo sapiens* might be persons: for example, dolphins. And certainly, this suggestion captures much that is at the core of religious contentions to the effect that the professed deity is a person. The only entities excluded will be those that lack the potential in the requisite sense.[87]

However, even if acceptable, as it stands the definition is still far from being clear. Precisely how is the notion of a constitutive potential to be understood? What is it "to be aware in a manner characteristic of rational beings" or to "have the present capability of rational awareness"? Furthermore, how is this rational awareness—or worse yet, the capability for rational awareness—to be recognized? In short, the definition needs to be clarified and supplemented by criteria.

All of these difficulties can be met by considering first this last question. The initial temptation is to fall back on physical states of affairs as indicator phenomena, to argue that the means whereby we can recognize actual or potential rationality must be accessible to us within the context of the world in which we move. And here, physical behavior immediately comes to mind: An entity will be deemed a rational being if and only if it engages in the sorts of activities—behaves in the sorts of ways—that traditionally have been associated with rational thought. Such a criterion, however, would be intolerably restrictive. It would permit us to include all and only those entities that actually evinced physical behavior of the requisite sort. In other words, it would allow us to consider as persons all and only those entities that actually behaved rationally in some recognizable way. But what of those who are comatose, catatonic, simply do not act in a physical manner, or are actually insane? Furthermore, the criterion neglects the fact that

87. The definition will force us to admit nonliving, nonbiological entities as persons so long as they satisfy the definition. I do not think that this constitutes a difficulty; quite the contrary.

one man's rationality may be another's insanity; indeed, that rationality vis-à-vis behavior can be recognized only by those within the same phenomenological culture group. Finally, what would this do to the clause about potential awareness in the original definition?

Fortunately, a solution to the difficulties is forthcoming. Again, it will involve physical manifestations. After all, these do constitute the only publicly accessible means for evaluating personhood. This time, however, the criterion does not involve the performance of some act or other, but instead centers around the constitution underlying such (possible) acts. In other words, the constitution of the entity itself is taken as an indicator phenomenon.

Let me give an example of what I mean. In biological entities of the species *homo sapiens,* that part of the organism which is generally considered to be the generative and originative part governing activities is the nervous system, in particular, that part of it which we call the central nervous system, with special emphasis on the brain. The nervous system in general and the brain in particular evince electrical activity of varying degrees of intensity, frequency, and complexity. This can be recorded by means of electroencephalographs. The electroencephalograms (EEGs for short) that result have a characteristic nature which—whether the human being is asleep or awake—can serve to distinguish his nervous activity from that, say, of a cat, a frog, or even a monkey. EEGs, then, reflect a difference in neurological activity of man vis-à-vis other animals. Furthermore—on a slightly different tangent—the brain of a human being has certain structures, particularly in those parts of it that are termed the nonlimbic cortex, which are characteristic of the human brain. They are thought to be the physiological basis for symbolic processes and self-awareness. If, then, we take a normal human being as our paradigm case of a rational being,[88] we can establish the following as an operational criterion for being a rational being:

88. Ignoring the difficulties in defining the notion of the normal human being.

All and only those entities are rational beings whose
neurological activity or relevant analogue thereof has a
mathematically analyzable structure that is at least as complex as that of a human being, or whose brain or relevant
analogue thereof has a structural and functional similarity
to that of a human being, particularly with respect to those
substructures that are the relevant analogues of the nonlimbic cortex.

With this criterion we can once again approach the problem
of the sleeping, of the comatose, and so on. So long as their
neurological systems or the relevant analogues thereof are sufficiently complex to support a type of activity (or analogue
thereof) that compares favorably with that of our standard
case, they will count as persons. Or, alternatively, so long as
their brains or the relevant analogues thereof have the requisite
substructures and possess a structural similarity to those of a
human being—whether the system is actually functioning or not
—then the entities in question will be persons. Another slightly
different way of putting the point would be by appealing to the
Aristotelian distinction between first and second degree of
actuality: An entity will be in a state of first degree of actuality
vis-à-vis rationality if its neurological system (or analogue
thereof) is capable of supporting neural (or analogous) activity of the requisite degree of complexity. It will be in a state
of second degree of actuality if the potential inherent in the
system (or its analogue)[89] is actually realized. Thus sleeping
or comatose beings will be in a state of first degree of actuality
with respect to rationality, simply in virtue of possessing nervous systems that are sufficiently similar in structure to permit
them to enter into a state of second degree of actuality as defined, should the proper stimulus and so on be forthcoming.[90]

89. Henceforth, this parenthetical phrase will be understood in this and
similar locations.

90. Where—it must be noted—this stimulus does not effect a structural change in the neurological net or its analogue.

This criterion also has two further advantages: It recognizes that the human model might not exhaust the class of types of rational awareness. That is why there is the "at least" clause in the requirement on complexity. Also, it does not beg questions as to the precise constitution of the being in question. That is why there is the "analogue" clause.

The Moral Status of Abortion

Being in possession of a criterion of personhood—a criterion, be it noted, that may overlap with, but need not be coextensive with, that of humanity—we can now return to our initial definition of moral acts as directed toward persons, and can proceed to the question of the moral status of abortions. The solution will take the following form: If the abortion involves the termination of life of a fetus whose neurological system either actually does or potentially could evince neurological activity whose structure is of the type of a human being, or, alternatively, whose brain has the relevant structures definitive of a rational being, then the act of killing it will be that of killing a rational being. In which case, as per our preceding discussion, the act of killing it will be the act of killing a person. Whence, given our analysis of moral vs. nonmoral action, it follows that the act permits of moral evaluation, possibly even that of murder.

This, of course, squarely confronts us with the question with which we began: Is it one of murder? In the light of the preceding argument, it seems to follow that it is. It seems to follow, that is, unless we can show either that such an act was not premeditated or that some one or other of the excusing and extenuating circumstances generally admitted in the case of homicide obtain.

Unfortunately, neither of these alternatives seems to hold. As to the first, it is a simple fact that an abortion is not something which is done in the heat of passion, where, for the moment, one has lost one's head, and where one is swayed solely by the emotions of the moment, unable to stop and reflect. Abortions, after all, require time, both with respect to preparation and execution. Furthermore, in all but the most unusual circumstances, they are performed by someone else in situations where the possibility for sober reflection does obtain. Finally, when considering this first alternative, we must not lose sight of the one point on which our present discussion hinges: We are talking here about a pregnancy that is sufficiently advanced in order for the fetus to qualify as a person. In other words, a pregnancy that has lasted several months. In any ordinary understanding of the term, the abortion of a pregnancy so well established can hardly be said to be an unpremeditated act.

This, then, leaves the second alternative: the possibility of mitigating and extenuating circumstances. And, here, all the various arguments and considerations adduced by what we have called the proponents of the new morality will be deemed relevant. Various extenuating factors—or what are thought to be extenuating factors—may be singled out for special attention: What if the woman, as a result of finding herself pregnant, is emotionally so distraught that she exists in a world of utter despair and does not know what she is doing? What if the pregnancy is the result of a rape? And what of the really tough cases: those involving mothers whose lives are threatened, deformed fetuses, and so on? Can our position really handle them? And, is it really fair just to dismiss considerations such as these as irrelevant?

In considering these points, our work is lightened by the fact that many of the possible considerations that we have just glossed over have already been discussed in the preceding, detailed sections. Therefore we need not deal with them here. In fact, only the four major sorts of considerations just mentioned really merit our special attention at this stage of the discussion: (a) the claim that the act was done in a state of mental depression resulting from the pregnancy, and that therefore a plea of diminished responsibility ought to be admitted; (b) the claim that the pregnancy is a result of a rape, and therefore merits abortion, no matter what the circumstances; (c) the claim that the threat to the life of the woman is always an extenuating circumstance; and (d) the claim that radical fetal deformation of the fetus—or a good likelihood thereof—is always an indication for abortion.

Two of these—(a) and (d)—can indeed be dismissed as irrelevant, stark and extraordinary as that may seem. For, as we had occasion once before to observe, considerations of these types entirely miss the moral point at issue. We are dealing here with the question of aborting a fetus that is sufficiently developed to be a person. The existence of this person is the result of an act of intercourse engaged in by other moral agents. As moral agents, the participants in that activity are responsible for the results of their actions. In engaging in this act which could—and did—lead to the existence of a new person, the participants have assumed responsibility for the existence of another repository of moral rights; that is to say, they have—either tacitly or explicitly—assumed responsibility for the existence of another person. In that sense, they have subordinated their rights to its rights—particularly in view of the fact that the existence of such a person may be attended by certain risks: precisely those risks which they are now unwilling to accept: threat to life, mental depression, socioeconomic hardship, and the like. Furthermore—and this is a telling factor—in not aborting the pregnancy prior to the fetus's attainment of the status of a person, the individuals have confirmed that cession of rights which they now wish to withdraw. Therefore all other things being equal—the intercourse not being one of rape—the participants cannot now plead extenuating circumstances, whether these involve reasons of health, socioeconomic condition, psychological well-being and stability, or what have you. Nor could the unwanted nature of the pregnancy be introduced as an excusing factor. Quite the contrary: It would only serve to heighten the charge of culpable negligence in not taking the proper precautions which would have prevented the pregnancy in question. Therefore, in the cases of (a) and (d) excusing circumstances for aborting the pregnancy will not obtain. Whence it follows that aborting a fetus of the sort under discussion will be an act of premeditated and inexcusable killing of a person. It will be an act of murder.

As to (*b*) pregnancy resulting from rape, in this case, too, abortion will be an act of murder, since, in the situation under discussion, the crucial threshold to personhood has already been passed. The element of premeditation exists here as in all other cases, and the temporal consideration is just as relevant. As to the fact that the pregnancy was, so to speak, forced, the reply here is that this is not to the point in considering the question of abortion. It is to the point in awarding damages to the individual who has thus been used and who has suffered as a result of the action. It is also to the point when examining a society that would permit such a thing to occur, and, above all, which would permit such a pregnancy to proceed until the fetus has attained personhood. But, as we said, it is not to the point when examining the question of whether a person—the fetus at this stage of development—may be murdered.[91]

Finally, there is point (*d*), the tough cases involving fetal abnormality or high likelihood thereof. In particular, cases like Down's syndrome, Tay-Sachs disease, rubella, and thalidomide come to mind. In such cases abortion, surely, is warranted? Once again, the reply must be in the negative. Once the fetus has become a person in our sense of the term—and by the criteria which we indicated, the fourth month of the gestation period would seem to be a reasonable point on which to focus —aborting it would be nothing less than killing a person because of its handicaps, without even obtaining the consent of the person in question, a factor that just barely might change the whole situation to one of (requested) euthanasia. And that, we submit, no matter how considered, is murder. Therefore even cases of type (*d*) do not afford an escape from the indictment.

Before concluding, we should consider briefly one type of case which, so far, we have neglected: that of accidental pregnancy resulting from contraceptive failure, where otherwise due care was taken that conception should not occur. In such a case —it is frequently argued—abortion should be permitted; all

91. Largely, be it noted, for the sake of convenience.

the more so, since the charge of culpable negligence cannot be raised against the individuals involved, and therefore no moral blame attaches to them. Furthermore, so sentiment has it, to deny them an abortion would be to punish them for an accident over which they had no control—something that goes against the grain of every legal and moral consideration.

Nevertheless, even in these cases abortion would be murder. That is to say, abortion under the conditions we have outlined. The fact that due care was taken to prevent conception is beside the point. The point is that here we have a person, and no matter how or under what circumstances the person came to be—whether on purpose or by accident—that alters nothing in his personhood. It is this fact of personhood that is morally decisive. Therefore, under these circumstances to perform an abortion is to commit murder. As an aside, I might add that if the pregnancy was really unwanted all along, it should have been aborted at an earlier date prior to the acquisition of personhood by the fetus. No moral gravamen of a murderous sort would then have attached to such an act. Waiting until the threshold of personhood has been passed is to play games with a person's life.

These last comments focus the discussion on a qualification that has run throughout all of the preceding: namely, that an abortion will be an act of murder if and only if it occurs after the fetus has passed the threshold to personhood. Does this mean that, so far as our analysis is concerned, abortions performed prior to this time are not murderous? Much as it may grate on some sensibilities, I see myself forced to answer yes. The logic of my position demands that I deny that abortions performed prior to this crucial point are murderous. Nor am I loath to accept this consequence. However, in this context, two further points are worthy of explicit mention. First, this does not mean that no moral gravamen is attached to an abortion performed prior to this point of development. That would follow if and only if it was assumed that only acts done to persons are attended by moral qualities. Although this was assumed throughout the foregoing discussion, it was done for the sake of the argument only. In point of fact, I subscribe to the thesis that the wanton taking of any sentient life is morally reprehensible. Therefore, in reply to the question of whether or not abortions performed prior to this critical period are without moral parameters, I can do no better than to quote what I said at the beginning: that the moral gravamen attaching to such an act is commensurate with the stage of development of the fetus.

The second point—and this is the note on which I shall conclude—is this: I have spoken a great deal about a threshold to personhood, about a critical point in the development of a fetus, about its becoming a person, and the like. Given our working criterion for personhood and our analysis of murder, that is natural enough. But in so talking, I may have fostered the impression that this is a temporal criterion only: that it is the same for all fetuses, and that the transition occurs at a particular, definite point in time. Both of these impressions must be corrected. The point of development is not the same in all cases. It depends on the particular nature of the pregnancy and of the fetus involved. And it does not occur with momentary rapidity, as it were, taking merely an instant. It is a gradual development spread over some time—a development where only the beginning and the end are clearly discernible. There is an indefinable, unclassifiable middle ground, where we do not know whether our criteria apply or not: whether or not to call the entity in question a person. To abort or not to abort? Here we will be in an area of grave moral risk.

2

Suicide

THE PROBLEM

If I kill you, in full knowledge of what I am about, with full intent to commit the deed, and in complete possession of all my faculties, am I guilty of murder? All other things being equal, the answer must be a resounding yes. However, if I kill myself, in full knowledge of what I am doing, with full intent to commit the deed, and in complete possession of all my faculties, am I guilty of murder as well? In this instance, the answer is likely to be no. We do not generally think of such cases as instances of murder. Why?

Let us consider another example. If I hire you to kill someone for me, knowing full well what I am doing and doing it with the express purpose of rendering that person dead, am I as guilty of murder as you? By any ordinary standards—and even by those sanctioned by law—the answer is in the affirmative. However, if I hire you to kill me, again in full knowledge and with express intent, I shall not be guilty of murder although you may be.[1] Once more, the question arises, why such a difference between the two cases should obtain.

In one fairly obvious and clear-cut sense, the answer lies at hand. In both sets of examples the second sort of activity is one which we generally designate by the term 'suicide', and we accord it a special category, distinct from that of murder. That is to say, by the term 'suicide' we understand the act of a person deliberately and with full intent and purpose bringing about

1. See the Statutes of Texas, Massachusetts, Michigan, Ohio, Illinois, Oregon, etc. on this point.

his own preternatural death, either immediately and directly by his own agency, or indirectly by the agency of someone or something else especially employed for that purpose.

Suicide we generally place into a moral class all by itself, distinct from murder and other heinous actions of that sort. The question is why that should be the case. Is not murder the deliberate and purposeful killing of a person with the express purpose of rendering that person dead? And is not the recipient of the action in the case of suicide a person? But when we address ourselves to these and similar questions, we must take care to exclude a possible misunderstanding over the notion of suicide, a misunderstanding which, unless corrected at the very outset, may lead to a serious misunderstanding of the whole issue.

The misunderstanding I have in mind is actually a confusion between two closely related notions: that of suicide on the one hand, and that of a suicidal act on the other. Let me put this by way of an example. Consider a person who systematically engages in a type of activity, knowing full well that this activity will lead to his premature and unnatural death, but who persists in engaging in the activity in spite of this knowledge. Is such a person not committing suicide? Certainly, in ordinary discourse, we frequently talk as if that were the case—yet our definition would have us reject this sort of case. The sort of activity that I have in mind here is that of someone given to the excessive use of alcohol, tobacco, drugs of various sorts, and the like. Is such a person not a suicide? Or, to consider a slightly different sort of case: What of the person who, in full knowledge of the circumstances enters into a situation where, as he knows full well, he will immediately be killed, but who ignores that fact and proceeds with the action anyway? The sort of situation that would be an instance of this would be someone's participation in the Charge of the Light Brigade. Is that sort of action not suicidal? And, by that very token, is the person engaging in it not a suicide?

To reply briefly and to the point, the answer is no. These examples, and others like them, rest on the confusion indicated above, between something being an act of suicide on the one hand, and being suicidal on the other. An act may be suicidal without being suicide if at least one or both of the following conditions are met: (*a*) The action must, with reasonable certainty, lead to the death of the person engaging in it; (*b*) it must be known to the actor that his death would be a virtual certainty were he to engage in that act. However, in order for the act to qualify as suicide, one further condition is indispensable. (*c*) The actor must engage in that action for the express purpose of bringing about his own death. If this condition is not met, the action will not be one of suicide, although it very well may be suicidal.[2]

THE NEGATIVE ARGUMENT

Having excluded this possible misunderstanding, let us return to the question with which we began: Why should suicide not be murder? And of course the answer is, that it is not at all universally accepted that it is not. On the contrary, it is frequently contended that, like ordinary murder, suicide is something preternatural which carries not only religious but also social and moral condemnation.

The Religious Argument

To begin with, there is the religious argument. In actuality, of course, like any matter of religious significance, it is a series of arguments, each with its own separate premise, but all leading to the same conclusion.

First, there is the argument based on the commandment "Thou shalt not kill!" Just as an act of murder constitutes a contravention of this explicit command by God, so an act of suicide—since it is the act of killing a *person*—will fall under the same rubric. To be sure, so the argument continues, there

2. Another way of putting the point would be to say that suicide involves an intentional element which suicidal acts lack. The class of suicidal acts has as its proper subset that of suicide. This intentional element is clearly reflected in the expression used to designate suicide in some languages: "self-murder" as, for example, in German (*Selbstmord*).

are biblical instances of people who did in effect commit suicide
without divine disapproval. The case of Samson is a good instance. However, in such cases we must postulate a divine
command to that effect which, although unknown to us, nevertheless was quite explicit to the person in question.[3] In other
words, this line of reasoning has it that unless explicitly commanded by God, suicide is an act of murder and is punishable
as a direct contravention of divine law.

However—and this is the second line of argumentation—
suicide is also a contravention of natural law, that is, of the
natural state of affairs. As Thomas Aquinas so clearly put it,
"Naturally, i.e. by its very nature, each thing loves itself, and
this implies that each thing naturally preserves its existence and
as such opposes as much resistance to its destruction as it can.
Therefore someone who kills himself goes against natural inclination and against that love which everyone owes to himself.
That is why killing oneself is always a mortal sin, since it
opposes natural law and love." [4] Therefore, even from the point
of view of natural law, suicide is morally unacceptable.

Third—and we are still within the Christian context—there
is the argument based on the premise that life is a gift from
God.[5] Such a gift cannot be denied or perverted except at the
cost of eternal peril to one's soul. And in a similar connection
—although by rights it ought to be considered a fourth argument—there is the thesis that all men are the property of God.
Consequently, to kill oneself is tantamount to destroying a
piece of God's property.[6]

Furthermore, a thesis common both to the Judaic and the
Christian tradition is that God is the ultimate judge. As it is
said in Deuteronomy 32:39, "I kill and I make that there is
life." To commit suicide, therefore, is to usurp this decision-
making function in a morally reprehensible manner which, even

3. Cf. Augustine *De Civitate Dei* bk. 1, chaps. 16–26. See also Aquinas
Summa Theologiae II-II, Q. 64, A. 5.
4. Aquinas *Summa Theologiae* II-II, Q. 64, A. 5.
5. Ibid.
6. Ibid.

if nothing else were at stake, certainly could not be condoned.[7]
Thus, as the Judaic tradition has it, whereas each person has
a right to his death,[8] this does not mean that a person has a
right to procure it.[9] To those not of a Judeo-Christian persuasion, the considerations just indicated will lack a probative
force. Not only that: given the postulate of a rewarding and
punishing deity—of a deity, that is, who punishes transgressions
of his commands and who rewards those who observe them—
the whole train of speculation seems to have a more or less
quid pro quo character. If the religious arguments were all
there were to the thesis that suicide is morally unacceptable,
that position would collapse for want of support—at least for
those who do not share the religious assumptions on which the
preceding arguments are based. However, the religious approach is only one facet of a much more complicated position.
There are at least two other lines of reasoning that are representative of the position against suicide: what we have called
the social and the moral arguments respectively.

The Social Argument

The social arguments originate from an entirely different set of
premises than those we have considered so far. Whereas religious arguments, by and large, agree in maintaining that suicide is not a right but a crime against God, his commands, or
the laws that he has set, the social arguments also begin by
accepting the premise that suicide is impermissable—but with
a difference, namely, that the basis of the immorality of the
act is not to be traced to a deity, but to the sovereignty of the
society over the individual.[10]

7. Judaic condemnation of suicide is quite explicit. See Midrash Rab-
bah 34. See also Rabbi Solomon Ganzfried, *Code of Jewish Law* (Kitzur
Shulchan Aruch), H. E. Goldin, trans. (New York: Hebrew Publ. Co.,
1961), vol. 4, chap. 201. See F. Rosner, "Suicide in Biblical, Talmudic
and Rabbinic Writings," *Tradition* 11 (1970): 25–40.

8. *Sefer Chasidim,* nos. 314–18.

9. Cf. *Schulchan Aruch,* Yore Deah 339:1

10. Cf. Aristotle *Nicomachean Ethics* bk. 5, chap. 11 (1138a6–14).

The thrust of this series of arguments can be put simply, like this:

> If all of us had the right to commit suicide whenever we pleased, we could always escape the consequences of our acts, no matter how heinous, simply by removing ourselves from the scene. That, however, would be to undermine the basis of all social authority which resides in the domination society has over the lives of its members. If that basis were removed, social structure and authority would be threatened and would ultimately collapse. Consequently, suicide cannot be condoned as the right of an individual. In fact, it must be regarded as a crime: as murder.[11]

A variation of this argument—there are countless others—is found in the *Summa Theologiae* of Thomas Aquinas. We mention it only because it has had some influence on the formation of later laws on the subject.[12] Blackstone substitutes "king" for "society," but the content of his argument is the same. Briefly, it runs like this:

> Every person is a member of the society in which he lives. As such, what he is belongs to the society. Therefore, if a person kills himself he will be harming the society, and in that sense will be doing something immoral.[13]

The Moral Argument

Finally, there is what we have called the moral arguments against suicide. As the name indicates, they are wholly moral in nature. As in the case of all other arguments or series of arguments, there are of course variations. By and large, however, they all fall along the following lines. The argument generally begins by assuming the definition of 'murder' as the

11. It will be noted that nothing was said about suicide as a duty. In this context, that falls into the rubric of euthanasia.

12. Cf. Sir William Blackstone, *Commentaries on the Laws of England,* 4:189.

13. Aquinas *Summa Theologiae* II-II, Q. 64, A. 5.

voluntary and expressly intended killing of a person. To this definition, the argument adds the consideration that we ourselves fall into the rubric of persons. Therefore, so the argument continues, the act of killing us in the aforesaid manner would, by that very token, also be an act of murder. As to the consideration that in the case of suicide it is we ourselves who perform the act, this argument counters that that makes no difference. Murder, by definition, countenances no consideration as to the identity of the agent. All that it requires is that the act be directed by a person toward a person and that it be performed in a certain way. Both requirements are met in the case of suicide. Consequently, suicide is an act of murder.

Nor—so the argument continues—does it matter that in performing such an act, we effectively place ourselves beyond the possibility of human retribution. The moral nature of the crime is not thereby reduced nor even removed altogether. The two —possibility of punishment and moral status of an act—are two entirely distinct things and ought not to be confused. Suicide, therefore—so far as this argument has it—is merely a subspecies of murder and by that very fact is morally reprehensible. A well-known variation on this argument is found in Kant's *Foundations of the Metaphysics of Morals,* section 2 (421–22). Kant sees the immorality of suicide not merely in the fact that it is an act of deliberately killing a person in a murderous manner, but also in the fact that the act abrogates the universality of the law against killing, in fact involves a contradiction in the will that wills it.

THE POSITIVE ARGUMENT

It would be foolish to suppose that the preceding arguments exhaust what there is to say on the subject—or even what has been said about it. After all, there is the position of those in favor of suicide: the positive side of the issue. Those who array themselves on this side of the question will generally accept the definition of 'murder' that we have given, as an act that has as its primary and explicit objective the rendering dead of a person, where that act is done with full knowledge and intent. They will also agree that these conditions are met in the case of suicide. Nevertheless, they insist that suicide is not an act of murder. Once more, why?

Popularly, several reasons are given. These can be ranked under seven general headings: (1) the argument from legal self-stultification; (2) the argument from psychological incapability; (3) the argument from human dignity; (4) the argument from bearability; (5) the argument from private ownership; (6) the argument from social responsibility; (7) the argument from relativity.

The Argument from Legal Self-Stultification

The argument from legal self-stultification is really quite simple. It finds its roots in the fact that, traditionally, murder was an offense punishable by death. Obviously, if suicide were classified as a species of murder, the punishment for it would have to be in keeping with the nature of the offense. In other words, the punishment for the act would have to be an act materially identical with the act itself and therefore would not constitute a punishment. Abstracting from the pragmatic impossibility of implementing this punishment, there is also this consideration to be borne in mind: In thus punishing the act, the executioner and those materially and intentionally responsible for the execution thereby become willing executors of the suicide's own purpose where this purpose was the procuring of his own death. Consequently, since that purpose is one of murder, the executioner and all others thereby become accessories to the fact— an intolerable situation. Therefore, both from the pragmatic point of view of the enforcement of punishment and from the theoretical point of view of the interrelationship between punishment and crime, to classify suicide as murder would be legally self-stultifying. Hence, the drive to classify suicide not as murder but as a species of action in its own right.[14]

14. However, in British law, as well as in some states of the United States (e.g. New Jersey, Washington, North Carolina, etc.), it is a criminal offense. Attempted suicide is likewise adjudged a criminal offense, albeit not one bearing as grave a charge as murder.

The Argument from Psychological Incapability

The argument from psychological incapability is slightly different both in tenor and basis. It hearkens back to what is alleged
to be a universal truth about all living beings: that, consciously
or unconsciously, they all have an instinctive and insuperable
will to live.[15] That is to say, it is alleged that normally this is
the case. Where this drive or will does not obtain—or does
not seem to obtain—we are so struck by this deviation from
an apparently universal norm, that in the case of the lower
animals we blame ourselves for having an insufficient understanding of their behavior;[16] in the case of *homo sapiens* we
postulate insanity.[17] The conclusion of this line of reasoning,
therefore, is that suicide cannot be a species of murder because it involves deliberate self-destruction; and deliberate self-
destruction is the result of an insane disposition. Suicide, therefore, is free from the extreme moral gravamen attaching to
murder and falls into a species all its own.

The argument from legal self-stultification and the argument
from psychological incapability have one factor in common:
Both seek to minimize the moral gravamen attaching to suicide
by arguing that there are external circumstances which prevent
that sort of action from being one of murder. That is to say,
neither argument questions the correctness of the definition of
'murder' nor denies that at least to all appearances, the pre-
conditions for calling suicide a type of murder are met. Instead,

15. A good traditional statement of this position that has had considerable influence on the Western world is found in Aquinas *Summa Theologiae* II-II, Q. 44, A. 5.

16. As an example of the sort of suicidal activity found among animals, we can cite the behavior of lemmings which, periodically, migrate
to the ocean only to jump in and drown.

17. Examples of this position are easily come by, if we but consider
contemporary medical and psychological analyses of suicide. A good bibliography of the available literature is found in Eberhard Lungershausen,
ed., *Selbstmorde u. Selbstmordversuche bei Studenten* (Heidelberg:
Hüthig, 1968). See also Norman Farberow, *Bibliography on Suicide and
Suicide Prevention* (Chevy Chase, Md.: National Institute of Mental
Health, 1969).

both try to alleviate the charge by arguing that, somehow, the conditions involved are so special that the charge should not really apply.

However, there is a series of arguments claiming a special status for suicide, which do not take this route. These arguments do deny that suicide is murder—not, however, because of some sort of special and extenuating circumstance's being operative, but because they contend that suicide is an inalienable and fundamental right of any person. In other words, there are several stances on the issue of suicide which assume as a fundamental premise that everyone has the right to terminate his life at his own discretion, and that suicide is merely the exercise of that right. The difference between this sort of position and that encountered in the arguments from legal self-stultification and psychological incapability is as great as it is obvious, for it involves the refusal to see suicide as a type of murder—indeed, as a reprehensible sort of act at all. We mentioned these various positions in the introductory discussion to this section, and labeled them (3)–(7) respectively. Let us now consider the various arguments in more detail.

The Argument from Human Dignity

The argument from human dignity is as old as philosophical and religious speculation on the subject of death itself. Thus, we encounter it as an already well-established philosophical position at the time of Plato,[18] and even the Old Testament seems to admit it as an acceptable consideration.[19] Nor was the acceptability of this reason confined to earlier centuries. Suicide for reasons of dignity was enjoined by the moral code of continental European nobility. In fact, the concept seems

18. *Laws* book 9. See also the general Stoic and Epicurean positions on the subject of voluntary death. Cf. Marcus Aurelius *Meditations* viii:47, x:8; Seneca: *Ep.* 70; etc.

19. Cf. 2 Sam. 17:23, where the suicide of Ahithophel for reasons of dignity (he could not live as a disgraced counsellor) is accepted without moral dissent. See also Judg. 9:54, 16:30; 1 Kings 16:18; 2 Macc. 14:41, on related biblical failure to condemn suicide.

to have been something of a cultural universal, finding analogues in almost every society with which we are familiar. If
one cannot live his life with dignity—or even as a mere human
being—then he has the right (even the duty) to end it. Of late,
this argument has been refurbished by those who maintain that
the mere fact of existence is not enough: that life must also
be worth living in purely human terms, from the point of view
of a *person*—a rational human being.

It is this last train of considerations that brings out what is
important in the argument. Its basic assumption is that we must
distinguish between two things: the fact that someone is alive,
and the fact that the life of that individual is worth living.
Life, so this argument contends, is like any other state. The
mere fact that it obtains does not give it any special value in
virtue of which the balance of things should be adversely affected were it to be discontinued. In point of fact, a positive
value attaches to being alive if and only if it is of such a nature
as to be described by the term 'human', that is, if certain
conditions as to the personal condition and dignity of the individual living it are met. In other words, the quality of life
is deemed important. If the life we lead is one of degradation
and indignity, if we are downtrodden and treated like animals
in every sense of that word and our dignity as persons is
trampled into the dust—and if, furthermore, there is no prospect that the future will change this state of affairs for the
better—then that life is not worth living, and we have the right
to terminate our existence.[20]

The Argument from Bearability

Closely related to the argument from human dignity is the
argument from bearability. Like the former, it assumes that the
mere fact that there is life is insufficient to imply that this life
ought to be conserved. That is to say, it, too, considers the

---

20. Indeed, it could be argued that in such circumstances we have a
duty to do so. But to do justice to this thesis would carry us too far
afield.

quality of life a determining factor in deciding whether or not
a particular life is worth living; and, like the argument from
dignity, in the eventuality of a negative answer it attaches no
moral gravamen to the voluntary termination of that life. However, unlike the argument from human dignity, it addresses
itself not to what makes a life worth living in a properly human
—and in that sense perhaps aristocratic—sense, but focuses
on the felt experience of that life itself. That is to say, the
argument gravitates around the question, Is the life bearable
in a psychological or a physical sense? Are the psychological
factors such as to make that life a "living hell," a "nightmare,"
or simply so depressing that to continue to live would be sheer
torture? If so, and if there is no perceivable way out of that
situation for that individual, without losing his identity, then
suicide is justified.[21] Is the physiological condition of the individual so fraught with pain and extreme discomfort that continued life merely promises a continuation of already unbearable
agony? If so, and if informed hope for the future promises no
betterment—in short, if all he has to look forward to is more
of the same—then that sort of life is not worth living, and he
may terminate it at his own pleasure. Nor—so the argument
continues—need the present state of the individual actually be
one of pain and debilitation. The certain promise of such a fate
to come is sufficient to permit the exercise of the right to terminate one's life. And lest it be thought that this right obtains
only in those cases that we have just indicated, let us be more
explicit. The principle of this argument is that any medically
extremely debilitating state, or the certain promise of such a
state to come (whether that state be interpreted in psychological, neurological, or general physiological terms), permits
the exercise of the right to suicide. The certainty of becoming a
"human vegetable," as in some cases, as well as cases of Huntington's chorea or similar illnesses, would therefore also fall

21. In this context, it should be noted that the person living that life
is not necessarily the right judge to decide whether or not there is an acceptable way out. On this point psychological unbearability may differ
slightly from physiological unbearability.

under this provision. In other words—so this argument has it
—in these and similar situations, suicide will not be morally
reprehensible but instead our right.

The Argument from Private Ownership

The last two arguments agree in their basic stance that suicide
requires no excusing consideration, simply because suicide is
a right. However, as we indicated some paragraphs ago, these
considerations by no means exhaust the positions that fall under
that general premise. There is also what we have called the
argument from private ownership. Like the preceding two, it
considers suicide an individual right; but unlike them, it contends that this right is neither basic, nor that it is the outcome
of a premise concerning the quality of our lives. Instead, it
maintains as its *point d'appui* that we have a right to our own
life, indeed, to ourselves as property and that we can do with
ourselves whatever we please.

Put somewhat differently, the argument amounts to this:

> Each and every one of us stands in a peculiar and unique
> relationship to his life. Our life is our own in the way in
> which nothing else is. We could characterize this relation-
> ship by calling it, perhaps somewhat tendentiously, a rela-
> tionship of nontransferable ownership. But we do own
> it: that is the major point. And as with anything that we
> own in the full-blooded sense of that term, we have the
> right to dispose of it as we please. In particular, we have
> the right to advance it, to ruin it, or even to dispose of
> it altogether. In short, we have the right to end it if we
> so please, to commit suicide. Nor do we have an analogous
> right with respect to any other life. It is solely in virtue
> of the peculiar and unique relation of nontransferable
> ownership that we can have such a right—and that rela-
> tionship we have only to our own body: our own life.
> Suicide, therefore, is our right simply in virtue of a much
> more general right: the right to do with our own property
> as we please.

The Argument from Social Responsibility

From talk of right we turn to talk of duty; that is to say, from arguments based on the contention that suicide is the right of every individual, we turn to arguments to the effect that suicide is a duty incumbent upon us. Argumentation here divides into two streams: one concerned with ecological considerations and another concerned with matters of the common good.

The argument from ecology is fairly easy to state. Hearkening back to Malthusian considerations and to ecological theories daily substantiated as fact, it argues that any particular society, and indeed the world as a whole, can support only a finite and quite limited number of persons. Consequently, and primarily, we have the duty to prevent the conception of new individuals whose birth would strain the resources of the community beyond the breaking point.[22] And even if that breaking point has not already been reached in our particular ecological enclave, still, for the world as a whole that point has been attained. Only a planned replacement of population will prevent slow starvation for all, due to an exhaustion of the finite resources available to us.

Population control, therefore, is absolutely mandatory. Contraception is the obvious and easiest method. However, accidents do occur. That is to say, exercising even the greatest of care, conception accidentally does happen. In such cases, abortion seems to be the logical solution; particularly if, as we suggested at the end of the preceding chapter, the abortion is performed very early on. On the other hand, there is this consideration: the young of a species are its potential for survival. Therefore to kill these is to attack this potential at its very roots. Humanity is no exception to this general natural principle. It, too, survives through its progeny. Therefore, if there is some other method of controlling the population within ecologically safe limits, which does not at the same time attack

22. Here considerations drawn from the arguments from human dignity and bearability would clearly be apropos.

the basis of the population, then that method would be more acceptable.

As we already know, there is such a method. It hinges on the fact that in any human population there is a class of people who, for some reason or other, are not necessary for the survival of the community (for the species as a whole). The physiologically debilitated, the deviant, and above all the old fall into this category. Consequently—so the argument continues—in the interest of the survival of the community or the species, these people have a duty to remove themselves from the scene so that an ecological place can be provided for new members of much greater significance to the survival of the whole. In other words, it will be the duty of these to commit suicide.

The argument we have just sketched maps a particular direction that admits of several variations. What we have called the argument from the common good is one particular variant. Unlike the preceding argument, it does not consider the question of the number of human beings that can be supported by a given ecological environment. Instead, it centers around the quality of the life thus supported. Therefore, over and above accepting the ecological underpinnings of the preceding argument, it adds the premise that only a certain quality of life is worthy of being called human and that, given the ecological considerations just adduced, this quality can be maintained only at the price of death. Once more, for the reasons indicated, abortions and similar expedients are out of the question. These strike at the very base of the community as a whole. But there are those who lead no useful existence whatever. Not, at any rate, in any ecologically acceptable sense. The incurably ill and those who have already "led a full life" are obvious instances. They are unnecessary and also constitute a disproportionate and irredeemable drain on the resources of the community, which could otherwise lead a better life. Therefore, in the interest of the whole, these individuals ought to terminate their existence. In other words, basing itself on the premises of social function and ecology, this particular version of the argument maintains that it is the duty of all people who have reached a certain age or who have ceased to contribute productively to the quality of life of the remainder to commit suicide.[23]

The Argument from Relativity

Finally, we come to an argument which is totally distinct from those we have considered so far. Previous arguments viewed suicide as either positive or neutral on the moral scale, where this scale was thought to have absolute validity. The present argument denies that the concept of morality applies in any absolute sense at all. In our initial discussion we called this argument the argument from ethical or moral relativity. The appropriateness of this denotation now is immediately apparent for its basic premise is that there are no absolute moral standards: that moral predicates like 'good' and 'evil', or 'right' and 'wrong' carry no absolute weight. It is the fundamental premise of this sort of argument not merely that there are no absolute moral standards, but also that the moral evaluations that we all want to make—or, at any rate, what we take to be moral judgments—are really nothing other than expressions of tacitly codified modes of behavior sanctioned by the community in which we live. In that sense, such evaluations are relative to a given society and hold only within that context. They hold only because of the tacit agreement among the members of that society to adhere to those mores.

In other words, the argument is based on the premise that moral judgments neither have universal validity nor are sui generis. From this the argument goes on to contend that, all other things being equal and considering the pragmatic nature of our society, we are at liberty either to reject such mores or to amend them. Since we ourselves are the decision makers of the community, we may decide that suicide is permissible for us or within our society; in fact, that it has no deeper moral significance than a sneeze. And if we so decide, given the thesis

23. It is clear that in this argument we have an overlap with arguments for abortion, senicide, and euthanasia.

of relativity, it will be so. And if we decide it is not morally acceptable, then, mutatis mutandis, in that context it will be reprehensible. Suicide, therefore—according to this argument —is in itself morally neutral. As neutral as any other act is in itself. It is we who decide what value it has or ought to have.

The conclusions of the argument are by now patent. If we decide that suicide is our right, then within the context concerned by our decision, that will be the case; and if we decide that it is our duty, then likewise. Under no circumstances can it be morally evil if we (or the society in which we live) decide that it is good.

EVALUATION

We now face the task of evaluating these various positions on suicide. However, to do so by means of detailed analyses of the various arguments would be tedious and, quite frequently, repetitive in the extreme. The best way to avoid this is to consider the issue of suicide in itself, referring to the various arguments only in passing.

Is suicide murder? There are only three ways of avoiding an affirmative answer: (a) by saying that the individual who is killed is not a person; (b) by saying that exceptive conditions are operative which prevent it from falling into that category; (c) by changing the definition of 'murder'.

As to (a), clearly, it is unacceptable. If it were true that the victim of a suicide is not a person, then the victim of a murder would not be a person either. It is only an accident, as it were, that makes the agent of the demise the victim itself. However, if the individual who is killed is not a person, it would also follow that there would be no murders, for a murder requires a person as its victim. Now, it may just barely be the case that there are no murders;[24] but the reason for that will not be lack of persons or victims, but something about the nature of the act itself.

24. For example, if one rejects ethics entirely, or if one argues for a complete determinism. See the discussion of alternative (c) on pp. 119–21.

As to alternative (b), it argues that exceptive conditions are operative which remove suicide from the category of murder. One of these exceptive conditions might be that of insanity. And, in fact, insanity has generally been accepted as an excusing condition, whether we consider the matter from a religious, a social, or a moral point of view. The reason for accepting it as excusing is to be found in the definition of a moral act: Whether of a positive (good) or negative (bad) nature, an act, in order to fall within the sphere of the moral, must be a voluntary act.[25] In order for an act to be voluntary, however, the actor must know what he is doing. More colloquially, he must be in full possession of his senses. An insane individual, of course, is no such thing. Either he is unaware of the nature of the act itself, or of its consequences, or of the very fact that he is engaged in that act. He may also be unaware of the moral parameters attaching to the act by virtue of its very nature. In any case, the act of an insane person is not considered to be voluntary in the proper sense of that term, and consequently is thought to fall outside of the domain of the moral. Therefore, while the act may still be very much an act of homicide—the act of killing a person—it cannot be an act of murder. It is clear that the plea of insanity neither applies nor is intended to apply across the board to every suicide. And in any case, it does not disprove the contention that suicide as such is murder. It is on precisely this issue, however, that we come across what is sometimes adduced as a morally excusing condition: Suicide is not murder because of the very nature of the act. It is an act directed by the actor against himself. This peculiarity we noted before, when considering the argument from private ownership. Let us now look at it more closely.

However, when we do look at it more closely, it begins to emerge that the thesis of private ownership as applied to our lives can hardly constitute an acceptable reply; if for no other reason than that, as it stands, the notion on which it is based

25. This notion goes back to Aristotle, *Ethics*, bk. 3, chap. 1, for the classic statement of that position.

is logically incoherent. What we own—in any full-blooded sense of that term—we can disown, give away, sell, or otherwise dispose of so that it becomes the property of someone else. We cannot do this with our lives. Therefore whatever the unique relationship this bears to us, it cannot be one of ownership. In an extended sense of the term, that of *identity* would be a better candidate.

Let us, therefore, construe the argument to that effect: It is because of the relationship of identity which obtains between actor and person acted upon, that suicide is not murder. Of course, the argument does not proceed to this conclusion immediately. It does so by several distinct steps: The reason why identity is here seen as a distinguishing factor is that it brings into play a further thesis—that of the inherent freedom of the individual. That is to say, it is assumed that each individual has a right to self-determination. Therefore, insofar as the individual is an actor, he has the right to decide what to do; and insofar as he is the recipient of that action, he has a similar right. Now, as is generally accepted, one person may cede a right to another, thereby turning what might otherwise have been an immoral or morally reprehensible situation into one above reproach. In the present context, however, no such ceding of rights is necessary. Actor and person acted upon are identical, and the will of the one is that of the other. Consequently, this act of homicide does not involve the infringement or deprivation of any right. Therefore, despite the fact that it is a voluntary and explicit act of killing a person, in virtue of the identity between actor and person acted upon, it is not one of murder.

We cannot fault the claim that all individuals have certain rights, the right to life among them. Nor can we deny the identity between actor and person acted upon. Nevertheless, we can and must say that, given the above definition of murder, all of the preceding arguments are no more than sophistic contentions that do not change the outcome of the issue. The act of suicide will still be a voluntary act of killing a person and by that very token an act of murder.

However, perhaps this conclusion is premature, for there is

still possibility (c), that of changing the definition of murder. Nor is this an altogether fanciful suggestion, made only to save the suicide's position from moral collapse. It dovetails quite neatly with the previous suggestion that we can give up or cede our rights. If so, then we could also cede or give up the right to life. Not *to* someone, but simply abandon it. Let us, therefore, redefine 'murder' as follows:

> Murder is the act of voluntarily, with full intent and knowledge, violating someone's right to life.

If this definition is accepted, then we must distinguish between homicide on the one hand, and murder on the other. Homicide will merely be the killing of a person—of a member of the species *homo sapiens;* murder will involve the violation of his right to life, in other words, the deprivation of his life without his consent or some such relevant cóndition.

This is one way in which we could argue that suicide is not a species of murder. There is another way, which is equally above reproach. Like the preceding, it seizes on a factor introduced in one of the arguments: the fact that lives can be arranged hierarchically according to quality, so that some are and others are not worth living. With this as a premise, the argument then continues as follows:

> Life, in and by itself, is nothing of intrinsic value. It gains whatever value it has from its content, from the quality with which it is imbued. Therefore if a life is unalterably unbearable in nature, it is not worth living. To the individual who lives it, it has no value. Therefore if that life is deleted from the universe, the world would not have suffered a loss, nor would the person living it have been deprived of a good. Consequently, the performance of such an act of suicide, rather than being morally reprehensible, is morally at least neutral and probably to be praised.

If we now return to the traditional definition of murder, as the voluntary and intentional act of depriving someone of his life, we can see immediately that there will be two kinds of murder: those which consist of the taking of a life that had positive value and was worth living for its liver, and those which consist in the taking of an unwanted and unlivable life. If the deliberations of the preceding argument are correct, only the first will be morally evil; the second one will be morally neutral or even good.

However, as should be quite clear to everyone, the suggestion just made sounds peculiar, to say the least. It also meets with a certain amount of inveterate resistance. Part of it stems from the conviction that whatever we may say, life does have an intrinsic value, and that therefore the deliberate taking of a life is morally evil. This, however, mainly amounts to an unargued denial of the premise of the argument, and we shall simply ignore it. The other part of the resistance stems from the fact that the concept and indeed the term 'murder' have a certain history which has left an indelible association for that term. For one reason or another, murder has traditionally been associated with the morally reprehensible and felonious taking of a life. Therefore the concept of murder is, almost by definition, the concept of a morally reprehensible homicide. This traditional association is too strong to permit an attempt at separation. Consequently, in order to avoid confusion, let us not distinguish between the two types of murder, but instead between two types of homicide as we did above. The one, which traditionally has gone under the heading of murder, will be the act of voluntarily and expressly depriving an individual of his life even though he considers that life worthwhile or merely as worth living. Such an act will retain all the negative moral valuations traditionally put on it. The other sort of act will be one of relieving an individual of the burden of an unbearable sort of life. No morally negative valuation attaches to this act, nor does it fall under the heading of murder. Traditionally, another term has sometimes been used for the latter: euthanasia.

Suicide, then, will be not murder but homicide in the strict sense of that term: the killing of a human being. But—and this places suicide squarely within the same category as certain other species of homicide which frequently go under the heading of murder—the principle which thus licenses, even enjoins suicide is not confined in its ambit to acts of self-killing. By its very nature, the principle will count as mere homicide, unattended by any blame, all acts which have as their aim the relief of all genuine suffering that can be ended in no other way. In other words, suicide emerges as nothing more nor less than a species of euthanasia. To be sure, it is a unique species, differing from all others; but it differs only in that (1) agent and person acted upon are identical; and (2) the possibility of moral error is reduced almost to nil in that here, as nowhere else, the agent has privileged and, in principle, unfalsifiable access to the information of whether the life-style in question is in fact unbearable.

This brings us back to one of the initial arguments in favor of suicide: that everyone has the right to self-determination, in particular with respect to his own body and life. If our investigation up to this point has been correct, this thesis is mistaken. To be sure, everyone is in a privileged and unique position vis-à-vis the disposition of his own life. Not, however, because it is his and his alone to dispose of, for that would imply the exploded myth of nontransferable ownership. Instead, he is in a unique position because he and he alone has a privileged access that permits him to determine without fear of error, whether the quality of his life is sufficiently unbearable as to warrant termination. By the very nature of things, only the individual himself can determine with accuracy how this world is experienced by him—how it is felt. It is because of this that the right to termination rests primarily with the individual himself. It is not a reflection of a peculiar and unique right, but a result of the availability of information. The right is a universal one. Nor does it remove the possibility of moral error from a situation of suicide, thereby making it unique as a species of euthanasia. To be sure, it removes the possibility of error in regard to whether the world is experienced as unbearable, and in that sense closes an avenue of moral mistake. But it does leave open the possibility of error in evaluating the future—in judging what the chances of changing the situation are—and in that sense a grave moral risk remains. If the evaluation is not carried out carefully, under consideration of all relevant data, or of data that reasonably could be expected to be considered, what would otherwise be an act of euthanasia becomes an act of manslaughter, no matter by whom it is performed.

Before leaving this analysis of suicide and its attendant argumentation, we should consider briefly several points that arose in our presentation of the arguments pro and con. One of the points was that human beings, even though persons, are property: either of God, as the religious arguments have it, or of the state, as the social arguments implied. Another point raised was that life is a gift from God; and in this context, too, it was mentioned as a telling consideration of some moral import that to try to stay alive is a natural inclination: a natural desire, as the argument put it. And, finally, there was the thesis of the quality of life as a determinant.

There is no question but that other assumptions are also involved in the various arguments we have presented; just as there is no question but that there is a plethora of arguments on both sides of the issue that we have not even mentioned.[26] However, the themes we have just mentioned are so common to argumentation surrounding the concept of suicide, that we feel that in their case a special consideration is warranted.

The first thesis—that human beings are property—is not confined merely to the contrasuicide context; nor is it to be found only in the form we have just indicated. It is also advanced by those who are in favor of suicide and, in fact, is involved in the argument from private ownership of one's own body and life. But no matter by which side this thesis is advanced, it is unacceptable, and not merely for the reason we have already considered,[27] namely, that it involves an incoherent

26. For an introductory discussion of some of these, see St. John-Stevas, *The Right to Life,* chap. 4. For a bibliography, see Farberow, *Bibliography on Suicide,* as well as Norman St. John-Stevas, *Life, Death and the Law* (Bloomington: Indiana University Press, 1961), pp. 356–59.

27. Cf. discussion on pp. 118–19.

notion of ownership. In essence, after all, that is a nonmoral, perhaps even purely legalistic consideration. This thesis is also morally unacceptable precisely because it considers persons as pieces of property. Perhaps 'unacceptable' in this context is too strong a word. A utilitarian might well argue that. But this much of the point does stand: that the notion of persons as property cannot merely be asserted as a moral truth. It has to be shown. And here it does not matter whose property a person is supposed to be, whether of himself, of another person, of society, or of God. The point is that from a moral point of view this thesis of property is highly questionable.[28] And given that it is questionable, any argument based on it, whether for or against the moral permissibility of suicide, will lack probative force until this premise is finally established one way or the other.

The second point—that life is a gift from God—in many ways overlaps with the preceding thesis. In that sense, it shares the latter's shortcomings. However, even considered on its own, it is not what we should call an indubitable premise. It is a religious premise, and like all religious premises requires for its acceptability that we accept the religious framework in which it is at home. Minimally, it requires the acceptance of a creator God. But, of course, that is not enough. It also requires a peculiar understanding of 'gift'. This point can best be brought out as follows. As we noted some time ago, a gift may be rejected, returned, or whatever. The giver of a gift may be hurt or even insulted by our treatment of the gift, but in no instance is the destruction of the gift, if we find it bothersome or even painful, sufficient ground for a morally justified retribution on us by the giver of that gift. After all, the gift is ours now; otherwise, it would not be a gift. And it is a characteristic of that which belongs to us that we have the right to dispose of it as we please.[29] Therefore, if the thesis that life is a gift from God

28. Kant, for instance, would question it, as would G. E. Moore, to mention but two instances.

29. The argument would have to be rephrased if utilitarian considerations were to enter the picture.

is meant at all seriously, then, while it *does* follow that we may not take the life of anyone else—that would be tantamount to robbery—it *does not* follow that we may not take our own, that is, that we may not reject the gift from God. A gift which we cannot reject is not a *gift*. It also follows that if retribution were to be visited upon us because of such a rejection, mistreatment, or destruction of the gift from God, we should have no alternative but to conclude that it would be the individual who visited the retribution and not we ourselves that would be morally guilty. In fact, the very threat to visit such retribution would be immoral, for it would be a calculated threat or actual attempt to interfere with our liberty.

Before going on to the third and last point, let us note two more things. First, we have just discussed the thesis of life as a gift from God on its own merits. We did not take into account consideration of the further thesis that this gift is conditional: namely, on the observance of the laws laid down by God as conditions of acceptance. We did not consider this because it does not change the outcome of the argument. For the point is that a gift which we cannot refuse is not a gift; a gift which is not ours to dispose of is not a gift either, especially if we had no choice in accepting it.[30] Second, and this is in a less polemical vein, we should be quite clear on what it is we have here considered as a gift. It is not the person—for that would make no sense—but the life of the person. For the concept of a gift to have any relevance at all in the context of suicide, these two must be kept entirely distinct. But if they are, then we are faced with a radical difficulty, not to say incoherence, in the concept itself. A gift can only be given *to* someone. It cannot *be* that someone, where both receiver and what is received are one and the same entity. Differently, what is given and the individual who receives must be distinct entities. In the present context, however, it is rather difficult to see how that

30. Lest the concept of gratitude be thought relevant in this context, we should also recall that gratitude for an unsolicited gift is not a moral obligation—especially if the gift is of the nature we have just indicated.

could be the case, unless the individual preexisted his own existence. Therefore, to put the point quite bluntly and leaving all considerations about the moral implications of the gift aside, the concept of life as a gift, no matter what else it may be, is logically incoherent.

Lastly, the thesis of natural desire in this context holds that going against a natural desire is immoral, particularly in the case of life. The concept of a natural desire is itself a curious one. As it stands, it goes back at least to the thirteenth century, but probably finds its ultimate antecedents in the writings of Plato and Aristotle. Nowadays, we talk about instinctive drives, unconscious but universal drives, and the like. But no matter whether understood in the ancient or the modern manner, two things apply. The first was already enunciated by John Duns Scotus in the Middle Ages and reiterated after him by William of Ockham: In order for any argument from natural desire even to get off the ground, it has to be shown conclusively that there *is* such a natural desire—that it is a specifically universal characteristic. In the case of the desire for life, that might prove difficult; not merely does the example of lemmings usually come to mind, but there is also the fact that Freudian and post-Freudian schools have postulated the existence of a death wish for all human beings—in more or less pronounced degrees, to be sure, but nevertheless it is said to be there. Therefore the hurdle of the *naturalness* of this desire first has to be cleared.[31] The second point that applies is that all this has absolutely nothing to do with what is really at issue. Let us recall what is at stake—whether suicide is immoral, perhaps even a species of murder. The question of whether or not someone has a natural desire or an instinct for self-preservation is absolutely out of place in such a context. There is no reason in the world to suppose that going against a natural desire or denying an instinct is morally good or evil. In point of fact, religious and social tradition have been inconsistent on this issue. It is said

31. The danger here is to define such a desire as natural—i.e. as a characteristic of the species. Clearly this would be an invalid procedure: a *petitio principii*.

to be morally praiseworthy to abstain from giving in to lust, aggressiveness, and similar instinctive modes of behavior; just as it has always been presented as morally praiseworthy—even by Saint Paul—to go against the natural desire for sex and to conquer the sexual, natural desires which invariably hit us when we, as it were, contemplate "our neighbor's wife." [32] But in any case, and to return to the moral point at issue, from the fact that something is a natural desire—that it flows, as it were, from the nature of the thing—it no more follows that a denial or frustration of that desire is morally good or bad than from the fact that we are naturally subject to gravitational attraction it follows that to try to break or even stop our fall is morally good or evil. A natural desire, being the outcome of our nature, is—like our natural desire for sex—something inherent in us by our very nature. It has no moral parameter in itself whatsoever.

Before passing on to the remaining few points in our discussion, there is one thesis that has common currency in contemporary and traditional discussions of suicide, and which at times has been closely linked to the concept of a natural desire, but which has also enjoyed some vogue apart from it. Indeed, if there is any element of popularity to be found in any of the arguments dealing with suicide—particularly on the side opposed to it, but also on the side that denies its moral gravamen —it is that suicide involves insanity. Frequently, when a coroner's jury's verdict dealing with suicide is brought in, the reason for the act is said to be insanity. Far be it from us to question the correctness of the verdict thus proffered. However, purely for the sake of conceptual completeness, we should like to point out that in a great many cases, the reasoning that is adopted

32. This point cannot be met by stating that we have misunderstood the notion of a natural desire, for see note 31. For an easily available and coherent discussion of the efficacy of natural desire, see A. B. Wolter, O.F.M., *Duns Scotus: Philosophical Writings* (New York and Kansas City: Bobbs Merrill, 1962), chap. 6. Aquinas's discussion of natural desires is inconclusive, since when taken consistently, it leads to the conclusion that there is no evil. See *Summa Theologiae* I, Q. 103, A. 8r.

in order to reach that conclusion is invalid: Because the person in question saw death as the only way out of his difficulty, therefore the person must have been insane. For, so the tacit reasoning seems to continue, under no natural, sane, and normal circumstances would a person who was wholly aware of what he was doing commit such an act. Nor is this sort of reasoning confined to analyses and judgments of suicides. Suicide attempts are frequently treated in the same manner; such attempts are said to be the results of psychotic conditions because, clearly, no normal person would consider such an act as an acceptable way out of a difficulty.[33]

Aside from the questionability of its logic, this sort of argument suffers from a further shortcoming. It depends on two premises, both of which may be questioned. First, it assumes that what is normally the case is in fact correct. In other words, it assumes a definition of insanity on the basis of what is statistically normal. Such a definition need only be stated in order for it to be obvious that from a moral point of view, as well as from the point of view of rationality, there is little to recommend it. It was normal, and indeed rational, to think that the earth was flat, that the earth was the center of the universe, and that to burn witches and heretics was good. For all their statistical normalcy and rationality, these opinions were wrong. We need only think of Hitler-Germany, of Southern United States racial discrimination, and similar other instances to become aware of modern counterpoints. Therefore, that suicide is not generally recognized as a sane way out of a difficulty does not show that in fact it is not. Second, even if we did grant that suicide is no way out but instead hurts more than it helps, the argument still does not establish insanity. Unless, that is, we accept the thesis that no normal person harms himself willingly. This thesis is of venerable ancestry. It goes back to Aristotle, Plato, and even Socrates. But for all that, it is of questionable truth. We may be curious, or we may be bored, or whatever.

33. Most contemporary literature dealing with suicide and suicide attempts listed in Farberow, *Bibliography of Suicide and Suicide Prevention,* argues along these lines.

And thus, we may do ourselves harm on purpose. Such reasoning will not indict us of insanity—unless, once again, by definition. And there is this to ponder in the present connection. If the underlying Socratic thesis is correct, then there cannot be a voluntary wicked act.

But to return to the mainstream of our account. A fundamental premise throughout the preceding discussion was the assumption that the quality of a life is a relevant, even determining factor in assessing the moral acceptability of a particular suicide. Such an assumption, however, is far too momentous merely to be thrown into a discussion. It requires proper analysis and defense. The subject itself is so portentous for the remainder of ethics that proper treatment would require a book in itself. Obviously, we cannot consider it in anything approaching such detail. A brief, superficial discussion must suffice.

The assumption that the quality of a life is relevant in considering whether that life is worth living does not exist in an ethical vacuum. It is part of a much more extensive position which maintains that (a) the individual takes moral precedence over the welfare of the society within which he then finds himself or, differently, that all persons count equally; and that (b) the life of a person has, as such, absolute value. Both of these contentions can be and have been questioned in various quarters. So, for instance, utilitarianism has generally maintained the very opposite of (a); it has argued that the welfare of the majority takes precedence over that of the individual and that in all cases of conflict it is decisive. Utilitarianism admits that, in some instances, what fosters a happy and fulfilled life for a particular individual is in agreement with what benefits society as a whole. But, so far as utilitarianism is concerned, this need not be the case; and if it is, it is a matter of accident, not design.[34] And should the eventuality of a conflict arise, so far as utilitarianism is concerned, the individual would not have the right to dispose of himself as he saw fit. Instead, he would have

34. For a classic statement of the utilitarian position, cf. John Stuart Mill, *Utilitarianism*. There are various modern restatements and redefinitions of the general theory.

to bear his lot and do what is best for the majority. It goes almost without saying that if this sort of theory is correct, the analysis of suicide proffered above would become untenable. In fact, suicide for any reason other than that of advancing the common good will be morally wrong and therefore attended by all the traditional gravamen of murder.

As to (b), it has also been questioned, not merely in the philosophical tradition, but also in the realms of religion and speculative thought in general. Nevertheless, to this we must oppose the following: If morality and ethics are not merely our own invention, games which we play because we so choose, then there must be absolute values, and these will attach to rational beings. The very existence of such a being—its life—will possess a value in itself. Therefore, so far as this position is concerned, the destruction of even one of these would constitute a moral transgression.

Having indicated the existence of a current counter to our own exposition, we must leave matters here. Not because discussion would not be worthwhile—for surely it would—but because it would become too prolonged. In conclusion, let it be noted that my own favorite analysis of suicide involves both (a) and (b), and that I believe both of these to be correct.

3

Euthanasia

Philosophical issues have the frequently disturbing characteristic that they are rarely isolated within a well-defined context. Instead, they ramify in all directions, until whatever solution the particular problem may receive, it will have repercussions far beyond its immediate domain.

The problem of abortion is a good example. The general issue underlying it was seen to be the question of what, precisely, counts as a person. And, considered from that point of view, the problem itself could be put in the form of the question

Is it (the fetus, or the as yet unborn and undeveloped child) *already* a person?

This question, however, is merely the other side of the question

Is it (the individual in question) *still* a person?

In other words, the problem of abortion is merely the other side of the problem of senicide—the killing of the aged—and whatever the analysis in the case of the former, the latter will also be affected. But the question of what right we have to commit feticide inevitably entrains the question of what right we have to kill people; and this issue immediately ramifies further: into those of suicide, euthanasia, infanticide, and even legal homicide, such as execution.

In the preceding chapter we took a somewhat detailed look at the issue of suicide and concluded that the only way in which suicide can be rationally and consistently defended as

131

the right of each individual is to construe it as a particular species of a much more inclusive kind of act: the act of alleviating the unbearable and inescapably unalterable suffering of a person. In other words, we construed it as a species of euthanasia—of mercy killing, to use the colloquial term—and placed the two acts on the same moral plane. We also suggested that this sort of view necessitated a redefinition of the concept of murder. For, although intentional, premeditated, and a species of homicide, euthanasia (at least on this view) is attended by none of the moral gravamen attached to an instance of murder.

It is now time to consider the concept of euthanasia more closely. To begin with, however, we need a definition. The following, already hinted at in the preceding paragraph, is sufficiently neutral to serve as a working model:

> Euthanasia is the mercy killing of a person, that is to say, the intentional and express termination of a life whose quality is such that it is not worth living.

However, this definition, perhaps because of its neutrality, is ambiguous. For instance, it leaves open such questions as, for whom the quality of life is not worth living, and how, ultimately, the decision for termination is to be made. But it does have advantages. So, for example, it makes it quite obvious that suicide is a form of euthanasia. It therefore has the considerable merit of bringing out a unifying element inherent in what would otherwise be a series of disjointed practices of death. And on that theme it serves one further purpose: It shows that whatever we decide in one area of life and death will have repercussions in another. Accordingly, we shall adopt the preceding as a working definition and go on from there.

THE NEGATIVE ARGUMENT

The tradition opposed to euthanasia falls essentially into five categories: a religiously motivated one, a category determined by moral considerations, arguments based on our ignorance of other minds, a group of arguments centering around the pragmatics of social practice, and an argument from appropriateness. This division does not of course imply that any particular argument might not straddle rubrics. In point of fact, some do. Nor does it imply that the considerations of any particular argument are confined to the category from which it is drawn. Frequently, considerations are overlapping. The division is merely a heuristic one, for ease of analysis, and implies no more.

The Religious Argument

Confining ourselves mainly to the Christian tradition, the religiously motivated arguments, by and large, are variations on the following themes: (1) the argument from the command of God; (2) the argument from the general moral code given by God; (3) the argument from the chance for merit; (4) the teleological argument; (5) the argument from the gift of God; (6) the argument from the appropriateness of death; and (7) the argument from eschatological considerations.

The argument from the command of God is actually a variety of arguments centering around one common theme: the claim that God has forbidden us categorically to take human life. With this as a common basis, one version of the argument then runs as follows:

(1a)   It is the express command of God that we take no human life. On this point his command is quite explicit. Nor do either wording or context of "Thou shalt not kill!" allow of exceptions. Euthanasia, however, is the deliberate killing of a human being. Consequently, it is a deliberate transgression of an explicit command by God. Therefore it is religiously unacceptable, and any like act will be punished by eternal damnation.

A variation of this theme of explicit command emphasizes less the unequivocal nature of the commandment and instead concentrates more on the nature of the life that would thus be taken. As such, it would be expressed like this:[1]

(1b)   God has commanded us that "The innocent and just man thou shalt not put to death!"[2]; and "The innocent and just thou shalt not kill!"[3] We, however, are finite human beings who are unaware of the true nature of the persons with whom we deal. In particular, we do not know whether the persons in front of us are innocent and just in the sight of God—are saved—or whether they are wicked and condemned. Lacking such knowledge, we have no way of deciding whether or not we may—indeed should—put people who, to the best of our knowledge have committed no crime, to death. Therefore, no matter what the medical or human reason, we may not kill. And if, in spite of this, we do kill, we shall be subject to eternal damnation.

The reasoning in the preceding arguments is unquestionably of a religious character. Based on religious and revealed premises, they each go on to reach the same conclusion. Further variations, especially in the premises, are of course possible. Thus, the premise could be changed to read that, by his very statement, God and God alone is the arbiter of life and death, that any usurpation of his prerogative by us brings with it the visitation of an eternal nemesis. However, all these arguments have two things in common: They begin with an appeal to God's command, and they point to God's activity as an enforcer. As such, these arguments carry no essential moral weight. Unless, that is, we are extreme voluntarists in ethical matters.

The second sort of argument that we mentioned at the beginning of this section does have a moral parameter. In fact, it is constructed around it. It is what we have called the argu-

1. Cf. St. John-Stevas, *Life, Death and the Law*, p. 272.
2. Exod. 23:7.
3. David 13:53.

ment from the general moral code given by God. In outline, it goes something like this:

(2)   There is a certain general moral code enjoined by God which holds absolutely. This code—this system of ethics—contains as a fundamental tenet the law that it is immoral to kill, deliberately and of set purpose, any person except an unjust aggressor, and then only in case of absolute necessity of self-defense. There are no exceptions to this. Any other act will be murder and hence morally evil; God will punish any transgression of his absolute code with eternal damnation.[4]

From talk of moral codes enjoined by God and of commands enforced by his actions, we turn to an argument of a slightly different variety: the argument from the chance for merit, which goes something like this:

(3)   God has planned the universe down to the most minute detail. The agony of the incurably ill, the nonawareness of the "human vegetable," and the anguish of the spectator all have their place in the scheme of things. Part of that scheme is that each and every one of us be afforded the opportunity to acquire virtue—in particular, so far as the present context is concerned, the virtues of patience, perseverance, humility, and compassion. Therefore, instead of attempting to hasten the day of someone's demise when agony and extreme disability occur, we ought to accept this as an opportunity to develop those very virtues that God finds pleasing. Once more, therefore, euthanasia would be a grave mistake.[5]

4. Cf. Franz Walter, *Die Euthanasie u.d. Heiligkeit d. Lebens* (Munich, 1935).

5. Lest this be thought a non-Christian argument, see the address of Pope Pius XII to the Italian anesthetists, February 24, 1957. See also St. John-Stevas, *Life, Death and the Law*, p. 272.

The next argument on our list—the teleological argument—
is premised on the assumption that God, as the supreme creator
of the universe, is also the planner for the procedures and situations as they obtain in it. Thus,

(4)   There is no question but that life is full of trials and
        tribulations, not merely of the momentary kind of
        agony, but also of the prolonged kinds of pain and
        anguish. In a word, life is full of situations which
        "test men's hearts." However, this is not haphazard.
        It is according to God's plan. To be sure, we, who
        are insignificant and finite creatures, do not have an
        understanding of the coherence of all things. In par-
        ticular, we cannot understand what to our finite gaze
        seem to be nothing more than sadistically prolonged
        lives of incredible agony; nor do we see the point of
        a life of complete unawareness, lived—if that is the
        term—like a vegetable. But there is a purpose in
        all this, both for the person who himself is the sub-
        ject of this way of life, as well as for the person who
        suffers empathetically as onlooker. We must trust.
        It is not our place to interfere. There is God's plan.
        Therefore all concerned must endure. It is our duty
        as creatures of God. Ultimately, everything will turn
        out for the best.[6]

More commonly encountered than any of the preceding arguments, however, is the argument from the gift of God. More
explicitly, the title ought to be "argument from the premise
that life is a gift from God." With this as a fundamental assumption, the argument proceeds as follows:[7]

6. This sort of argument seems to underly the Christian position of
perseverance in faith because of God's plan, as it is to be found in various
places in Augustine's *City of God*. On the flat assertion of God's plan,
see Aquinas *Summa Theologiae* I:103, A. 1–8.

7. Cf. St. John-Stevas, *Life, Death and the Law,* p. 272. See also Frank
J. Curran, "Religious Implications," in Harold Rosen, ed., *Therapeutic
Abortion* (New York: Julian Press, 1954), pp. 153–65.

√(5)   Man's life is not his own to dispose of, nor is it the
       prerogative of anyone to shorten it or to take it
       away. For this life is not his own but something
       which he holds in trust from God. He may use it
       wisely, even prolong it, but he may not destroy it
       because to do so is to destroy what essentially be-
       longs to God.[8]

The argument from the appropriateness of death once more
is a relatively simple argument. Based on the premise that God
is the master of life and death, it continues:

(6)   The prerogative of giving life belongs to God; nor
       may that prerogative be usurped. Conversely, the
       prerogative of taking life. It is God's and God's
       alone. In his wisdom he has decided who should
       live and who should not; who should die, and when.
       That time, at which death would naturally occur, is
       the time set by God for that event. Therefore we
       must not interfere—certainly, not hasten it. Con-
       sequently euthanasia, as a preternatural hastening
       of the appointed time of death, constitutes an unac-
       ceptable interference in the work of God.[9]

Finally, there is the argument from eschatological considerations. In essence, it is no more than a collage of the various
other arguments, but it states more explicitly what appears
only in veiled form in some of them:

(7)   God is the giver of laws, not merely the creator of
       the universe. As such, he has given us explicit com-
       mands on what to do and what not to do. We may
       not agree with these commands, if only because as
       finite beings we lack sufficient insight into their rea-

8. Cf. St. John-Stevas, *The Right to Life,* p. 50.
9. This sort of argument also lies at the basis of Jewish and Islamic
injunctions against suicide. Cf. chap. 2.

son and nature. However, we can and do understand the following: that we shall be punished in the
next life if we do not obey them. "Do not kill in
any instance except self-defense against an unjust
aggressor," is one of these. In other words, if for
no other reason than that of a hope for the eternal
life to come ought we to refrain from killing—and,
a fortiori, from euthanasia.

This last argument brings out clearly what underlies a great
deal of the various religious arguments against euthanasia as
cited above: a simple and direct appeal to the power of the
being postulated by religious thought. But of course we would
be sadly remiss if we suggested even for a moment that this is
all there is to the various religious strands. Even the most
cursory glance at the various arguments we have sketched
above will show that the moral parameter also plays a large
role. And this last provides a transition to the next category of
arguments against euthanasia, drawn from the realm of ethics.
However, prior to considering these, let us cast a brief analytic
eye over arguments (1) to (7).

When doing so, several things immediately strike us. The
first is that the various reasons given for not allowing euthanasia are extremely and surprisingly diverse. Not merely are we
told that it is our duty to suffer, as in (1) and (2); we are also
told that it is our privilege, as in (3); and that all the suffering is a necessary part of God's plan, as in (4); and finally
that it does not matter what we think, since we are merely the
recipients and administrators of a gift. It is not at all clear how
—or even that—all of these reasons are mutually compatible.
Nor are matters helped any by the claim that death can be
allowed only at an appropriate time, as in (6), or by the simple
appeal to raw power, as in (7). The problem is perhaps not
so much that we have a question of internal consistency, but
that we have a serious difficulty of how to reconcile all this
with the characteristics that God is supposed to have: supreme

mercy and compassion, infinite love and justice, and a good-
ness that knows no bounds.[10]

Second, there is the fact that every single one of these arguments assumes as true some version of religious revelation
concerning the existence and nature of God, as well as his
relationship to man.[11] However, for the sake of clarity and in-
tellectual honesty, we must insist that these are merely assumptions, that they are in no way substantiated by what
ordinarily goes under the name of proof. Hence the conclusions
based on these assumptions cannot lay claim to absolute and
unconditioned correctness.

Third, and closely related to the preceding, there is this consideration: Even if the existence of a God were, somehow, to
be proved, there would still be no guarantee that what such a
God commands is necessarily good. Nor, for that matter, that
he has a plan which involves the ultimate reward and/or punishment of man. The truth of eschatological theories is not
automatically substantiated by the truth of existential claims
about God. Consequently, barring further proof of this matter,
it is not at all clear that arguments based on eschatological
considerations carry any weight. But even if they did—and
this is a fourth objection—it could be argued with great cogency that acquiescence in these expectations constitutes the
morally incorrect reason for refraining from euthanasia. If we
generalize the schema on which (1) to (3) and (5) to (7) are
based, it has the form "If you do x, then God will punish you!"
From a moral point of view anyone who acts on that sort of
principle proceeds on a quid pro quo basis—on a basis of
bribery, to put it crudely—and what he does lacks moral merit.
A refusal to engage in euthanasia will be morally good if and

10. At this stage, an appeal is generally made to the analogical character of all statements about God. Without going into detail, it is safe to
say that the difficulties with the theory of analogy are notorious.
11. Strictly speaking, the last phrase is incorrect. It ought to read,
"and/or the relationship of man to God." But hereby hangs a theological
tale too complex for our present considerations.

only if it is not done out of self-interest—as the religious arguments all have it—but for moral reasons. In the present context, these are conspicuously absent.

Fifth—and this objection is specifically directed toward (3) and (4)—even if all the assumptions concerning God and his plan for the universe were granted, is that plan a good one? Is the amount and degree of suffering it entails in the case of euthanasia candidates really necessary? Can the virtues that their condition is alleged to make possible not be inculcated in some other way? If yes, need we really prolong their agony?

Finally, and perhaps most important of all, there is the fact that all of these arguments ignore the quality of the life led by an individual as an irrelevant factor of no concern to the present issue. That is to say, they assume, one and all, that considerations as to the nature of life led by a person count as nothing in the face of the dicta of God. One could argue, and very properly so, that it is far from clear that such a disregard for the quality of life is acceptable. If how we live is not a relevant datum, then surely something is wrong with the ethics of God. Nor will it do to reply as per argument (5), that life is a gift of God and therefore cannot, without incurring grave moral guilt, be taken away. The reasons why this will be unacceptable have already been amply shown in our previous discussion of a similar thesis in the context of suicide, and we need not repeat them here. Suffice it to say that if life really is such a gift, then we, who are its recipients, have the right to do with it as we please. It is a right which as such holds for all. The giving of the gift may make for gratitude—but it does not, either logically or morally, require it. And it certainly does not entail that, when, as by someone's own statements or relevant considered indication, that life has become an unbearable burden to that individual, we do not have the right—indeed, the duty—to relieve him of it. On the contrary. If there are moral indications in this case at all, they all go the other way.

The Moral Argument

So much for the presentation, analysis of, and counterarguments to the religiously motivated approaches to the question of euthanasia. There is no question but that we have simply glossed over important issues on both sides of the problem; but in the main, the heart of the controversy is there. Therefore, let us now examine those arguments against euthanasia which are based on moral considerations alone. In other words, let us turn to the issue of euthanasia as considered from the point of view of ethics. And again, we are faced with a plethora; but as before, the various particular arguments can be grouped around three general lines of reasoning: (1) the argument from personhood; (2) the argument against qualitative considerations; and (3) the argument from the likelihood of mistake.

The argument from personhood is really a misnomer. More properly, the title should be "the argument from the assumption that persons are ends in themselves." As such, the argument is based on the further assumption of an absolute and universally applicable set of moral standards and values for the universe—an assumption which, in this context, entails that any deliberate form of killing a person is morally reprehensible and prima facie tantamount to murder. Euthanasia, like suicide and abortion, is then presented as one species of this genus. More specifically, the argument generally takes something like the following form:[12]

(1)   All rational beings, no matter what their particular physiological or psychological states, are ends in themselves. Therefore it is morally reprehensible to take the life of such a being (except, possibly, in self-defense) if that action occurs with full knowledge, purpose, and intent. An act of euthanasia does not fall under the exceptive circumstance indi-

12. The thesis of persons as ends in themselves is best brought out by Kant in his *Foundations of the Metaphysics of Morals,* esp. sec. 2.

cated, yet definitely is the taking of such a life. Consequently, an act of euthanasia—which, by definition, cannot be performed by accident—is morally reprehensible. In fact, it is an act of murder.

In evaluating the cogency and probative force of this particular train of reasoning, let us always keep in mind that what we have just presented is only a schema, and as such may be fleshed out in different ways. But in whatever way the bare bones of this argument may be clothed, the following facts remain: First, this argument contains the overriding assumption that all rational beings have an absolute value—more precisely, that they are ends in themselves. But how is this proved? The argument in question does not attempt to furnish even the beginnings of a proof. In fact, it is difficult to see how, short of an appeal to intuition, such a proof could be furnished. As to intuition, we need say little about it: One man's intuition is another's prejudice, and the whole amounts to no more than a state of psychological conviction. Second, even if the assumption of the absolute value of rational beings were granted, the conclusion still would not follow. Only by a confusion between a rational being on the one hand and its life on the other could we conclude from the fact that the former is an end in itself that the latter has absolute value as well—without any qualifying considerations. It is entirely compatible with the thesis of rational beings as ends in themselves that only a certain quality of life is deemed livable for them, and that in the eventuality of its nonrealization, the life of that being ought to be terminated. Third—and this point was already touched upon in the last consideration—there is the general assumption that considerations as to quality of life are irrelevant to the question of whether or not that life has value, and to the further question of whether the intentional termination of a negative life by an outside agency is murder.

This last consideration encapsulates an objection to the second sort of argument that we mentioned at the beginning of this section: the argument against qualitative considerations. By all standards of fairness, therefore, and before we proceed any further in considering this objection, the argument itself ought to have a say.

> (2)   Arguments in favor of euthanasia are premised on the assumption that the quality of life led by a person is a relevant parameter when considering the question of whether or not it is moral for us, as external agents, to terminate that life or by our inaction to allow that life to come to an end. However, qualitative considerations are not to the point. We are dealing here with the life of a person, and such a life is an absolute—something that must be preserved at all cost. To end it in any way, either actively or by inaction, is murder.

As will be obvious at first glance, this argument depends for no small part of its cogency on the thesis of absolutism—in particular, on the hypothesis of the absolute value of the life of a person.[13] Herein we have a profound overlap with the argument from personhood; and herein we also find the reason for the fact that any objection brought to bear against the argument on that score at the same time reflects negatively on the present one. One further thing will be apparent, a point that really exhausts the import of the whole argument: The claim that the quality of life led by an individual is irrelevant makes sense only in the context of this absolutistic assumption. Otherwise, it amounts to no more than a blatant, incredible, and unargued contention. But it is not at all clear that the absolutistic hypothesis can bear the burden thus imposed upon it. In a logical sense, it is not at all clear that the latter entails the former, or even that they go together. We need scarcely point out that the absolutistic thesis itself is in need of proof, for that is obvious from our preceding discussion. All in all, there-

---

13. This is a thesis common to all absolutistic moral theories.

fore, this particular argument against euthanasia at best rates a "not proven"; at worst, it fails.

Finally, there is the argument from the likelihood of mistake. In a nutshell, it goes like this:[14]

(3)   The human mind is not omniscient. Among other things, what this means is that in assessing a particular situation with which we are confronted, we are liable to error. In matters of small moral importance, such errors can be forgiven; in matters of high moral stakes, we cannot afford to err. Potential euthanasia situations are situations in which the moral stakes are as high as they can be. Therefore we cannot afford to err. For if we are wrong, we shall have killed a person. Therefore, we must be sure of both the moral facts of the case as well as its material aspects. In neither case, however, can we claim absolute certainty. As the preceding arguments have shown, the moral verdict is far from in; and as to the material facts of the matter, even physicians of the highest order have been shown to be mistaken. Therefore only one course of action is open to us: to continue in our efforts to keep the person alive. For only in that way will we escape the risk of murder.

The argument just sketched has an air of cool reasonableness that may strike us as disconcerting. And well it should. For, as it stands, it amounts to no more than the following injunction: Unless absolute certainty obtains in all situations, refrain from acts that have moral consequences. What is disconcerting about this is not the thesis itself—although that, too, may be the case—but rather that it is impossible to implement the advice thus proffered. Even to keep a potential candidate for euthanasia alive is to engage in a moral act. Or, at least, it is

14. Cf. St. John-Stevas, *Life, Death and the Law*, p. 273 and passim, for a similar argument.

to engage in an act that has moral parameters. The argument merely *tells* us that it is potentially murderous to kill him or let him die. But with equal degree of likelihood there is the possibility that matters may be the other way around: That *not* to kill, *not* to let him die, is immoral. Furthermore, from a purely moral point of view, this argument is based on what most charitably can be described as a utilitarian premise: When in doubt choose that alternative that runs the least risk of moral error. The acceptability of that premise is not in doubt. What is in doubt is its application to the present case. For, while denying knowledge of the moral parameters on the one hand—with respect to euthanasia—it assumes that knowledge on the other—with respect to keeping a person alive. If not a logical inconsistency, at least this constitutes an inconsistency in practice.

To sum up, what the various moral arguments amount to is this: a series of unproven assumptions about the moral structure of the universe, about the value of the life of a person, and about the refusal to take risks. All this is coupled with the further assumption that it is better to err on the side of life than that of death—an assumption that shows a sublime disregard for the quality of life which it supposedly honors. In the light of this it would be foolish for us to assume that the moral case against euthanasia has been proven.

The Argument from Ignorance of Other Minds

From arguments based on moral considerations, let us turn to arguments based on the facts as we find them. One of these facts is that for each and every one of us, our awareness is confined to the limits of our own mind. That is to say, none of us can have anyone else's sensations, thoughts, or feelings as that other person has them. We are, as it were, locked in the prison of our own mind. The only escape from this prison is by means of public communication: by using signs which, hopefully, mean to the other person what they mean to us. Another fact is that we have our own attitudes about all sorts of things; and, lacking any explicit indication to the contrary, we frequently ascribe these attitudes and opinions to others only because we deem it reasonable, because we have them.

These facts form the basis of the following, somewhat complicated argument against euthanasia:

> Frequently, when considering the fate of people in comatose states or conditions of apparent and prolonged agony, we forget that we are not really aware of what goes on in their minds, what they really feel. We forget that our assessment of their plight is nothing more than an autobiographical report: an analysis of what we think we would feel were we in that situation. But we have no guarantee whatever that the people in question actually do feel the way we think they do; nor can we be sure that if they could communicate with us, they would agree with our assessment. Consequently it is highly presumptuous, to say the least, to kill people under such circumstances or to let them die, solely on the assumption that that is what they would —or do—wish. It amounts to setting ourselves up as the final and infallible arbiters of what is the case. And for that, we have no warrant.

The main force of this argument is directed to those cases where, for some reason or other, the person in question is not of sound mind. Comatose states, delerious states, states of severe mental aberration, situations of infantile regression and the like would be good examples. One side of the argument has it that in such cases euthanasia would be felt as a blessing—even though the persons affected are unable to communicate such a sentiment to us and are unable to tell us that from their point of view this would be the case. The thrust of the argument itself, however, is in the opposite direction. It is to the effect that even in such cases—or especially in such—we have no grounds to press for euthanasia. As the argument's major premise puts it, How could we possibly know what such a person would want? All of us are inescapably trapped within the prison of our own minds. The only way out is by means of overt communication. And in order to be effective in achieving the desired result, this communication must be sure. Certainty, however, does not obtain in the present case. There is no communication; or, what there is is of an unsure if not incomprehensible form. Any assumption that communication has occurred, and that its content is of a specific nature, amounts to pure guesswork. And here, where a person's life is at stake, we cannot afford to guess. Nor can we afford to let our feelings about what we think we would want in situations of this sort stand as an analysis of the wishes of other persons. It amounts to an assumption of omniscience on our part. And that is inexcusable—as well as morally fraught with danger. Therefore euthanasia, as based on the putative wishes of the comatose and so on, is morally unacceptable.

This argument could be expanded in the following way:

> Nor will it do to appeal to a "living will"—a blanket request for euthanasia composed by the euthanasia candidate prior to his (her) entering upon the particular debilitating state in question. For, if the wishes of the individual are at all relevant, surely the wishes *as had now* are more relevant than the wishes as had at some previous time. But how can we know that those wishes which are expressed in the living will still obtain? Lacking all insight into another human mind, how can we know that the person has not changed his or her mind?

If we consider this argument as a whole, there is no faulting its fundamental premises: We do not have a direct acquaintance with the minds of other people, nor, lacking such an acquaintance, can we know whether or not such a person has changed his mind. At least, that holds true in situations of the sort we have envisioned, where the individual is unable to communicate properly with us. But in spite of this fact, the argument as a whole is inconclusive. For, against it we can array the following considerations: First, it is simply not true to say that we have no objective basis for saying that under such circumstances the persons themselves would not or do not wish their demise. It is simply false to claim that our desire to administer euthanasia

—whether actively or by a withdrawal of life-support systems—reflects no more than our own momentary personal bias. For there are a great many people who find themselves in similar debilitating conditions but are able to communicate, and who tell us that they do wish to die.[15] Consequently, our warrant for the decision in favor of euthanasia is quite good and is not merely an autobiographical report having purely subjective validity. Second, it is questionable whether those who are candidates for euthanasia but who refuse it really are the right people to make that decision. To put the point somewhat differently, the argument assumes that the individual himself is the final arbiter as to what should be done with him. That, however, is an assumption of extremely dubious status. Not only does it assume that the individual is of greater significance than the society of which he is a member; it also assumes that from a strictly moral point of view, what makes the killing of a person morally unacceptable is that the person does not wish it. Both these assumptions can be, and indeed have been, questioned. Third, the claim that possibly by now the individual in question has—or, if conscious would have—undergone a change of heart and therefore would no longer want to abide by the decision of his living will is really quite irrelevant. As indicated previously, it is quite possible to argue from the point of view of a utilitarian position that the decisions and wishes of the individual are irrelevant from the moral point of view and that, no matter which option the wishes and desires of the individual favor, we ourselves are morally duty-bound to act for the common good. Therefore this whole issue of our inability to know the wishes of the individual, of running the risk of being mistaken, is irrelevant. It is we, the objective observers, who have the responsibility to decide on the basis of the common good. And if it

15. For literature on this, see the various publications of the Voluntary Euthanasia Society. However, it should also be said that the claim we have just reported is not the result of proper scientific investigation. The whole problem still awaits careful and analytic statistical study. Let us also add that such a study would not solve the moral problem.

should turn out that no useful purpose would be served by keeping the individual alive, if there are more worthy competitors for our medical care and attention, then we should allow such an individual to die.

Argument from Social Praxis

The thesis of social utility mentioned above brings us to another, closely related series of arguments. They are what we shall call the arguments from social praxis. In a nutshell, they reject euthanasia as running the real risk of endangering the very nature and existence of society. Three arguments in particular stand out above all others.

(i) The individual who requests euthanasia or the person who orders it on the grounds that the situation is not merely unbearable but also—and mainly—cannot be alleviated or improved is simply not omniscient. He does not really know that what he thinks is the case at the present time in fact is true. Nor, assuming for the moment that he is correct, does he know that in the very near future the apparently hopeless state will not become curable. Furthermore, there also are such things as "spontaneous recoveries." All this will be made impossible if euthanasia is administered. The person making the decision can only go on what seems reasonable to him at the time. But what is reasonable is a relative thing, very much dependent on the intelligence of the decision maker and the availability of data. Nor is there any guarantee that what is reasonable is in fact correct.

(ii) There is no objection to euthanasia when administered at the behest of society or of those responsible for the common good; but euthanasia given at the request of the individual himself sets a dangerous moral precedent. It is a de facto admission that the individual is more important than the society. Such an admission is not merely morally inadmissible but also dangerous to the survival of the society as a whole.

(iii)   The administering of euthanasia, no matter how well controlled and no matter how carefully legislated, very easily lends itself to misuse. In fact, it invites it. The state may use it as a means to whip people into line, to enforce its own doctrines. In other words, euthanasia, once permitted, runs the very real danger of becoming merely another version of legalized murder or execution.[16]

As to the first argument, there can be no question but that it has a point. It is simply true that the decision to administer euthanasia must be made on the basis of what seems reasonable at the time, and that there is no guarantee that what seems reasonable at one time or to one person will seem reasonable at another time or to another person. But that problem is not unique to the case of euthanasia. It obtains in all cases involving choice. If the principle underlying this sort of consideration were to be enunciated, it would be that we should refrain from acting in all cases where we do not have all the data that are or can be had—where we do not know beyond the possibility of error which course of action is correct. But that would mean that we ought to refrain from any sort of action. And that is absurd. Therefore, unless we wish to be guilty of inconsistency, this principle cannot be accepted. Furthermore, the argument suggests that we do not know what the future will bring. True enough. But again, if this were to be taken consistently, it would mean that we ought to engage in no activity which might conceivably be affected by a change in the present state of affairs.

16. Cf. St. John-Stevas, *Life, Death and the Law*, p. 273. See also Yale Kamisar, "Some Non-religious Reasons against Proposed Mercy-Killing Legislation," *Minnesota Law Review* 42 (May 1958): 969–1042. Kamisar also presents versions of (i) and (ii).

Once more, this would result in almost complete inactivity on our part and ultimately lead to social collapse.

The *second* argument does not reject euthanasia completely. It merely wants to take the decision-making power away from the individual and place it where—according to this theory at least—it belongs: into the hands of society. The underlying assumption here is, of course, that the welfare of society takes precedence over that of the individual, that the individual's importance is secondary to that of society. This, clearly enough, is an ethical theory of value and obligation. As such, it cannot just be stated. It has to be argued and proven. Nor is it quite obvious that this particular theory is correct. Therefore, as was said in the context of suicide—unless and until this theory is proven, it is on a par with any other theory of value and obligation, and consequently its tenets cannot be used to establish a point. They can only make it appear reasonable and even true, if the theory itself is. In other words, the conclusion of this sort of argument has only heavily conditioned validity.

The third sort of argument seems to espouse a nonutilitarian position, and in that sense is apparently opposed to (ii) in its basic assumptions. It is therefore difficult to see how (ii) and (iii) can be reconciled. But that aside, there is this further consideration: There is no doubt that legislatively permitted euthanasia would lend itself to possible misuses. There is even less doubt that legislatively enjoined euthanasia would lead to such misuses in precisely the manner envisioned by the argument. But, as we already had occasion to note, that is the fate of any moral choice and power: It may be misused, even perverted from its true nature. In this sense, euthanasia is not unique. But to argue that since euthanasia may be misused, therefore it is morally unacceptable, is to argue invalidly—to commit a non sequitur. Practically speaking, of course, it may be a reason to forbid it, but this consideration of what is pragmatically the correct thing to do ought not to blind us to the fact that this is not necessarily correct from the moral point of view. Nor, does this entail that euthanasia ought not to be permitted. It merely follows that, for pragmatic reasons, it ought not to be enjoined.

The Argument from Appropriateness

Finally, there is what has sometimes been called the argument from appropriateness. It is very brief and goes like this:

> Death must be allowed to occur at the time appropriate to it, not at the will of the individual.[17]

It is not at all clear precisely how we are to take this argument. In fact, it is not even clear that it is an argument. It resembles more the expression of a particular view, bald and unargued, to the effect that we ought not to interfere in the workings of nature. But however reasonable that may seem on the surface, one thing is clear: Those who advocate this sentiment most probably would be unwilling to apply it consistently. For, what exactly does it mean not to interfere in the workings of nature? Surely nothing other than that we ought not to introduce artificial, man-made factors into the chain of events. In short, we ought not to interfere in the natural course of events. But let us be quite explicit on what that means: We ought not to practice medicine of any sort; nor ought we to engage in any commerce nor in the manufacturing of any tools. We should live as we did when man was a primitive animal. Anything else would constitute interference in the workings of nature. It is highly unlikely that those who propound this particular sentiment would want to see it applied this far. But if not, they must explain why an exception to this principle ought to be made in cases other than that of euthanasia. Barring a reasonable answer on this score, the argument against euthanasia cannot be deemed consistent. Moreover, we ought not to lose sight of one fact: It is not at all clear what is meant by the phrase "the time appropriate to death." What constitutes an appropriate time? Is it the time when it occurs on its own? In that case, it will be the time of birth—for, unless we interfere, the baby, untended and uncared for, will surely die. Is it the time when in the normal

---

17. This argument finds explicit religious statement in the *Shulchan Aruch*, Yore Deah 339:1. For a contrary current in Judaism, see *Sefer Chasidim*, nos. 315–18.

course in the life of the animal called *homo sapiens,* death would occur? That would be to degrade man to the status of a mere animal, to refuse to recognize that he is rational as well. And that, in fact, would itself be an extremely counternatural procedure. Is it the time when, in the natural course of events of the rational animal called *homo sapiens,* death would occur? But that would permit us to use our reason, and thereby our decision-making powers as to what is appropriate and what is not. In effect, understood in this last sense, this so-called argument places no real restrictions on euthanasia whatever. It merely gives the appearance of doing so. Therefore, this concept of appropriateness is so hopelessly vague that it is of no use as a basis on which to found a decision on life and death. Criteria of application are lacking. And lest it be said that an "appropriate time" for death obtains when ordinary methods fail and extraordinary methods have to be employed, let us recall what we have had occasion to observe once before: 'Ordinary' and 'extraordinary' are relative terms. They depend on the relative level of sophistication of the society in question. What is ordinary for us—say the use of open-heart surgery to install a new heart valve—would be extraordinary to the Azande of Africa. Therefore my death would be appropriate in the latter society, whereas it would be inappropriate in our own. But surely this is unacceptable, for the only thing that has changed in this context is the social situation, not the problem itself. The facts of the matter also have remained.

THE POSITIVE ARGUMENT

Having considered the traditionalists' approach to euthanasia, it is now time to consider the more contemporary point of view: the position of the neomoralists. Again, let me emphasize at the outset that in a very definite sense, the claim that this favorable attitude toward euthanasia is representative of the new morality is not intended as a purely historical claim. That is to say, we do not wish to argue that hitherto euthanasia has been condemned as immoral or impractical by all who have thought about the matter. For that is false. People have always toyed with the idea of mercy killing, and some have even advocated it. The point of presenting this as part of the position of the new morality—indeed, of calling it by that name—is that at no other time in the recent past of our Western culture has the thesis of euthanasia been advanced so vociferously or enjoyed such apparent popular support.

The arguments for euthanasia are at least as diversified as those against it. By and large, however, they fall into the following four groups: arguments from personal dignity; arguments from moral considerations; arguments from biological considerations; and arguments from social praxis.

The Argument from Personal Dignity

The argument from personal dignity is well summed up in the following statement of what has been called a living will:[18]

18. A famous variant of this is encapsulated in the "form of declaration under the Voluntary Euthanasia Act, 1969," which was appended to the Voluntary Euthanasia Bill presented to the House of Lords by Lord Raglan and defeated on second reading. Cf. House of Lords Official Report, *Parliamentary Debates* (Hansard), vol. 300, no. 50 (March 25, 1969), cols. 1143–1254. In part, it reads as follows:

> If I should at any time suffer from a serious physical illness or impairment reasonably thought in my case to be incurable and expected to cause me severe distress or render me incapable of rational existence, I request the administration of euthanasia at a time or in circumstances to be indicated or specified by me or, if it is apparent that I have become incapable of giving directions, at the discretion of the physician in charge of my case.
>
> In the event of my suffering from any of the conditions specified above, I request that no active steps should be taken, and in particular that no resuscitatory techniques should be used, to prolong my life or restore me to consciousness.
>
> This declaration is to remain in force unless I revoke it, which I may do at any time, and any request I may make concerning action to be taken or withheld in connection with this declaration will be made without further formalities.

For a detailed discussion of this bill, see Jonathan Gould and Lord Craigmyle, *Your Death Warrant?* (London: Geoffrey Chapman, 1971).

To whom it may concern: If it should ever occur that I can no longer participate in making decisions as to my own future, the following is a testament of my wishes for such an occasion: If, all things being considered, there is no reasonable expectation that I shall recover from my extreme physical or mental disability, I request that I be allowed to die, that I not be kept alive only by dint of heroic measures. I do not fear death as much as the indignity of physical and mental deterioration, utter dependence and, hopeless pain. I ask that if necessary, drugs be administered to me to end my suffering, should my condition reach such a state. I make this request while in good health, in sound mind, and good spirit.

As is generally admitted, such a living will at present has no legally binding force. That fact need not concern us. What should concern us is the actual content of such a document and its underlying assumptions. To begin with, the point of such a will—and the point of the argument from dignity which underlies it—is fairly clear. As one eminent theologian has put it, today's expiring patients in hospitals frequently die "comatose and betubed and sedated and aerated and glucosed and *non compos mentis*." [19] This state of affairs is deemed undignified. The life led by such an individual is considered to be subnormal and beyond ordinary moral considerations. The right thing to do is to prevent the individual from sinking into such a state, voluntarily or otherwise. In other words, the person ought to be allowed to die.

This argument has an air of extreme reasonableness about it. Certainly, such a state as the one described is not very pretty, nor is it comfortable for any of the parties concerned. But that is not really the issue, unless we let a question of aesthetics rule the issue of life and death. The issue is whether it is undignified for an individual in the throes of death to fight by any means at

19. Dr. Joseph Fletcher, as reported in "Governor McCall's Views on the Death with Dignity Issue," press release from the Office of the Governor of the State of Oregon, February 28, 1972.

his disposal; for the society of which that person is a member to attempt to save him or, failing any immediate hope of that, to attempt to keep him alive in the hope that in the near future a cure will be discovered or a spontaneous cure effected. The question is also precisely what 'dignity' here means, if not the convenience of those concerned in preserving that life or the absence of pain for the patient. And even more fundamentally, the question is whether any considerations such as those of dignity are relevant to the present context. The claim that for the sake of one's own dignity one be allowed to die—even be *made* to die[20]—is the claim that the quality of our lives is a morally relevant factor. And that has yet to be shown. In fact, it very much seems that those who propound the argument from dignity frequently do not know what dignity is, nor can they give any reasoned explanation as to why dignity should be important.

Furthermore, if the argument from dignity were to be admitted, its consequences would be grave. It would entail that all who live an unalterably undignified form of existence ought to be killed. On the surface, this seems to be innocuous enough. The term 'unalterably' seems to prevent us from depopulating the underdeveloped countries and our own ghettos. But a moment's reflection will show that this is appearance only, that in fact just such a consequence would ensue. For the thrust of the

20. The argument is sometimes made in medical circles, that there is a difference between permitting a patient to die by abstaining from the use of extraordinary means of prolonging his life and actually killing him. There is no question that there is a difference between the two sorts of acts. However, it is a difference which, from a moral point of view, is inconsequential. Physically, the two sorts of acts are distinct. Morally, they have the same status since, from a moral point of view, failure to do something is also to do something; the absence of an act is also an act. This moral fact lies at the basis of the legal concept of culpable negligence: the failure to perform an act which, morally speaking, the individual was duty bound to do. Therefore, whether the euthanasia practice consists in an overt act of killing or the withdrawal (or refusal to administer) life-support systems, the moral status of these procedures are on the same level. Nothing is solved by pointing to their physical difference. The real issue—the moral issue—is still to be decided.

argument from dignity is that if, "all things being considered" —that is, given the present state of affairs—"there is no reasonable expectation" of being cured—that is, of this state of affairs being ameliorated—then the person ought to be killed. The crucial phrases are those in quotes, and they apply to the underdeveloped countries just as much as to our own ghettos. At the present time and for those who are presently alive, the currently existing state of affairs is such that for them there is no reasonable expectation that their lot will be altered, that they will be released from their extremely undignified mode of existence. Therefore they will fall into the same rubric as the medical candidates for euthanasia, and consequently they, too, ought to be killed.

The reply to the preceding is generally that it completely misconstrues the issue. What is at issue is not every and any state of undignified existence, but specifically such a medical state of utter dependence that without great efforts on the part of other people, the person in question would die. However, this reply is itself quite insufficient. Why should a state of utter medical and/or psychological dependence be considered sufficiently undignified so as to warrant euthanasia, and why no other state? By what criterion does the one count but not the other? Unless, of course, the matter is thus by definition.

Furthermore, and quite apart from any ethical considerations, there is the question of what is to count as "heroic measures"— and to whom. Surely both are relative matters. Relative, that is, to the society, the availability of resources, and the state of technology. Consequently, lacking any clearer definition of this phrase and its analogues, the request itself is useless.

Finally—although much more could be said about the matter —the structure of the argument from dignity seems to be this: If I am not satisfied with the life I live, kill me. Suitably amended, it holds for euthanasia recommended on behalf of others. Stripped thus to its bones, the argument loses much of its appeal. Certainly those who claim that we have a duty to society should think twice about accepting this argument, for its repercussions in that area are grave.

The Moral Argument

The argument from moral considerations is really a series of arguments that may be reduced to two types: one, dealing with the rights of the individual; another, centering around the rights of society. The argument arising from the rights of the individual maintains that each individual has the right to decide whether and under what circumstances he wishes to live. If the individual so decides, it is his privilege—his moral right—to request that his life be terminated. In other words, the individual has a moral right to suicide even by means of some agency other than his own. Therefore he has the moral right to prepare a living will and to see it executed.

This argument is in fact a veiled—or not so veiled—argument in favor of agent suicide. Since we have already dealt with this case in the preceding chapter, we shall let matters rest there and go on to the second kind of argument: that centering around the rights of society.

> It is simply a basic and unarguable moral fact that the welfare of the society takes precedence over the welfare of its individual particular members. In fact, that act and only that act is morally good which promotes the greatest amount of good for the greatest number of people. If it should happen that an individual should become hopelessly comatose, a burden on the society and a source of constant anguish for those who are in contact with him, then it is not merely the right but also the duty of society to terminate the existence of that person. Any other act would be morally wrong, not right. Therefore, even from a purely moral point of view, it will sometimes be the duty of society to administer euthanasia.

The basis of this sort of argument is the ethical theory of utilitarianism. Encapsulated in the first few statements, it would indeed entail that in at least some cases euthanasia is the morally appropriate course. But as we have said so many times before, what guarantees that utilitarianism is correct? The matter is ethically far too important merely to be left to the claim of obviousness. Moreover, suppose that the thesis of utilitarianism were granted: Euthanasia is not the only practice that would thereby be licensed. Infanticide, suicide, abortion, senicide—in fact, any killing that would benefit society—would thereby become morally above reproach. Conceivably, we could thereby justify not merely capital punishment, but also the extermination of any and all minority groups whose existence is a source of difficulty to the majority. In the interest of consistency, are those who propound the preceding argument willing to go that far?

Finally, quite aside from the ethics of the matter, there is the question of how the principle underlying the argument is to be applied. By what standards are we to judge that an individual is in a "hopeless" state which imposes only a burden upon society? By the standard of convenience? In that case, why not come right out and say that the reason why we think that a person in such a state should be killed is that we find it inconvenient to keep him alive! To say anything else would be to hide behind a moral facade. If the standard is not that of convenience, is it that of the present state of the art? Who, then, is to make that decision: the doctor? Doctors disagree—or at least frequently do. What are we to do in a case like that? And what about the constant advances being made in medicine? Can the potential for these not enter into our calculations?

Furthermore, and perhaps most important of all, there is the following counterargument which could be adduced against the present thesis: By what token can we claim that the burden of the comatose is *not* for the good of society? It is merely assumed by this argument and never once proved that the killing of the comatose, the "betubed and sedated and aerated and glucosed," is in the interest of society as a whole, that to kill these people is to perform an act which will—or at least most probably will—produce the greatest amount of good for the greatest number of people. Unquestionably, such killing—or euthanasia—will result in a state of affairs where the material resources otherwise committed to the care of such individuals need not thus be engaged and hence could be used to alleviate the lot of the remainder. But that merely means that euthanasia would result in the greatest amount of *goods*—of material amenities—for the greatest number of people, a different thing entirely. In order for the argument to succeed, it has to be shown that euthanasia in fact results in the greatest amount of *good*—in the moral sense—for the greatest number of people. Or, failing that, that it will most probably result in the greatest amount of good for the greatest number of people. On the surface, at least, it is not at all clear that euthanasia is a likely way to achieve this. Patience, perseverance, and so on are virtues— moral goods—and they are much more likely to be developed by rejecting euthanasia than by engaging in it. In short, so the counterargument would run, the argument from the common good as it is here presented is guilty of a fundamental confusion between good and goods and therefore remains a non sequitur.

Hitherto, we have given the impression that the moral argument for euthanasia, considered from the point of view of the society, necessarily requires utilitarianism as an assumption. Strictly speaking that is not correct. We could argue for euthanasia from the social point of view simply by claiming that the function of society is to benefit its members. In a nutshell, the argument would proceed something like this:

> It is the function of society to benefit its members. Sometimes it happens that the members of the society are in such a state that continued existence for them is agonizing and unbearable. In such a case, pursuant to the initial premise, it will be the clear duty of society to ameliorate such a state. Euthanasia is the only means of doing so. Hence it will be the duty of society to administer euthanasia.

Quite clearly, the premise underlying this argument—the ethical theory on which it is based—is diametrically opposed to the utilitarian sentiment underlying the preceding discussion. In fact, the moral theory at hand is to the effect that utilitarian considerations come after considerations dealing with the welfare of the individual. As such, the theory of course needs proof.

None is provided. It is merely assumed to be true. This is the first shortcoming of this argument. The second shortcoming is a common failing, one which we have encountered several times before. Who, precisely, is to make the relevant decision? And, on what basis? Finally, all the moral objections based on the assumption of an absolutistic theory of value can again be adduced against the present argument. That is to say, we can ask, When was it ever shown that there are not absolute values in the universe and that the life of an individual does not have intrinsic value? When was it shown that a deliberate killing of a person is not murder?

The reply to this critique is not lacking. It is a reply that takes us to the very heart of the euthanasia controversy. In an abbreviated form, it goes as follows:

> The concept of murder and the notion of a right to life are predicated on the common assumption that the individual in question is a person. However, to be counted as a person, certain criteria must be met. That is to say, the individual in question must give some evidence of rationality, of freedom, and indeed of capability of choice and self-determination. At the very least, more than merely a primitive stimulus-response type of reaction to the environment must be present: The individual must evince what we call rational awareness. None of this is present in the extreme sort of case under consideration. Betubed, sedated, aerated, glucosed, mechanically manipulated, the individual is totally without awareness. In short, it is not a person. Therefore such an entity exists outside of the realm of moral.

The first thing to note about this reply is that it is not really a reply to the above critique. It shifts the argument from whether or not anyone has the right to decide on the intentional and explicit killing of a person, to the question of whether or not what are commonly assumed to be candidates for euthanasia actually are persons. And this brings us to the very heart of the matter. When considering the issue of abortion, we saw that a major part of the problem centered on the question of whether or not a fetus is a person. We concluded that if it is, then at least on one clear and definite understanding of the nature of ethics, abortion is murder—unless, that is to say, utilitarianism is true. In that case, *anyone* could be killed without moral opprobrium and indeed with moral approval just so long as his death benefited the community more than his staying alive. We also concluded that if a fetus is not a person, the problem of abortion would resolve itself. The issue would leave the realm of the moral and devolve into a question of pure pragmatics.

In the problem of euthanasia a similar dichotomy faces us. The candidates for euthanasia are divided into two groups: those who are incurably ill, in agony, and merely physically extremely debilitated, on the one hand; and those who are mentally debilitated, on the other. It is then argued with respect to the latter that they are no longer persons. That is to say, it is claimed that since, to the best of our knowledge, they no longer meet the criteria of personhood, such individuals no longer are persons nor, by that very token, do they enjoy the moral status of persons. Consequently, it is claimed, the entities in question need not be treated with the moral concern and attention due to persons. In other words, and more particularly, the argument concludes that we are as much at liberty to kill them as we are to kill a debilitated, comatose, and otherwise unresponsive dog.

The logic of this reasoning cannot be faulted. If the debilitated are no longer persons, then the act of killing them with deliberation and of set purpose cannot be an act of murder. In fact, no serious moral gravamen would attach to such an act of killing. The question, however, is whether the criteria of personhood proposed in the preceding argument are unacceptable —even more important, whether they are correct. Furthermore, as a related issue, there is the question of whether the criteria, if acceptable, can be and have been correctly applied in particular cases. This is not the place to decide whether or not these criteria can be or in fact are met. Suffice it to point out that unless the answer is in the affirmative, the case of euthanasia as based on this whole argument collapses.

Furthermore, there is this to be considered: Undoubtedly it is true that if an individual who is kept artificially alive is no longer a person, then removing the life-support system or indeed administering a drug to kill him is not an act of murder. In that sense, as we said, the argument is undeniably valid. However, as before, the question is whether or not such an individual in fact is a person. It could be argued that by the very criteria of personhood professed in the argument itself such an individual may very well be a person. That is to say, if what makes an individual a person is the presence of rational awareness in the sense described, then how that awareness is maintained will be irrelevant. Therefore, it cannot be argued that without exception, *all* betubed, sedated, aerated, glucosed beings are no longer persons and hence are beyond the pale of the moral law. Some such individuals might very well be rational beings in the sense we have indicated; in which case, by the very criteria of the argument itself, to deprive them of their life-support system would be an act of murder.[21]

The preceding brings out quite clearly what concerned us before: What, precisely, is it to be a person? Is it a matter of mere definition? Or is it a matter of possessing certain characteristics which, as a matter of fact, a group of other individuals have? Unless that issue is resolved, the issue of euthanasia no more admits of a solution than did the problem of abortion.

The Biological Argument

The arguments from biological considerations fall into two general rubrics: the arguments from clinical death, and the arguments from eugenics. The former sort of argument concentrates on those cases that we might describe as persons in extremis, that is, persons who survive as living organisms only because of the very sophisticated life-support machinery to which they are connected.

21. This conclusion can be avoided only at the cost of making personhood, by definition, a matter of independently supported rational awareness. Again, however, such a position would have to be argued.

Biologically speaking, many individuals in the last stages of their life are kept alive artificially and in fact are really dead. Therefore, so far as ordinary standards of life and death are concerned, they constitute dead bodies with artificially induced life. To cease such an activity cannot be murder. Therefore, in such cases at least, euthanasia ought to be supported.

This argument is essentially like the argument dealing with artificially maintained rational awareness, which we discussed earlier. Hence it is open to the same kind of objection. It should also be mentioned that, like the argument from artificially maintained awareness, this argument incorporates a factual mistake. The life of such people is not artificially induced, as the argument has it, but artificially maintained. The two are quite distinct. Whereas artificially induced life might, just barely, not really count as life at all, artificially maintained life must count as life in the ordinary sense. It is just that in order to maintain it, unusual means are necessary. The onus of proof lies on the proponent of this argument to show that artificially maintained life is by its very nature of a different moral status. Without such a proof, the argument collapses.

The argument from eugenics is essentially similar to the eugenic argument in favor of abortion. The two differ only in the time at which the proposed killing is to take place.

All of us know that there are certain congenital disabilities, indeed certain congenital diseases of a serious sort, which make people incapable of leading normal lives. One such disease is hemophilia; another, extreme epilepsy; and so on. Not all of these are discovered at birth.[22] Therefore no moral gravamen attaches to the fact that the individuals who have that disease are not killed at that time. However, it would be more than merely criminal if these disabilities and defects were to be passed on. In fact, such genes ought to be deleted from the gene pool. Consequently, unpleasant

22. Diseases like Huntington's chorea here come to mind.

as it may be—in fact, indubitably will be—the individual having such genes ought to be killed. Euthanasia, in the traditional and precise meaning of that term, ought to be administered.

Like the eugenic argument in favor of abortion, this argument for euthanasia suffers from several major flaws. First, it assumes that the only way in which the avowed aim of preventing the defective genes from entering the gene pool can be effected is to kill the person who has them. It should be clear by now that this assumption is factually mistaken. There are other, equally effective methods that do not incur the moral charge of murder: for instance, contraception and sterilization.[23] This, of course, is based on the assumption that there is no moral problem attaching to the claim that the genetic structure of a man can be or even ought to be interfered with. It has been argued that to do so is to interfere not merely in a natural process, but also in the handiwork of God. Whatever the strength of the religious contention, it can be recast into a nonreligious form: How do we know which genes are deleterious and which are not? The mere fact that they lead to death or temporary disability—even the fact that they ultimately impose a burden on society—cannot count as decisive in view of the fact that many people who have carried such genes have lightened the burden of all of us by their inventions and contributions; and that, in any case, the cure seems to be as bad as the disease itself. Furthermore, from a purely practical point of view, we are just beginning to become aware of the crosslinkages that obtain among various genes. Until we know more about it, any interference in the genetic pool of mankind might well prove disastrous. And very much along the same lines, there is the fact that genes which may be lethal or debilitating in one context are survival factors in another. The gene for sickle cell anemia is a good example. The point, then, is that what counts as a defective gene is very much a relative matter. In the light of these circumstances the

23. The future might even add a further alternative: genetic engineering.

argument loses much of its initial support. Furthermore, there is this, essentially pragmatic, series of points: Advances have been made in the medical art. We can treat, or at least correct as harmless, diseases that would once have been extremely debilitating and fatal. Therefore, unless the argument carries some premise as to the noninterference in so-called natural processes, the effects of genetic damage referred to could be corrected by less dramatic means. Or, at least, frequently this could be the case. As to the thesis of noninterference, but a moment's reflection will show that very few who advocate it in this context do so consistently. For, by that very token, anyone who is not born perfect but requires medical attention as a baby—even as an adult—in order to survive, should be killed. With the exception of those exceedingly few disease-resistant individuals among us, we all fall into that category. As to the claim that this involves the susceptibility to disease, rather than a genetic condition, to this we must reply by asking precisely what the difference is. After all, a different genetic makeup would have freed us from this susceptibility. Furthermore, in the interest of consistency it ought to be pointed out that all of us carry recessive genes concerning which we know little but which manifest themselves in certain situations. That is to say, almost all of us are the possessors of deleterious genes. If the underlying assumption of the present argument were to be applied consistently, it would follow that, in the end, all of us would be killed. Finally, it should not go unnoticed that once again the moral theory underlying all of this is a version of utilitarianism. In light of what we have already said about the admissibility of such an assumption, we need only mention this fact in order to achieve a verdict: not proven!

The Arguments from Social Praxis

The arguments from social praxis have two things in common: They are distinguished by an utter lack of moral considerations —they dismiss these as irrelevant—and they deal with the long- and short-term aspects of the functioning and survival of a so-

ciety. One of the most popular arguments in this category is the
so-called argument from usefulness.

> A society can survive and function properly if and only if
> its members fulfill their assigned roles. It is in the very na-
> ture of the thing that some of these roles—such as that of
> doctor or nurse—can be fulfilled if and only if some of the
> members of the society are physically and/or mentally in-
> capacitated. Therefore the incidence of such incapacities is
> essential. What is not essential, however, is that this inca-
> pacity be of a permanent or an indefinitely prolonged sort
> with no hope of cure. In such cases, the prolongation of the
> individual's existence serves no useful purpose to the so-
> ciety. There are sufficient cases of otherwise productive in-
> dividuals requiring temporary medical attention, that the
> function of the medical profession can be usefully dis-
> charged without endeavoring to exercise it in that field.
> Consequently, from the admittedly pragmatic point of use-
> fulness, no purpose is served keeping such individuals alive.
> Therefore they are either to be killed or simply left to die.

The pragmatic concern of this argument is obvious, and we
remarked on it before. Consequently, we shall not consider it
further. As to the factual assumptions, once more these cannot
be faulted. From a productive point of view, the terminally ill
and comatose, the mentally incapacitated, and the like serve no
useful function whatsoever. They merely tie up productive en-
ergy that could be employed otherwise. Nor is there any way in
which we can object to the claim that the professions necessary
to the survival of our society can survive without the existence
of such nonproductive entities. There is nothing wrong with this
part of the argument. Nevertheless, the argument does have a
flaw. What is wrong with it is that it presumes to deduce a
prescriptive conclusion from factual premises. In other words,
the logic of the argument is at fault. A prescriptive conclusion
can follow only from a prescriptive premise, that is to say, from
a premise of an imperative sort. In this particular context, the

intended conclusion can follow only if we add the premise: We ought to do all and only those things which redound to the productive effort of society. Only then will the conclusion follow. But of course, such a premise changes the whole picture entirely and certainly needs arguing.

The second type of argument under the rubric of arguments from social praxis involves ecological concerns:

> The world has only a finite amount of resources, as does any society within it. Therefore, sooner or later, every society must ask itself how much of a population it can support and in what style. Inevitably, the answer will be that the ideal stage of life can be maintained only if, all things being equal, population is maintained at a certain maximal level. Once that level is attained, the surplus members must be deleted: killed. The logical candidates for death are those who are old, debilitated, and so on. Why these? Because their existence places an incomparably greater burden on the resources of the society than any other group— and for an incomparably lesser return. Therefore, in their case at least, euthanasia ought to be practiced.

Once more, the initial premise of this argument is unexceptionable: The earth's resources, and a fortiori the resources of any society found on it, are finite. It is also true that the strain placed on the resources will rapidly become too great unless certain things are done. What this argument proposes is that the debilitated, the aged, the infirm, and the otherwise superannuated be killed as a matter of course, as a population control measure. The argument presents this course of action as the only reasonable and effective one. It could doubtlessly be bolstered further by the contention that only the terminally infirm and superannuated are in a position where they have already enjoyed the most pleasant aspect of their normally-to-be-expected existence, and therefore that to kill them would not be to deprive them of the most rewarding aspects of their lives. To put it briefly, "They have already lived." Such would not be the case with those otherwise possibly falling into the same bracket: those who would be candidates for abortion.

But whether thus bolstered or not, the argument still fails and remains a non sequitur. To be sure, resources are limited and space is finite. Indubitably, the manufacturing waste products required to keep such people alive are incomparably greater than under ordinary circumstances and force a reduction in ecological viability. But there are several other ways in which the same results could be achieved. Birth control is one of them, an alternative that is here completely overlooked. As we said, the end proposed by this argument could be achieved by such means—and without any danger of comparable moral risk. Feasibility, certainly, is not an obstacle either. Consequently, the argument must be adjudged unsuccessful. In fact, perhaps it ought to be remarked parenthetically here that this and similar sorts of arguments, by the very fact that they concentrate on the solution of euthanasia, abortion—killing in general—to the exclusion of all other possibilities, seem to be motivated more by considerations of convenience on the part of the healthy than by anything else. If true, that is hardly a commendable motive, morally or otherwise.

EVALUATION

This brings to a close our discussion of arguments on euthanasia. Indubitably, there are other arguments, both pro and con. And it may even be that some one of those which we have not examined is logically impeccable and has unquestionably true premises. The ones we have discussed here, however, do not fall into such a category. Like the arguments we considered in the first two chapters, they fail, or at least do not establish their conclusions, either because the premises are not indubitably true or because their logic is faulty. Those that are exempt from these critiques fall prey to another shortcoming: They are based on premises of such a nature that, were they consistently applied, the conclusion would be so far-reaching as to affect every part of our lives in a way that would be unacceptable even to the proponents of the arguments themselves. In other words, those which escape logical invalidity are beset by inconsistency or unacceptability in practice. Ordinarily, if we were asked to engage in a course of action on the basis of arguments having such characteristics, we should be hard put to determine who was the greater fool: ourselves, for listening to such advocacy, or the proponents, for propounding it. Yet in the case of euthanasia, we are asked to proceed on the basis of just such arguments. The situation requires no further comment.

But it is also too important merely to be left at this juncture. The prospect of death is one which faces all of us. Sooner or later, all of us die. But not all of us die in the same way. If the inductive evidence based on past experience is anything to go by, the death of some of us will be anything but pleasant. It may in fact be exactly as described by some of the proponents of euthanasia: betubed, sedated, glucosed, aerated, drugged, and *non compos mentis*. But even that would be preferable— at least for some—to the prospect of prolonged months of incredible agony which could no longer be alleviated by drugs. In such cases, our personal preference might very well be euthanasia. But is preference enough for the moral person? In the arena of ethics, is the claim of pain and at least felt indignity sufficient to carry the day? The matter is too important to be left merely to a statement of preference. For, why—morally why —should preference count at all?

We must therefore take a close and dispassionate look at euthanasia itself. Our effort will be divided into three parts. In the first, we shall deal with the definition of euthanasia; in the second, we shall consider some of the moral and pragmatic difficulties besetting the notion; and in the third, we shall reach a tentative conclusion.

Definition of Euthanasia

'Euthanasia' comes from the Greek and, taken literally, means a pleasant death. It is the practice or act of intentionally killing a person in a manner that is not painful to the person to be killed but instead, if anything, is supposed to be pleasant. This definition immediately presents the moral problem with which we have already wrestled: the fact that the act is the intentional killing of a person without the excuse of self-defense. Does this make it a species of murder?

Several replies here come to mind. The first is that actually euthanasia is different from murder because, unlike the latter, it does not have the personal good of the actor but that of the recipient of the action at heart. Thus, to take but one example, the deliberate killing of a terminal patient in unbearable agony for the sake of relieving the obvious suffering of that individual is not murder. The motive here makes all the difference in the world. It must be admitted at the outset that this sort of case is quite distinct from the run of the mill case of murder. We lack what in legal terminology we should call a *mens rea:* an evil will. But we lack it only in the sense that we do not wish, at least not overtly, personal gain or indeed gain for anyone else. We do not lack it in the sense that we do want to kill.

This definition, however, is not inclusive enough to take care of those cases referred to by the living will mentioned above, where neither agony nor awareness is present. Nor does it quite fit the case of euthanasia for people who are "human vegetables," either congenitally or through some later development. Such individuals are not aware of anything, and therefore do not require release from suffering. Nor is it sufficient for us to lack evil intent for personal gain in order for our action not to be one of murder. I may kill you in full awareness of what I am doing, and allegedly for your sake, simply because I subscribe to the belief of metempsychosis and wish to hurry you along the road to perfection by killing you now, before you can be tempted and become morally guilty. Still, however noble my intentions, we should still want to say that I am guilty of murder. Finally, as to the generic premise that euthanasia is never committed for private gain, we stated before that this was true; nor do we wish to retract that claim now. Any similar act done in the expectation of private gain would be an act of murder. But this consideration suggests another: What of euthanasia done for nonprivate gain: for the public good instead. All acts of euthanasia done for reasons of biology and social practice fall into this category. The only major reason operative in these cases is the present and future welfare of the species or of the society. That, however, is a gain—perhaps not for the individuals directly involved in the euthanasia, perhaps not even for the society at that time; but it is a gain nevertheless. Are we, therefore, to reject as murder those acts done for private gain and to accept as euthanasia those done for the public good?

Herewith we come to the crux of the whole matter. By all accounts euthanasia is different from murder. This seems to be almost a matter of definition. However, accounts do diverge as to why and how it is different. Without prejudging the question of whether or not this assumption of difference is correct, we can pinpoint at least one major reason why appraisals of this difference diverge so radically: We are faced with at least four fundamentally distinct ethical theories—that is, aside from the absolutistic ethical position which identifies euthanasia with murder and the religious position which (by and large) condemns it outright. One position, utilitarian in outlook, excuses and indeed commends certain acts of homicide, such as euthanasia, insofar as they advance the common good. That is why they are morally acceptable. Another moral position, individualistic in nature, exhorts the performance of euthanasia as morally commendable if and only if the individual to be killed has a disability that makes his survival unbearable to the individual himself. That is to say, the individualistic ethical position underlies the notion of a living will. A third ethical position is wholly relativistic in nature; and, to put the matter quite crudely, the distinction between euthanasia and murder is here the result of a particular moral code adopted by the individual. In other words, this position recognizes the difference to be arbitrary. Finally, a fourth ethical position maintains that there are no moral properties at all, that all ethical discourse is meaningless emotional twaddle and, consequently, that the notion of a difference between euthanasia and murder is itself empty as such and can be arranged at our pleasure.

These four positions, as well as the absolutistic and religious positions indicated earlier, are unalterably distinct. How, then, shall we resolve the differences among them and arrive at an acceptable definition of euthanasia itself: one that does not beg any moral questions? Essentially—so the reply must run—by fiat: by stating that our definition is intended to exclude all moral parameters in itself, and that the definition is to be taken at face value. Our proposed definition, then, is this:

> Euthanasia is the act of deliberately killing a person in as painless a manner as possible where the act of killing is the result of full deliberation and is for the sake of that person, rather than that of anyone else.

Moral and Pragmatic Difficulties

Given this definition we are immediately faced with problems. What of the case of the comatose, the sedated, and the "human vegetables"? How can killing them be "for their own sake"? Indeed, and much more important, how can the act of killing someone ever be for the sake of that person? Is that not a contradiction in terms? Furthermore, does our definition not definitely rule out a utilitarian premise?

To begin with what lies at the heart of the issue: How can the act of killing a person possibly be for the sake of or to the advantage of that person? Is it not flatly contradictory to make such a claim? Of course, this is not the first time that this question has entered our discussion. We have already encountered it several times, specifically in our discussions of abortion and suicide. Then, we forbore to comment. It is now time to give the issue detailed and explicit consideration.

The question itself purports to be neutral in character, merely exhorting us to consider the issue. In point of fact, however, it is not. It is based on an underlying assumption that to kill a person is always and invariably to that person's harm: that it is axiomatic that if I killed you, I would do you an irreparable injustice. This underlying assumption, as is the case with many such assumptions, is merely stated, not argued. Nor is it surprising that this is the case. First of all, from a purely psychological point of view, the fear of death is so deeply rooted in most of us that it is almost a psychological impossibility to consider our own demise with rational deliberation. Psychologically, our fear turns death into an evil, and that evil is transferred to all acts that bring about such a state. In other words, the nature of our psyche is such that our fear of death makes us consider the killing of a person as doing that person ultimate harm. This fear is only sublimated slightly in cases of religious commitment involving certain eschatological expectations.

Second, and from a purely philosophical point of view, any explicit consideration of this underlying assumption would have shown that the assumption is not quite as harmless and as obvious as it seems. It is based on the more general thesis that all human life has an intrinsic value, no matter what the quality of that life. In other words, it involves the thesis that considerations of the quality of a particular life are irrelevant to the issue of whether or not a certain life has value. This thesis, which we have encountered frequently before, is maintained to be obvious. However, as we have also had occasion to observe, obviousness is not a guarantee of truth, not even if that obviousness should turn out to be universal. In order to be rationally, morally, and above all philosophically acceptable the thesis has to be established by dint of a reasoned argument. As it stands, however, it is without a shred of proof. Nor does the fact that it is fervently believed, even acted upon, show otherwise. For people have fervently believed and acted upon falsehoods—the case of warlocks and witches provides a good example, as does the theory of the Pillars of Hercules. Furthermore, the contrary of this belief—the thesis that the quality of life *is* a relevant parameter when considering the issue of whether or not a life should be lived—has been and still is being maintained with just as much fervor and just as great (or small) a show of plausibility.

In point of fact, this latter thesis can be defended a great deal more easily than the thesis in question itself. So, for instance, we can adopt a hedonistic outlook and argue that what is good is what affords pleasure—where pleasure can be ranked as to intensity, kind, and distribution. We can then say that what is to a person's advantage is that which, all other things being equal, produces a greater proportion of good (pleasure) over pain than any other act. From this we can conclude that in some cases euthanasia—whether performed by ourselves, as in the case of suicide, or performed by others, as in the case of ordinary euthanasia—is to the advantage of the person to be killed. Why? Because failure to kill that person will result in a proportion of pain over pleasure that will not be altered in future times; whereas killing the person will put an end to such an increase of pain over pleasure. But even without adopting a hedonistic outlook or a utilitarian approach in general, we could still defend the claim that euthanasia can be to the advantage of the individual himself. We could assume with the absolutist that human life—in the sense of the life of a person —has absolute value because it is the life of a person. In other words, what gives it its value is the intrinsic value of the personhood attached. And from that point of view, lives can be ranked according to the degree to which the peculiarly person-making characteristics of the individual in question are realized. At the bottom of such a ranking would be the life where the personhood of the individual is completely frustrated; and at the top, the life where potential and realization coincide. We could then argue that although we have thus established a ranking, a value scale still needs to be imposed, and that it should be imposed in the following way: Those lives where the potentials are utterly thwarted and where there is an awareness of this frustration rank negatively; those where there is only moderate frustration or little or no awareness rank either neutrally or close to the neutral point; and those where realization is preponderant rank positively. We could then point out that negatively ranked lives impose a burden on those who live them; at least in a psychological sense. Consequently, it would be to the advantage of the individuals who lead them to be relieved of them. The ranking machinery we have just sketched would provide the moral decision-making procedure for effecting a cutoff point.

Therefore, even without adopting hedonism or utilitarianism it could be argued that it is simply false to say that to kill a person is always and invariably to that person's harm. To be sure, it is to do him harm in the sense of hurting him, but all things considered, that hurt is to his advantage.[24] Again, and in the interest of clarity on the issue, it ought to be made clear that the preceding does not amount to a disproof of the assumption with which the argument began. It merely shows that an attack on this assumption can be argued for and can be made to look plausible by means of reasoned consideration. It does not amount to proof, and thus to a disproof of the initial thesis. It merely shows that with respect to plausibility the two alternatives are, roughly, on a par. And it still leaves the fundamental moral issue untouched: whether or not euthanasia is morally acceptable. It does not resolve this issue because like the theories which it opposes, it is based on a fundamental and unproved premise: that what is good is what affords pleasure; that what is good is what has a greater ratio of self-realization over stultification. Or, perhaps in that what is good is a relative matter, since there are no hard and fast, intrinsic and absolute moral values. That issue still needs deciding. Obviously in these few pages we cannot decide which of the various hypotheses is correct.

While the preceding goes at least some way toward clarifying the issue in cases of euthanasia when the candidate is suffering or somehow in pain,[25] it is of no help whatever in respect

24. Furthermore, so the argument would continue, the claim that to kill someone would invariably be to his disadvantage rests on the assumption that if something is to our advantage, then we must be bound to enjoy its result. To this, it suffices to point out that such is not always the case. It may be to our advantage to cut our losses in order to prevent future grief—as when getting out of a particular business which threatens to go sour. The advantage here is a negative one—of absence of psychological pain. But it is an advantage nevertheless.

25. This does not rule out psychological suffering.

to the second sort of case: that involving comatose or otherwise completely unresponsive individuals where, from the data at our disposal, we can only conclude that they are not aware of their particular state. In their case, the arguments that it would be to their own advantage to be killed could not take the above forms. These arguments were premised on the assumption of awareness, for it makes no sense in the present context to talk about unexperienced (unperceived) suffering, pleasure, or pain. In the case of the comatose or sedated it is precisely this awareness that is lacking. Consequently it cannot be argued on this basis that to kill them would be to their own advantage. The only analogous sort of reasoning that comes to mind is based not on the pleasure or pain accruing to the euthanasia candidate, but on the pleasure or pain accruing to those who take care of them. For the sake of maximizing their pleasure or pain quotient, the individuals in question ought to be killed. Let us be quite clear on this point: The preceding train of reasoning amounts to an explicit abandoning of the initial thesis. That thesis, let us recall, was that it was to the advantage of the candidate for euthanasia himself that he should be killed. The present argument, on the other hand, is to the effect that it is to the advantage of the others.

As to the case of those who are "human vegetables"—or even those who are so supremely idiotic that their mental processes have nothing "high" about them—if anything, it should be argued that they are "happy with their lot." Certainly, the concept of psychological suffering and a sense of degradation does not apply to them. It is projected by those around them who, in a confused fashion, attempt to empathize. On the physical plane, their existence is no more painful than that of anyone else. Therefore, again, it cannot be claimed that the preceding argument is here applicable. That sort of reasoning will not show that it is to their advantage to be killed, although it may be to ours.

This brings out a factor we have encountered time and again: Consistent application of traditional arguments and of theses of the new morality is really quite impossible. It either runs head-on into what we are unwilling to do; or, in its theoretical basis, it contravenes fact.

Conclusion

The concept of euthanasia as we have defined it and as popular argument deals with it is thus beset by difficulties. Yet we must resolve them. A good place to begin is to decide that once we are convinced about the correctness of a fundamental premise, we shall follow its consequences even if they should happen to disagree with our own inclinations. In other words, we should begin with the resolve of consistency. A second thing to accept —without the hope of proof, but as merely reasonable and most probably true—is that all persons, in virtue of their personhood, have certain inalienable rights. One of these rights is the right to happiness; another that to life; and a third, that to self-realization insofar as the last does not infringe upon the corresponding rights of other persons. Another principle with which to begin is that in case of conflict that course of action ought to be adopted which, while not abrogating the right of the individual to life, self-realization, and happiness, does maximize the happiness in the world.

With these, we can now proceed to argue that euthanasia is permissible in several cases. First, it is permissible in those cases in which the individual in question is not yet a person. These cases would overlap with, and indeed be identical to, certain types of abortions. Second, it is permissible in cases where the individual in question is no longer a person. In such cases, as in cases of the first sort, no relevant moral rights accrue to the entity in question; and the killing of such an individual, although perhaps fraught with social and psychological consequences, may be at the discretion of society or of those persons performing or advocating such an act. However, here we must enter a cautionary note. Cases of euthanasia, by definition, deal with persons or with what may become or have been persons. In other words, the discussion of euthanasia is at home in the domain of personhood. Therefore, in all such cases as we have mentioned, the candidates for euthanasia are in the category of persons, may be in the category of persons, or have been in this category. It is not at all clear at the outset into what category the putative candidate belongs. Therefore the onus for showing that the various candidates are not yet or are no longer persons lies squarely on those who wish to show that in their case euthanasia is permissible. Examples of cases where this would not be in doubt would be, as we said, early abortions performed for the sake of the child; cases of babies born without a higher cortex; instances of severely and irreparably brain damaged individuals of a nonfunctional sort, and the like.

Third, euthanasia is permissible in all those cases where an individual, in full awareness of what he is about, asks to be killed or to be allowed to die because he finds life physically and/or psychologically unbearable, and where no other act would bring about an experiential alleviation of that state of affairs.[26] It would be a mistake to argue that acquiescence in such a request would be giving in to a request for murder. The act would simply not be one of murder. Homicide, to be sure, but homicide is not the same as murder. Murder, minimally, presumes an infringement of rights. In the present instance, such is not the case. What we have here is the voluntary giving up of the right to life. As we argue in the preceding chapters, if something is a right at all, then it can be given up; just as a gift, if it is a gift at all, can be renounced. Therefore, in cases where the quality of life has reached a certain subjective minimum, the individual has a right to give up that life: to request euthanasia. Consequently, in such cases euthanasia would be morally acceptable.[27]

26. Clearly, in almost all cases this will involve a medical reason. Equally as clearly, in many cases a readjustment of the socioeconomic context of the individual would result in better medical care which would bring about such an alleviation. This fact points to an interesting feature about euthanasia: that to a large degree, the issue may be one of social ethics—of what we, as a society, are willing to do.

27. The interesting question is whether such a right can be given up under any and all circumstances, or only in cases of the sort we have indicated.

Here we must interrupt our argument in order to interject a theoretical, definitional note: What we have just said brings out that in considering the first and second sort of case above we were not really dealing with cases of euthanasia: By definition, euthanasia must involve persons. If the antecedent conditions of the first two sorts of cases are met, however, we shall not be dealing with persons at all. Consequently, in their case the issue will be whether or not it is morally acceptable to kill personlike entities of this sort—a question on an entirely different moral footing.

And this, of course, brings us to the really difficult cases: cases where we are dealing with the comatose, betubed, aerated, glucosed, and otherwise medicated individuals who, but for the medical techniques employed, would be dead. In their case no expression of wishes is possible. Or, if it is possible, it is not at all clear that such an expression would be rational and coherent. This is the context in which the problem of euthanasia is usually posed, and this is the context that is assumed to be most difficult.

However, the conceptual machinery and distinctions that were developed in our discussion of abortion here stand us in good stead, particularly those developed in that part of the discussion which dealt with the notion of potential persons. There we argued that we must distinguish among three types of potentiality: pure potentiality, which leaves everything open; specific potentiality, where the genetic determinants of membership in a certain species are given, but the potential inherent in that genetic information is not realized; and determined potentiality, where the present constitution of the individual is such that his nervous system is structurally capable of sustaining rational awareness as we have defined it, but where at this point in time that potential is not realized. We can employ these distinctions to good advantage in the present case. An individual will be a person if and only if he is in the third state of potentiality. And if he is, he will have certain rights, the right to life among them. Therefore in some cases it would be morally wrong—indeed murder—to kill such an individual, despite the fact that he is glucosed, aerated, betubed, and so on. That is to say, it would be wrong to kill him unless, as per the third case above, he expressed a reasoned wish and/or gave his consent for such an action. In all other cases just mentioned we shall not have a person in our sense of the term. Therefore euthanasia—if that is still the right word—will be permissible.

As to cases where euthanasia would be to the advantage of the society, but would be performed on persons against their wish or without their wish and/or consent—cases where financial or analogous considerations are deemed relevant—such cases are morally indefensible, except, that is, on the assumption of a utilitarian ethics of the crassest sort. And that, by the very premises of right which we adopted several paragraphs ago, we find indefensible. In such cases, then, the right to life and sundry concomitant rights will have been infringed upon. Therefore such cases will be cases of murder.

"Such cases will be cases of murder." That is the conclusion we have just stated. But is that really true? What about senicide —the killing of the aged—and infanticide—the killing of babies and small children? Are these, too, murder? The law certainly seems to differ from us in these cases. At least, with respect to infanticide. It provides for a lesser sentence in such cases and in doing so seems to contradict our conclusions. Are we, then, mistaken? I think not. But to see why, let us consider these problems separately in the next chapters.

4

Infanticide

THE PROBLEM

Infanticide—the killing of children, especially of children before the age of puberty—is an old and almost universal custom, both in our own sociological complex and in societies elsewhere.[1] One look at our history will show that when the need was felt or it was deemed convenient, we have always killed our offspring. The myth of Chronos devouring his own children has more than merely mythological significance. But, so we feel tempted to argue, all that is in the past. Ours is a gentler society. We can no longer kill anyone with impunity, children not excepted.

However, opposed to this popular sentiment stand the following facts: If I kill your child, all other things being equal, I shall be held accountable for murder; whereas if you kill your child, all other things being equal, the likelihood is that you will not.[2] Ours is a gentler society? Perhaps—so the cynic might argue—*queasier* would be the proper word for it. We find babies too defenseless and cuddly when they belong to someone else, and we don't have the bother of caring for

---

1. Cf. Plato *Republic* 5.461.16; Augustine *De nuptiis et concupiscentia* 1.15; George Devereux, *A Study of Abortion in Primitive Society* (New York: Julian Press, 1955), pp. 173–74; Indian Penal Code, code 312 (1969); Alfredo Aguirre, "Colombia: The Family in Candelaria," *Studies in Family Planning*, no. 11 (New York: Population Council of New York, April 1966), p. 2 and passim., to mention but a few instances.

2. That is, if you are a woman, this is highly likely, especially if it occurs within twelve months after birth. Fathers and other persons are not treated in so preferential a manner.

them; whereas familiarity overcomes sentiment and breeds license.

Whatever the legal justification for this treatment of infanticide, the situation has an air of moral paradox about it. Are not all persons equal in the eyes of justice? Is not your action the same in nature as mine, and do we not therefore merit equal punishment? Apparently not. The cynic, remembering George Orwell's *Animal Farm,* doubtlessly will suggest that although all persons are indeed equal, some people are more equal than others; and that where children are concerned, parents and guardians will carry the day. The more traditionally inclined, perhaps even recalling some early religious training, will reply that the reason is different: Parents have a certain God-given authority over their children, and children owe obedience to their guardians and parents. Consequently, so these thinkers conclude, it is only natural that with respect to their actions vis-à-vis children, parents and guardians occupy a privileged position.

But such responses, whether cynical or otherwise, are far too glib. The situation in question hides a genuine problem which, like a thread of contradiction, runs through our current attitudes on the death of a child. The fact that my premeditated act of killing your child should count as murder implies—in fact presupposes—that a child has the moral status of a person. The fact that your act is considered nonmurderous implies that the child does not have this status. Nor will it be possible to evade this contradiction by postulating mitigating and excusing circumstances operative in your case as a parent, which do not apply to mine. For what difference could there be between the two cases except that you are more familiar with the individual? Or the fact that you are the (sole) supporter of the child? These cannot be extenuating because in no other instance of human intercourse are they deemed in themselves sufficient to ameliorate the charge of murder. And any other excuse—like that of emotional frustration at recalcitrant behavior—if at all acceptable, would apply in my case as well as yours.

Familiarity does not breed moral license—but ownership

might.[3] The point here is that whereas familiarity is morally insufficient to guarantee you as a parent a privileged status, that status would easily be assured on the following assumption: Whoever is in the position of parent or guardian has the right to decide, at least in part, on the future of that child. By dint of this principle, the actions of this one particular group of people therefore enjoy a privileged status.

The question is, why? And the only answer that seems at all reasonable runs something like this:

> Parents and guardians have decision-making power in these contexts because children, being immature and incapable of fending for themselves, require that most decisions be made for them. The reason why not just any adult is empowered to make these decisions, although he is frequently capable of doing so, is that children are the children *of* these persons: "Mine" and "yours" are concepts very much at home in this context. In other words, whether we realize it or not, the reason for this privileged position is that parents and guardians are deemed to stand in that sort of relation to their children or wards which is very much like that of owner to property.[4] The license an owner has in the disposition of his property, although not always universal and absolute, is very much greater than that of anyone else.

The preceding analysis of this particular situation may be fanciful, but it does point up the problem of the inconsistent treatment accorded the killers of children before the law. And this, in turn, brings us to the reason for including a discourse

3. This notion is more widespread than it may seem, especially among the so-called liberated. See, for example, Ti-Grace Atkinson, "Philosophical Argument in Support of the Human Right of a Woman to Determine Her Own Reproductive Process," quoted in Callahan, *Abortion,* pp. 262–63. The context is one of abortion, but the sentiment seems to be the same.

4. To be sure, love is generally given as the factor, but one look at biblical and Western legal pronouncements will indicate that the matter goes much deeper than that.

on infanticide in a book on engineered death. Our society makes provision for excusing the killing of children. The question, Is this morally correct? But if this were the extent of the connection between infanticide and engineered death, the link would be tenuous indeed. Nor is it the only link. A much more profound and cogent connection is that in our previous deliberations it emerged time and again that if any of the forms of engineered death are morally admissible, infanticide must be admissible as well. In particular, when discussing the question of abortion and euthanasia from sociological and eugenic standpoints, infanticide was seen to be one logical alternative to such courses of action. Consequently, in order to ensure conceptual completeness for our analysis, we must consider this alternative in some detail. Is it morally defensible? Are there arguments for it? And, do these stand up to examination? As usual, let us begin by considering the more traditional approach: the argument against infanticide.

THE NEGATIVE ARGUMENT

There are four generic sorts of positions which militate against infanticide: one based on religious contentions, a second based on moral contentions, a third having a pragmatic basis, and a fourth based on biological contentions.

The Religious Argument

The religious argument centers around the thesis that from the moment of birth, if not before,[5] a child is a person. As such, it has its gift of life from God; it is a repository of moral rights, just as is any other person, and consequently cannot be killed —except, that is, under circumstances of unjust aggression, which should prove to be extremely rare. And not merely would this injunction against infanticide enter into force. All those which we have considered in the context of abortion would do so as well.

The religious arguments, therefore, are essentially those

5. See chapter 1 of this book.

which we have encountered before in other contexts. Therefore they add nothing new. The only thing that has changed in this context is that here the subject matter is the infant and it is said to be a person, whereas in those other contexts the arguments concerned fetuses, the radically deviant, and the like. Nor is this lack of novelty a drawback with respect to the status of the position itself. If anything, it is a point in its favor, for it shows that the religious position as a whole, whatever its other drawbacks may be, incorporates a strong current of consistency in its treatment of those to whom it accords the predicate 'person', or, at least, that it tries to do so. Of course, this basic sameness in position and agreement does have some disadvantages. The religious position on infanticide is subject to the same generic criticisms, mutatis mutandis, that we have leveled against the religious arguments against abortion. The arguments may be valid, but that does not show that their conclusions are true. That would require the truth of their premises. And for these we have no guarantee other than faith. And that, as the religious individual is only too happy to say with respect to all beliefs other than his own, is a notoriously shaky foundation.

The Moral Argument

Moral arguments against infanticide follow pretty much the same pattern as religious ones; not with respect to content, of course, but with respect to the fact that, mutatis mutandis, they duplicate the relevant arguments against abortion and so on. The concept of a person is what is all-important here. Perhaps the importance of that concept can be brought out by sketching briefly a generic argument against infanticide from this point of view:

> Human children as soon as they are born (and possibly before) are persons. Consequently, they have all the rights and privileges that normally accrue to persons. In short, by definition, they enjoy the same moral status. That being the case, it follows immediately that if the deliberate

and intentional killing of a person is murder, the deliberate and intentional killing of a child will be so as well.

Here the argument rests. Nor need it go any further. If the premise concerning the personhood of a child is correct, then infanticide as we have defined it will indeed be nothing less than a species of murder. The question is, Is this premise correct? Are children persons? What was argued both pro and con in our discussion of abortion is relevant here, and we refer to it now. But there is also another, special argument designed to show that children are not as yet persons. It is an argument based on the notion of a voluntary agent. We shall discuss it when considering arguments in favor of infanticide. For now, it suffices that we have indicated the conditional soundness of this moral approach.

The Pragmatic Argument

The pragmatic argument against infanticide, as pragmatic arguments are wont to do, makes no appeal to religious or ethical considerations. It deals with what appear to be nonevaluative, hard realities:

> From a purely pragmatic point of view, the use of infanticide is to be eschewed because it leads to extreme social disruption. Parents have a natural feeling for their children and will resist any attempt to kill them, whatever the reason. They would rather see society go financially bankrupt in support of congenital cripples than to have their crippled, deformed, or otherwise deviant children killed. Consequently, for the sake of social equilibrium, such a situation of conflict ought to be avoided, and efforts are to be made to care for such children without imposing too great a burden on the whole. As to ecological considerations, the use of infanticide as a measure of population control would raise even greater resistance because potentially no one's children would be safe. The practice would therefore easily lend itself to the greatest political

abuses, and in that sense would be exceedingly dangerous and potentially disruptive.

Compared to the preceding two arguments, the present argument is logically a little less coherent and less tidy. In fact, two strains of reasoning seem to be intertwined. One deals with the social disruption caused by individual parents on the basis of parental attachment for their offspring; the other deals with the political misuse of power in regard to infanticide. But aside from this corrigible fault, there are several points that are not quite so easily emended. To begin with, there is the assumption that parents have an innate feeling for their children and that this feeling is sufficiently strong to produce social disruptive actions. In point of fact, this assumption is at least partly mistaken. While parental feeling may be instinctive, such feeling is not necessarily directed toward one's own child. Any child will do. As the example of other cultures has shown, the feeling we call parental love is very much a conditioned response in its particular manifestation. That being the case, at least this particular difficulty standing in the way of infanticide need not constitute an absolute and insuperable deterrent. As to the point of political misuse, any capital law or practice lends itself to such misuse. Institutionalized infanticide would constitute no exception. Therefore, if this consideration is intended as a special argument against infanticide, it fails. Furthermore, even if the point made were correct, the contention would still not be an insurmountable difficulty. Conditioning would be the answer. Demonstrably, very sophisticated societies have been able to condition their members into believing in the desirability of institutionalized death. War and ritual sacrifice are two good examples. This conditioning is and has been complete and without opposition of any really significant pragmatic sort. Consequently, that difficulty just mentioned is really illusory, and the argument that rests on it fails.

The Biological Argument

Finally, there is the biologically motivated argument against infanticide. Strictly speaking, it should be called the argument from the survival of the species. Stripped of its technical sophistication, it goes something like this:

> Each species has an innate desire for survival—a natural desire or drive, so to speak. That is to say, metaphors aside, each species includes as part of its genetic makeup the instinct for procreation. And that instinct can be realized in only one way: by having offspring. But the having of such offspring is not enough. They must also reach adulthood in order for them to be able to procreate and continue the species. Therefore, in order for the species' natural desire for survival—that is to say, in order for the species' innate potential for survival—to be realized, the young must not be killed. In the case of *homo sapiens*, this amounts—among other things—to an injunction against infanticide.

From a purely rational point of view, this argument has a sound core. That is to say, if we ignore the talk about natural desire and concentrate on the concept of survival, the central point seems to be all right. The young of a species do constitute its only means for survival as a species. However, from this unquestionable truth, the truth of the conclusion does not follow. First of all, there is the fact that the whole of the argument purports to be of a moral character. Or, at least, it purports to have some moral relevance, specifically with respect to its conclusion. Understood in that sense, the injunction against infanticide must be read in a moral sense. However, there is no moral premise in the argument at all. All we are given is a factual claim about species. In order for the conclusion to have moral import, we need the moral premise that the species *should* survive. But that, although comforting to assert, still needs proof, or at least reasoned defense. As it stands, therefore, the argument, if understood in a moral sense, confuses what *is* the case with what *ought* to be. The argument, therefore, is a non sequitur. At best, what it shows is that it would be pragmatically inadvisable to practice infanticide.

Second—and this ties in with the point just made—even if

we did grant that the species should survive, the conclusion would still not follow. What would follow would be that total infanticide would be morally wrong. In other words, nothing would follow about the morality of any particular case.

It is along these lines that we must also consider this third point: Even granted all premises, infanticide from purely eugenic and Malthusian considerations would still be permissible. For, let us recall the main premise: The species should survive. Therefore, infanticide, if it effects that survival or in any way facilitates it, would be acceptable by that very premise.[6]

THE POSITIVE ARGUMENT

The arguments in favor of infanticide are much more numerous and sophisticated than the arguments against it. In fact, there are about as many for it as there are for abortion. However, for the sake of brevity, we shall consider only six: (1) the moral argument, (2) the neurophysiological argument, (3) the sociodemographic argument, (4) the eugenic argument, (5) the historical argument, and (6) the personal argument. However, as we shall see, some of these are mere rubrics and require detailed analysis along several lines.

The Moral Argument

The title "moral argument in favor of infanticide" really covers three quite separate arguments: one based on the contention that children are not moral agents; another based on the hypothesis that either moral values are absolutely relative or there are no absolute values at all; and a third based on the notion of conflict of rights. The argument based on the claim that children are not really moral agents has an old and venerable history. It probably goes back to Plato and finds at least partial expression in the writings of Aristotle.[7]

---

6. This is not contradicted by the subsidiary premise that survival is only through the young. For, obviously, only viable and healthy young (in a genetic sense) would assure this.

7. Aristotle *Nichomachean Ethics* bk. 3, chap. 2 and passim.

The concept of a person is a moral notion, fraught with ethical overtones. Essentially is boils down to the concept of a being that is capable of independent, deliberate choice and action. Neither of these obtain in the case of children. Children are not fully rational agents capable of proper deliberation and choice. Consequently, they are not fully moral agents and do not enjoy the same moral status as persons proper. Therefore, the act of killing a child—any child—is morally not as heinous as that of killing a full moral agent. Children are just not persons in the moral sense of that term.

As we shall see in considering the neurophysiological argument, scientific support for this sort of contention is not lacking. However, even aside from this, the argument is powerful in its own right. If sound, it implies that any individual who does not engage in what we consider to be rational deliberation and deliberate choice is not a person in the moral sense. A human being he may be; a person he is not. In particular reference to the present context, children are not moral agents because they do not engage in deliberate and rational choice.

Are these contentions true? The first is simply a definition and, as such, is beyond check as to truth or falsity. But as a definition, it must be shown to be both non-question-begging and acceptable. Therefore this first point, instead of providing a solution, presents a program for further investigation. We can say without fear of contradiction that this sort of enterprise will not be without opposition. As to the second contention, pragmatically speaking it is somewhat dubious. Children do live in choice situations, they do reason, and even make reasoned choices. Their deliberations are limited by the amount of information at their disposal, but that is the only difference between their ability to choose and that of their parents.[8] To be

8. The investigations of Piaget, etc. are not really relevant in this context because what they establish is not that a child does not deliberate or reason, but that he deliberates or reasons in a way which is different from that of an adult. Therefore our argument would merely be complicated, not altered.

more precise, the only differences between the reasoning processes of a child and those of an adult involve the amount of
information at the child's disposal and the likelihood that his
rules of conceptual association will be different from ours.
However, neither of these differences is sufficient to establish
the point at issue. The first would make rationality and personhood a relative matter, depending upon the sophistication
of the society in which we live. By that token, many of our
ancestors and even some of our contemporaries do not count
as persons. As to the second, it not merely bespeaks a monu-
mental megalomania, but is also factually mistaken. It assumes
that our method of reasoning is the only rational one. This is
false. Although the particular principles of reasoning employed
by others may not be identical with our own, still, they are
employed in a logically consistent manner and hence indicate
what ordinarily we should call rationality.[9]

Therefore the contention that children are not rational agents
capable of deliberate choice, at best, stands in need of proof;
at worst, it is downright mistaken. Consequently the conclusion
based on this—that therefore they are not moral agents in the
full sense of that term and are not entitled to the moral status
and privilege of such an agent—does not follow. Therefore, the
antiquity of the argument and the names of Plato and Aristotle notwithstanding, it must be judged a failure.

The second version of the moral argument for infanticide is
based on the thesis of relativistic ethics or, alternatively, on the
naturalistic thesis that there are no moral absolutes at all. The
former argument is simply to this effect: Since all values are
relative to a given society and a given time, we cannot say
absolutely that infanticide is morally evil. The best we can say
is that our society has accorded it a negative status and that
according to this particular ethos, infanticide is unacceptable.
The second sort of argument merely goes one step further.
Instead of making moral values relative and without absolute

9. An obviously connected question is whether some of the insane are
nonrational, or whether they are rational but in a manner deviant from
the norm.

import, it claims that there are no moral values at all. Morally evaluative statements are construed as enunciations of preference. From this the argument concludes that no moral value attaches to infanticide in any case: What is at issue is whether we prefer the practice or not.

These two versions have their clear-cut differences. The first but not the second actually countenances moral values; the second but not the first reduces the issue to one of individual and/or social preference. But both versions are consistent; and in both cases, the conclusion does follow. The only shortcoming in both cases is one which we have encountered many times before: that of unproven moral assumptions. Both versions assume as true a theory of ethics that requires proof. No proof is forthcoming, either here or elsewhere. Consequently both arguments ultimately remain inconclusive.

Finally, there is the argument based on the notion of conflict of rights. This argument is very difficult to formulate clearly, since it involves diverse ethical parameters. Still, in the main it has something like the following structure:

All persons have rights, to be sure; and there is no doubt but that children—even neonates—are persons. However, not all persons have the same rights. And even when they do, it does not follow from the fact that they do have the same rights that they have these rights to the same degree. What rights they do have, as well as the degree to which they possess them, is a function of various things: minimally, of the duties which the entities in question fulfill; of the importance which they have with respect to the survival and functioning of the community in which they live, of mankind as a whole, and so on. But whatever the case, it is clear that by any of these criteria, the rights of children and neonates rank lower than those of adults. Consequently, when the threat of death arises in situations of genuine need and limited survival, the rights of children must take second place. Children may be killed —provided of course that no other way to survival except by killing a person is open.

This argument goes to the very heart of ethical theories because it forces us to deal with the question of the nature and ranking of rights. The position thus proposed is that the possession of rights is commensurate with the execution of duties. The logic of this does not seem to be in question. The problem, however, is the premises. We can begin by asking whether the very concept of the ranking of rights is legitimate. Can rights be ranked at all? Is a moral theory which ends up having to give an affirmative answer really acceptable? Over and above this generic critique, there is also the following more particular objection: Even if we were to grant the generic premise about conflicts of rights and their alleged ranking, it would still not be necessary for us to grant the further thesis that it is the rights of adults, and not those of infants, which take precedence. In other words, we might well wish to deny the thesis that rights are commensurate with duties. Instead, at least in this particular instance, we could invoke something like the principle of helplessness or the principle of innocence to make a case for the contrary claim. And so the criticism could continue in a similar vein. But there is really no need to go any further. The point has been made. Both the generic and the particular assumption on which this sort of argument is based are open to question. And that is sufficient to show that the certitude of the conclusion at best is up in the air.[10]

In view of these considerations, we may fairly ajudge the moral arguments for infanticide failures. This still leaves five other types of arguments. Let us see whether they are any more successful.

The Neurophysiological Argument

The neurophysiological argument, at least on the surface, is the most scientifically oriented of the lot. Like the moral argument

10. I here ignore further criticisms that could be raised, for example, that the argument claims that differences in rights obtain, but that the application of this thesis requires criteria vis-à-vis the different applications—criteria which are not given.

in its Aristotelian form, it is intended to show that a child is not fully a person and therefore cannot enjoy the full ethical status that a person enjoys. From this to the conclusion of the permissibility of infanticide is a relatively easy step.

> To be a person is to have a neurological system that is capable of supporting a higher, rational type of awareness. The only way we can be assured of the presence of such a system and of its functioning is to record it while it is in operation. EEGs—electroencephalograms—are the only means of doing so. However, when we examine the EEGs of babies and children, it emerges that they do not evince the amount of electrical activity typical of adult and fully conscious human beings. Nor are the electrical currents of the same wave lengths.
>
> After birth, the EEGs of babies resemble closely those of a frog, and with increasing age progress in complexity until at roughly age fourteen the individual's EEGs are of a typically human wave length and type. Consequently, by the neurophysiological criteria, it follows that until this particular age has been attained, the nervous system of the entity is not fully human. Whence it follows, by definition, that the being in question is not a person. In other words, babies and children are not persons until this age. Instead, they are on a par with those animals whose EEGs their own resemble. Consequently, to kill them prior to this stage of maturity is not murder.

From the point of view of electroencephalograms, this argument is certainly valid. If the EEGs of small children do not evince the amount of brain activity found in mature humans' EEGs—indeed, if on the point of complexity they do not even resemble those of the great apes—then such individuals do not here and now evince properly human brain activity. Therefore, the conclusion would certainly seem to follow that a small child is not yet a fully rational being.

But in evaluating this argument we must keep two things in

mind. The first is that amount of brain activity must be distinguished from nature or structure of such activity. The former is merely an index of the amount of material handled by the brain; the latter is an index to how this is done. This last is the important factor, for it is a key to symbolic rational activity; and on this score, the EEGs of small children are very analogous to those of other human beings. As to the wave length at which this activity occurs, to claim that it must occur at a certain frequency is not merely to ignore the otherwise distinctively human factor but also to legislate: to decide by fiat. The second thing to keep in mind is something that we said when considering the notion of a potential person. A distinction was made between the concept of specific potentiality, where a constitutive change is necessary for personhood in the full sense of that term to be attained, and the concept of limited potentiality, where all that is necessary is the actualization of an already existing constitution, indicated by means of the presence of a characteristic EEG. The present neurophysiological argument will be successful if and only if it is true that prior to age fourteen the neurological system is not merely immature and undeveloped from the point of view of amount of activity, but the structure of that activity is in fact not human. In other words, it will be correct if and only if it is also true that the immature EEG of a child is the result of an immature nervous system. On the surface at least, this seems to be the case. Completion of the central nervous system—myelination of the nervous fibers, attainment of the complexity of adult brain waves, and completion of intersystemic connections—is not fully acomplished until approximately five years of age; behavioral characteristics are not fully present and operative until age fourteen. At the fetal stage, certainly, fissure development in the cortex is not at all pronounced.

Nevertheless, these last considerations are not decisive. First, the evidence concerning neurological development and its detection in the early stages of human development is not all in, not by any means. Due to the nature of the subject matter, experimentation and analysis have been and continue to be slow. At the present time there are simply insufficient data to confirm or disconfirm any particular hypothesis.

Of course, this last argument cuts both ways. That is to say, it can be adduced with equal force and appropriateness by either side in the controversy. Therefore it does not settle the issue. In fact, it is more in the nature of a caveat, an injunction to go slow. However, there are two further considerations that may be raised against the preceding train of reasoning. One deals with the facts of the argument, with its premises; the other, with its logic. The consideration dealing with the premises is this: The argument as stated assumes, although it does not say so explicitly, that in order for there to be what we have previously defined as a properly human, personlike potential of rational awareness, the neurological base of that awareness (or its analogue) must be systemically complete and fully developed in all its aspects. That assumption is mistaken. It misses completely the crucial point of the concept of structural completeness which was central to our definition of personhood. It is not that the structure as a whole must be complete, down to the last nerve path and down to the last intercellular connection. What is important is that the structural makeup in its essential human blocks is there, that certain developments in the limbic and nonlimbic cortex are structurally present. It is structural completeness in this sense, not neurological completeness as to mass and axons, that is important. These structures, however, as we have stated before, are present very early on, in the fourth month or so of the gestation period. They may not be interconnected. But that is not essentially a matter of adding new cells and cellular structures. It is a matter of interconnecting, by means of the processes of cells already there, the structures that already exist. It is because these structures as we have defined them are there so very early on that even neonates are constitutionally capable of symbolic behavior, that children before the age of five are already perfectly capable of logical reasoning, and that the self-concept develops so very early in infancy.[11] Therefore the preceding argument fails because of a faulty premise.

The logical consideration that brings the argument to grief is the one which we already mentioned: Even if we ignored the distinction between amount of activity and structure, and even if we did grant that EEGs of the properly familiar, adult human variety indicate the presence of a human nervous system in the strong sense of that term, the conclusion advanced by the argument would not follow. That is to say, it does not follow that the absence of such an EEG—or the presence of an EEG of a different sort—implies the existence of nonhuman or subhuman nervous systems. The systems might not be operating in the usual way or at full potential. In other words, the EEG can only be taken as confirmation, never as disconfirmation, of a certain type or degree of neurological development. And the absence of a characteristic EEG certainly does not say anything about the existence or lack of existence of a certain neurological structure. Unless, of course, it could somehow be shown that the existence of such structures in the sense in which we have used that term must show itself in a human EEG and does not show itself in any child, fetus, or neonate. But that is far from being the case.

Aside from the preceding difficulties, other, less telling objections could be raised. Thus, it could be argued that the moral assumptions involved in the reasoning are not firmly established. It could also be said that the argument assumes what in philosophical circles is generally called the thesis of mind-body identity, which holds that the neurological system of a human being essentially *is* that person—that in that sense, his mind is identical with his body.[12] However, these objections

11. The problem with the self-concept of an infant is not that it does not have one, but that it is too inclusive—a different thing entirely. The latter involves self-awareness, but is mistaken in its domain; the former denies self-awareness entirely.

12. For a decent discussion of this, cf. D. M. Armstrong, *A Materialist Theory of Mind* (London: Routledge & Kegan Paul, 1968), which also includes a bibliography to further literature.

are not of any consequence, since like the first objection we discussed, they cut both ways, and in any case are themselves so hotly disputed that they can hardly serve as the basis for a counterargument.

The Sociodemographic Argument

As the name indicates, the sociodemographic argument is concerned with the living conditions of man within a society. As such, it presumes that the quality of life led by an individual is an overriding criterion as to whether or not that particular life is worth living.

> As we saw in the argument for abortion, any society can support only a finite number of individuals. Abortion and euthanasia, as well as senicide, certainly are answers. But they are only partial answers. Surplus population cannot always be gotten rid of by means of abortion. The sociodemographic conditions might—and sometimes do—fluctuate in such a way that what is considered to be an acceptable level of population turns out to be too great. Here, euthanasia and senicide would serve as effective means of lowering the population level. But even after these have been employed, the situation might still be critical. The question then arises, whom to delete. Since adults are necessary to the society because of their productive efforts, and since children—in particular small children under the age of puberty—contribute nothing, the latter are the most likely candidates. Consequently, it is they who should be killed. Nor should we fear that in thus doing away with our own progeny we should be dooming our population to extinction. The practice of infanticide need not be universal in its application and may be handled judiciously to prevent such an end. Furthermore, the fact that there are adults over the age of puberty will ensure the possibility of new members. In any case, this is a mere problem of detail and can easily be worked out.

Obviously, this sort of argument carries no brief for moral conclusions. In fact, moral considerations are here deemed irrelevant. In which case, unless the existence of a moral law can actually be shown, any critique from that quarter will be a pointless exercise.

But if that sort of criticism is obviated, what is left? If we ignore moral considerations, is the argument unexceptionable? Unfortunately or fortunately—depending on one's point of view—the answer must be in the affirmative. It is a fact that demographic conditions fluctuate, and it is a fact that adjustments to this fluctuation might require that certain members of the society should be killed if it is paramount that certain standards of living be maintained. It is also indubitable that from a completely amoral, completely pragmatic point of view, all and only those should be killed whose death does not interefere with or seriously threaten the survival of the community itself. Infanticide, therefore, emerges as as much of a live option for securing this end as do abortion and euthanasia. All three are on a par.

A particular version of the sociodemographic argument is even more detailed in indicating who should be killed. Basing itself on studies in the area of population dynamics, it argues that a certain proportion of male to female children is ideal, because only such a proportion would guarantee the ideal sex distribution necessary for effective functioning and survival. The reason why infanticide, rather than abortion, is recommended is one of pragmatics. Given the present state of the art, sex determination of a fetus just prior to its birth is not only costly, but also potentially dangerous in many cases. Consequently, birth is the only really safe time at which such determination can take place or can take place easily. Infanticide, therefore, is the only practical answer: All and only those children should be killed whose being alive would upset the ideal sex ratio.

Once more, the argument stresses the element of practicality. As we had occasion to note a moment ago, within the confines of the assumption that moral considerations are irrelevant, the argument again cannot be faulted. If, moral considerations aside, we feel a slight twinge of uneasiness, it must be ascribed to our conditioning, not to the facts of the matter.

The Eugenic Argument

The eugenic argument for infanticide is closely related to the sociodemographic one just considered. It is based on the contention that intrauterine inspection of a fetus is not merely costly but also dangerous. Consequently, so the argument continues,

> The only really safe time at which the viability of a fetus can be determined is when it is no longer a fetus: after it is born. Only at that stage can we determine with any show of accuracy and safety whether the being in question is deformed, genetically unsuited because of some hidden defect, or whether it is compeltely acceptable and "normal." Therefore, since this is the only time at which the decision on life or death can properly be made—because this is the only time at which all the relevant data are in—killing of the genetically unsuited or nonviable should take place at this stage. Of course, there are some genetic defects that do not manifest themselves until later in the infant's development as a child, just as there are some that are easily detected while the entity is in utero. That, however, should present no problem: The individual will be killed at the precise moment at which his genetic unsuitability is discovered. Except for these cases, therefore, infanticide in one form or another is the only workable answer.

The factual basis of this eugenic argument is not quite as strong as that of the sociodemographic one. Although it is indeed true at the present time that intrauterine examination of a fetus is by no means a commonplace and safe operation, it is increasingly becoming so. Furthermore, it appears that many congenital defects that would result in the birth of a marginal or nonviable individual can even now be detected quite safely simply by analyzing samples of the amniotic fluid in which the fetus lives. Furthermore, as the sophistication of our genetic knowledge and practice increases, we become more and more capable of determining the genetic characteristics of the future progeny, simply by analyzing those of the parents. Where unacceptability is then demonstrated, the course of action indicated would be that of contraception and, at worst, that of abortion. Certainly, infanticide would not enter the picture.

But there does remain the element of chance in predicting the genetic makeup of the progeny; and there remains the further fact that such precise genetic techniques are not available at the present time. The present is what we are concerned about. Forecasts of the future do not solve the problem. Therefore, if we confine ourselves to the present state of the art, it must be admitted that there are a great many defects of a serious nature which we do not want to see passed on and incorporated into the gene pool. There are also cases where the cost of keeping the individual alive would be immense, but where the fact of such a disability will not be known until after birth. In such cases, all other things being equal, infanticide seems to be the only workable expedient.

But *are* all other things equal? As we had occasion to observe in our discussion of abortion, on precisely this issue of eugenics, the phrase presupposes a great deal. It assumes that ethical considerations are either wholly irrational or, at least in their known utilitarian aspects, completely mistaken. This is a very large assumption and certainly requires proof. It also assumes that within certain more or less well defined limits we know what is eugenically correct and what is not, that we know what course human development should take. Again, this is a very questionable—at least, a very arguable—assumption. This much, however, we must grant the present argument—just as we had to grant it to the preceding argument from sociodemographic considerations: If the ethical premises previously alluded to *are* either false or irrelevant, then infanticide for eugenic reasons is as acceptable as abortion or euthanasia, when these are performed for similar reasons. However, until this assumption has been proven—and the onus of proof rests squarely on those who maintain it—the opposite is the more likely contender for truth.

The Historic Argument

Of all the arguments in favor of infanticide that we have discussed so far, what we have called the historic argument is by far the least credible.

> All previous ages and all cultures at some time or other in their development have advocated or condoned infanticide for various reasons. Furthermore, the practice has such able and penetrating philosophical proponents as Plato. Consequently, in view of the history of the notion, it is morally all right.

This argument is a gigantic non sequitur. To begin with, even if the initial premise of universality should be granted, from this it does not follow that the practice is morally right. It merely shows that people have in fact acted on this principle. But they might all have been wrong. At one time everyone believed that the earth was flat. Second, from the fact that otherwise revered thinkers have come out in favor of infanticide it does not follow that they were correct in doing so. They may have been just as mistaken as the majority of people who advocated burning at the stake. Furthermore, it should also be recalled that their advocacy has by no means gone unopposed. If the issue is to be settled on the basis of authority—and it certainly should not be —then the preponderance of philosophical thinkers have always been opposed to it.

The Personal Argument

"The personal argument" is a misnomer, since it is really a series of arguments which center around two generic approaches. Nevertheless, both approaches concentrate on the person of the baby and the simple question of whether we ought to supply the neonate with the requisite care necessary in order to ensure its survival, or whether we should let it die. The first line of reasoning deals with babies which, upon birth, are found to require special medical care and attention without which they could not survive. The second deals with what might be called normal babies.

(i)   The world is not an ideal place in which to live. It
       would be foolish to deny this. Therefore anything
       which we can do in order to minimize the amount of
       misery in it ought to be done. Now, sometimes babies
       are born which, if they are to survive, require special
       and intensive medical attention; those born extremely
       prematurely are cases in point. Only an affluent so-
       ciety, rich in resources, can afford to provide them
       with the necessary intensive care. In less rich societies
       that effort would be better spent alleviating the lot of
       those already on the scene. Therefore, in those socie-
       ties such babies ought to be allowed to die.

As it stands, this argument is straightforward enough. It bears
a certain similarity to another argument which we encountered
when we discussed abortion. Like that argument, it ignores completely the moral issue, the moral status of the baby as a person.
Or, from a slightly different point of view, it assumes that the
rights of the baby as a person—if it has any rights at all—are
subservient to those of the society, or of the people already on
the scene. In either case, the argument blatantly begs the moral
question. So does a variant of this approach which is less socioeconomic in character. Concentrating on the eugenics of the situation it goes like this:

The babies that require special medical attention sometimes
do so not simply because they are premature, but because
they evince certain hereditary defects. Hemophilia would
here be a good example. Or, alternatively, although their
present physiological debilities are not due to a genetically
inheritable defect, nevertheless such babies are known to
possess defective genes (e.g. for Huntington's chorea).
Since we do not want to saddle future generations with
genetic disabilities, such babies ought to be allowed to die.
That is to say, they ought not to receive that medical treatment and attention which is necessary in order to ensure
their survival.

As we said, this is a variant of argument (i) above; and like it, it begs the central moral question. But it does so not for socio-economic, but for genetic reasons. In that sense it is essentially similar to the genetic argument for abortion and shares many of its faults. In particular, it shares the flaw that it merely assumes that we know what the genetic norm *ought* to be (confusing genetic and moral considerations) and also merely assumes the correctness of utilitarianism. Finally, a third version of this particular approach considers the psychological outcome of permitting such a neonate to live:

> The later life of a deformed individual (e.g. thalidomide babies) or of a mentally severely handicapped person (e.g. Down's syndrome) is anything but pleasant—if not for the individual himself, then at least for the people who have to attend to him. Therefore, for the purely psychological— and in that sense, for the personal—welfare of the individual or of those other persons affected, the individual ought not to receive the necessary medical attention. We ought to let the baby die. If not for its own good, then at least for our own.

Once more, this particular argument has a familiar ring to it. We have encountered something very much like it before, in the context of abortion. Then, too, we found that the particular argument involved was invalid, just as we are about to see now. Quite aside from begging the moral issue, attendant on the personhood of the baby, there is the question of whether happiness —the baby's or our own—is a relevant consideration in an essentially moral context. Furthermore, it should be pointed out that not all deformed, feebleminded, or otherwise handicapped persons believe that they would have been better off dead, nor do all people who take care of such individuals have such an opinion. Therefore the pragmatic assumption—the thesis of psychological happiness—is not at all obvious or certain. Consequently, even if only on this basis, the conclusion ought not to be accepted.

The considerations with which we have dealt so far have all been premised on the assumption that the neonate in question required special medical attention in order to survive. We have shown that the arguments intended to deny it that attention fail. It might therefore seem a foregone conclusion that the second type of argument which we mentioned at the beginning of this section will fail as well. That is to say, that that line of reasoning which deals with medically healthy babies will also be invalid.

That appearance is in fact correct. Nevertheless, a brief consideration of the sort of argument involved will be instructive:

(ii)   Sometimes babies are born which, from a purely physiological point of view, are perfectly healthy. That is to say, without requiring special medical attention and given only "normal" care, they will survive as well as any other babies. However, the babies with which we are here concerned are defective in another way. They either carry a gene which will lead to a crippling neurological condition (e.g. Huntington's chorea); or they carry a recessive gene that might turn out to be lethal in later generations (e.g. female carriers of hemophilia); or while more or less healthy at birth, they will invariably die within the first two years of their lives (e.g. Tay-Sachs disease); or, finally, they are mentally feebleminded or otherwise defective. In such cases, the eugenic and/or socioeconomic implications of allowing such babies to live are unacceptable. The welfare of future generations would be jeopardized by allowing such genes to remain within the gene pool; and where there is no question of breeding, still the valuable care wasted on individuals who will either die or be of no use to anyone will spell deprivation or even death for other people. Consequently, such children should not be allowed to live. We should ignore them in the nursery, or in some other way make sure that they die.

This argument is of course very similar to all the other ones we have just considered. However, it has this crucial point of difference: The neonates in question are, at the time of birth, more or less healthy. The question is should they be allowed to live. And the reply is in the negative.

Once more, when analyzed, the argument itself turns out to be unacceptable. As before, it rests on unargued, moral, utilitarian assumptions. And, like the last argument which we considered, it is based on a mistaken pragmatic premise. It assumes that only the death of an individual will remove his genes from the gene pool. That is simply false. Such removal can be effected by many means. Sterilization is only one of them; contraception another. As to the argument that in some cases the babies will, with certainty, die within two years anyway, or that the individual which the baby will become will suffer a debilitating and fatal deterioration, these arguments are purely pragmatic and utilitarian in nature. As such, their basic premises have to be proven. But herewith we are back to the moral theme indicated earlier. It should also be pointed out that consistent application of the principle underlying this reasoning would force us to let all people who have a serious or terminal disease die without any efforts being made on our part to save them. It is not clear that this would be compatible with the professed ethics of the medical profession—some of whose members support infanticide on the grounds just indicated—or with the general beliefs of most people. In which case we have a flat inconsistency and contradiction. Whence it follows once more that if we are to be rational, we must either reject infanticide when proposed on these grounds or we must be willing to be consistent in our other relevant actions.

EVALUATION

We have thus reached the end of our critical analysis of the arguments pro and con. It is now time to enter the controversy ourselves. And here, in the light of our previous discussion on abortion and euthanasia, it is imperative that once more we draw attention to our notion of a person. A person is that sort of entity which evinces what, for want of a better term, we have called a characteristically human mode of awareness. We had also indicated that to a very definite degree, in many cases this could only be measured by EEGs as indicator phenomena of neurological processes. Our discussion of the maturation of the nervous system would now seem to indicate that this system is essentially complete only by age five and operative around age fourteen. It would therefore seem to follow that a human being is not a person in the proper sense of that term until it has reached the age of five. For only then is the constitutive potential in our sense of that term fully human.

It would seem, therefore, that by the logic of our own argument, we are committed to favoring infanticide; or, at any rate, to not condemning it as murder. In point of fact, however, this is not the case. The assumption that it is derives from a mistaken understanding of our definition of personhood. That definition does not tie us down to a complete cellular development of the nervous system as to axons, intercellular connectives, or whatever. What it does commit us to is the thesis that those neurological systems which are to count as potentially human in our sense of the term have those neurological structures which are characteristically human, and which are the repositories of self-awareness, of properly human awareness in the adult. Another way of putting this would be to say that it ties us down to the thesis that the cellular cores of the latter interconnected structures must be present. And these are present very early on.

Nor does our position tie us to the thesis that whatever does not evince a typically adult human EEG is not a person. For, as we have had occasion to observe prior to this, whereas the presence of such an EEG would establish the existence of *at least* a human nervous system (or an analogue thereof), the absence of such an EEG would not establish a corresponding absence. EEGs are merely indicator phenomena, in the sense we have suggested. Furthermore, their precise interpretation and sophistication will change as our understanding of human neurophysiology and psychology changes. Finally, we must bear in mind a distinction we have urged repeatedly: between the amount of brain activity evinced and the nature of that activity with respect to its structure. It is the latter that is indicative of personhood, not the former. To conclude, therefore, our position merely commits us to the thesis that whatever does not possess the constitutional capabilities for rational, symbolic thought and self-awareness is not a person. But as we stated before, the possession of such a potential is not the same as the possession of a fully mature brain. The brain centers (or structures) are important. And the "higher" centers of human awareness are characteristically present early in fetal development. In other words, the structural potential is there. Consequently, infants, as well as fetuses after a certain critical period, are persons. And to kill persons (except, possibly in self-defense) with set intent, knowledge, and purpose is murder. Therefore infanticide is—to say the least—morally reprehensible. In fact, it is murder.

The preceding also permits us to throw into relief an underlying theme of our earlier discussion, namely, that the transition from a nonperson to a person is not an abrupt transition, like a quantum jump. Instead, it is a gradual thing, beginning at the level of fertilized ovum and culminating at the status of an adult, normal human being. The initial transition is made at the fetal stage, when the higher centers are formed. The remaining stages, although important to the extent that they permit the characteristically symbolic human behavior, are as it were mere icing on the cake. Therefore while there may be some leeway for action in certain early fetal stages, there is none in later stages and certainly none after birth. At that point, babies are persons in our sense of the term, and as such possess all the moral rights and privileges that we possess. The deliberate killing of them is an act of murder, pure and simple. And if it is argued that this depends on the further assumption that there are absolute moral values, I must unabashedly admit that this is something which I hold to be the case.

5

Senicide

The Problem

The killing of the very young, whether fetus or infant, stands opposed to senicide, the killing of the very old. Like infanticide, but unlike abortion and suicide, senicide seems to be a very touchy subject among even the most liberal of the new moralists, to say nothing of those who are more traditional in outlook. And yet, it is not at all clear why this should be the case. If once again we listen to our cynic, we will of course hear a ready answer: Those who do the talking, by the very fact that they can even consider the issue, have passed the hurdles of abortion and infanticide. It is only natural that they not be worried about these any longer. Consequently, they can afford to adopt the more cavalier attitude on these issues. However, they all face the fact of old age and hence the possibility of senicide. Therefore it is only to be expected that they should be more careful. The cynic could also tell us that whereas most people have relatively few qualms about killing individuals they do not know, and certainly very few qualms about killing individuals they do not know *as persons,* the prospect of killing an old friend of long standing is downright unpalatable and unpleasant.

But egocentric and emotional cynicisms aside, this much is true: We find the prospect of killing acquaintances, relatives, and friends of long standing highly unpleasant, whereas we do not find the prospect of aborting a fetus nearly so bad. We should be fooling ourselves if we denied or ignored this state of affairs. But as we have reiterated in the preceding chapters, there is always the question of ethical import and the further question of moral consistency, both of which must be considered in these contexts. As to the first, it requires an independent analysis of the notion of senicide; and as for the second, it requires that whatever our decision on the first, it be consistent with the remainder of our practice of death.

It is precisely this question of consistency which poses a problem in the case of senicide. Whereas consistency of argument and application of principles is deemed well and good by those in favor of abortion, infanticide, or euthanasia, the very principles underlying such arguments are held to be inapplicable in the case of the aged. But we are already too far afield. Let us begin by defining 'senicide' and then proceed in our wonted course.

Senicide is the killing of the aged. As it stands, this definition is incomplete. Aged in precisely what context? What counts as an old individual in one society may not count as an old person in another. Old age need not even be a constant concept within the same society over periods of time. For example, what counted as old age in the Middle Ages does not count as old age now. Our definition, therefore, in order to be acceptable, must take account of this relativistic core of the notion and yet be applicable in every context. Accordingly, we shall define old age not by the possession of a precise number of years, but in terms of the physiological, and/or associated mental state of the individual—some "age more rapidly" than others—as well as the execution of the social function vis-à-vis the remainder of society. An old person, therefore, is one who is physiologically and/or mentally deteriorated past the point of social usefulness, where this deterioration occurs after attainment of physical maturity, and whose lack of social usefulness is not outweighed by the role played by him as a member of the age group in which he finds himself. In this sense, then, we are to understand senicide as the killing of the aged.

The Negative Argument

Is senicide morally acceptable? Is it murder? Once more, as in the case of infanticide, we are hard-pressed to give any detailed and coherent account of what the position of traditional ethics is really like. The reason is that traditionally we have merely assumed that to kill an aged member of our society, all other things being equal, is simply murder. We have never really stopped to think why we should hold this to be the case. Still, despite the absence of coherent and explicit argument on that score, let us see whether we cannot derive some defense of the traditional position from the principles underlying that position in other contexts.

The Religious Argument

Probably the easiest way to construct an argument against senicide is by turning to revelationary religious literature; in particular, to the Old Testament. There we find the express command "Honor thy father and mother!" With this as its foundation, the religious argument could then proceed as follows:

> God gave an explicit command to honor father and mother. One reason why this command singles out our parents is, surely, that they stand in a parental relationship to us. But it applies not merely to biological parents. Adoptive parents are covered as well. And if we take the New Testament into account, what emerges is that not even the exercise of a parental function lies at the heart of this injunction. For in the New Testament, parents are frequently equated with older people in general. In other words, what is really meant by the command to honor father and mother is this: That the old members of society ought to be honored. To kill, however, is not to honor, especially to kill for that very reason which puts the individual into the group which is worthy of being honored. Consequently, to kill the aged goes against the very command of God as thus understood.

This religious argument could be fleshed out by appealing to the fact that the aged, after all, are persons, and that as such they are entitled to the same moral treatment as all other persons. Consequently, to kill them in the aforementioned manner would be murder. In that sense, all the religious objections previously adduced against killing persons would also become relevant and could be used to flesh out the argument even more.

A religiously based argument, therefore, would not be too difficult to construct. As we have indicated, it would fit in very nicely with the various other religious arguments against killing persons, which we have considered from time to time. It would thus provide continuity with the remainder of the religious position. But it would also inherit many of the same problems we have already discussed. The religious premises themselves would require reasoned (and reasonable) defense to begin with; and it could also be argued that the very personhood of the aged is in question. Finally, it could be pointed out that the commandment on which at least one part of the argument is based has no moral force whatsoever, that when completed, the commandment runs: "that it might go well with you and you have a long life on earth!" When thus filled out, the command is a blatant threat and lacks moral persuasiveness. Therefore, even aside from all else, that part of the argument collapses.

The Moral Argument

But we need not confine ourselves to religious considerations in order to construct a traditionalistic argument against senicide. We can also turn to ethics proper. For, from the purely moral point of view, there is of course the argument that senicide is murder simply because it is the nondefensive, intentional, and explicit killing of a person. Any such act is murderous. That of senicide is merely one instance of a general sort of case. And in proceeding in this manner the traditional position is nothing if not consistent. If 'murder' is to be defined in that way at all, then consistent application of that definition will eventuate in the conclusion that senicide is murder. The question that an opponent of tradition would here raise is, By what token do we know that a person in his senescence is in fact still a person? Radically speaking, once calcification of the brain has set in or similar age-related physiological changes have occurred, a good case can be made for saying that the peculiarly human structures of the brain have deteriorated beyond functional usefulness, that thereby the peculiarly human potential for rational awareness (in our sense of that term) has disappeared, and that the individual in question, although undoubtedly human, is no longer a person. The physiological claims thus made may or may not be true. Certainly, however, in some cases they will obtain; and if they do, the personhood of some aged individuals will be in question. Another way of putting this point would be to say that "Once a person, always a person!" does not follow, any more than does "Once a fetus, always a fetus!" In particular, it does not follow if the ascription of personhood is functionally related to a neurological or other physiological base. We pass over without discussion the other moral assumption underlying this traditional argument: that under any and all circumstances (except that of justified self-defense against an unjust aggressor), the deliberate killing of an individual is murder.

The Pragmatic Argument

While the preceding traditional approach assumes the personhood of the aged and builds its moral case around this assumption, the next argument we shall consider has no ethical overtones whatsoever. To be sure, it is still on the traditionalist side. However, it stresses the pragmatic utility of the aged, the folly of killing them off, rather than the immorality of that sort of action. Briefly, it goes like this:

> The aged, by definition, have lived a long life, longer, at any rate, than the greater part of their particular society. Having lived comparatively longer lives, they have had a great deal more experience of the world. Therefore they are invaluable and irreplaceable repositories of experience and knowledge, both of which are essential to the proper functioning and ultimate survival of the community. Consequently, from a purely practical point of view, it would be bad policy to get rid of the aged.

But, we might ask, are the premises of this argument really correct? That is to say, does this argument really hold in our present society? To be sure, centuries and even millennia ago, when recorded forms of history were all but unknown or unavailable, the aged fulfilled this very vital function. With the advance of recording techniques, however, and the compilation of all sorts of records, this function has been superseded, at least so far as the passing on of information is concerned. Books, records, and other devices serve this purpose much more surely, in a much less distorted way, and for a much greater length of time. As to wisdom, or the practical application of theoretical knowledge, the aged will be of little help as teachers. Already Plato knew that this cannot be taught by anyone but must be acquired by each individual for himself in actual life. Once more, therefore, we must reply to the argument with a verdict of "not proven."

While on the practical side of the matter, we could try to point out that the older members of the community control most of the wealth of that community and hence are in an incomparably more advantageous position to control the mores of a given society. In particular, those against senicide. Therefore they could declare senicide immoral. But this does not really amount to an argument against senicide. At best, it could be turned into an argument from power, or into an appeal to fear. A little more cogent—and certainly a lot more common —would be the following consideration:

> The aged have performed their function in the community. Consequently, they have earned our gratitude, and it is our duty to show this by making their declining years as comfortable as possible.

However, even this argument, popular as it may be, lacks probative force. First of all, it assumes that it is our moral duty to show gratitude. Second, it assumes that gratitude should be shown in this particular way. Both of these assumptions sound reasonable enough; but that is no guarantee of their correctness. Third, the argument assumes that all who have reached a "ripe old age" have in fact benefited their society and have earned its thanks. Frequently, however, this is not the case. In which case, the argument itself would seem to suggest that those who have not thus contributed should not reap the benefit of our gratitude. In other words, there would be nothing wrong in having them killed. For, if the only reason for keeping the aged alive is as was just stated, and if that reason is absent, the conclusion to terminate that person's life follows.

A practical approach, however, is not confined to the preceding considerations. As a matter of elementary social dynamics it should be realized that any group which feels threatened in its survival fights to maintain it. This, we are told, is natural, given the instinct for survival found in the members of the group. These considerations could be integrated into the following arguments:

> If the aged were to face, one and all, the prospect of an untimely removal from this world, they would resist it to the best of their ability. And that ability would not be inconsiderable. Social upheaval would become the order of the day, if not on a group basis, then at least on the basis of individual action. In other words, if senicide were to become a social practice, we should be faced with the rise of a permanent class of social agitators whose disruptive influence might very well bring the society to ruin. Its membership could not be curtailed, since all things being equal every member of society sooner or later becomes a member of that class. Such a society would not be stable. Therefore, in the interests of social stability, we ought to refrain from instituting senicide as a social practice.

This sort of argument has whatever appeal it does have because of the way we feel at the present time. At the present time we recoil at the prospect of being killed when we have reached a certain age or when we have ceased to be able to fulfill a socially useful function. But, and we should be quite clear on this matter, it is not necessarily the case that we should invariably feel this way. To be sure, there is something instinctive about the fear of death. Instincts, however, are not like laws of logic. While there is nothing that we can do to change the laws of logic, there is something we can do to change or overcome our instincts: We can overcome them by means of conditioning. Our

conditioning—or lack of conditioning—at the present time is
such as to accord with or even enhance the instinct for continued survival. But this conditioning could be changed to result
in the conviction that death—artificially induced death—at a
certain age is not merely perfectly acceptable, but even morally
meritorious and psychologically desirable. Therefore, if somehow such an attitude could be inculcated (conditioned) in the
members of our society, the danger of social foment would not
exist. As to the possibility of instilling such an attitude, there are
historical precedents: For generations—indeed, for millennia—
young men were conditioned to believe in the desirability of
death "for their country." Or, to take a more germane example,
for hundreds of years people in the Aztec culture were conditioned to believe that death on an altar, as a human sacrifice,
was desirable. We need only look at our opinion of Christian
martyrs to find a relevant analogue.

THE POSITIVE ARGUMENT

By now it must seem as though the case against senicide is not
a very strong one—that is, if one discounts certain ethical premises. And of course, that feeling is entirely correct. If there were
no moral absolutes, anything which is practically feasible would
be right. The following series of arguments in favor of senicide
will demonstrate this point even more strongly.

The Ecological Argument

The first argument, the argument from ecology, is one with
which, by now, we are quite familiar.

> The resources of the earth are quite limited. Only a finite
> population can be supported in a way that we could prop-
> erly call human. Any population has one area of human
> surplus the removal of which will not threaten the sur-
> vival of that community but at the same time will lighten
> the demands on the ecosystem of which the community is
> a part: the aged. The young, unless they are physiologi-
> cally or mentally deviant or deficient, cannot be removed

because their existence ensures the continuation of the society. Those of mature years—adults in the years of productivity—are necessary for the existence of the society at the present time. Only the old are unnecessary and contribute nothing. They are only a source of demands. In fact, in virtue of their generally debilitated state, the demands they make are incomparably greater and lead to inordinate requirements of manufacture, which disproportionately upset the ecology. Therefore, in the interest of lightening the burden on the ecosystem, this domain of consumers should be removed as a matter of course.

As we said, if we disregard the ethics of the situation, this sort of argument is not entirely unreasonable. To be sure, we could argue over whether or not all infants ought to be permitted to survive to adulthood, or whether a practice of selective infanticide would not be within the guidelines of the present argument. We could also argue along similar lines for adults. But once that matter is settled—and really it is only one of detail—the rest of the argument follows. If, that is, the ethics of the matter count for nothing. And that, of course, is the question. The claim that this is so cannot merely be stated; it must be substantiated by argument.

The Argument from Social Welfare

A second line of reasoning, analogous and closely related to the first, is based on the concept of social welfare.

The style of life of individuals, the quality of their existence, is a direct function of the resources available to the society. That is to say, all other things being equal, the richer the society in material goods, the greater the likelihood that all members of the society will lead a happy and materially sufficient life. However, one of the prerequisites for such a state of affairs is that the goods necessary for such a life-style be produced. Only people who are capable of producing add anything to the society. If the number of nonproductive members exceeds a certain allowable maximum, the life-style will become depressed. Consequently, all those who have passed the stage of usefulness ought to be killed.

Obviously, this argument is very closely related to the ecological one. Its particular difference derives from the fact that, unlike the latter, it emphasizes the availability of material goods for a certain life-style without paying attention to ecological considerations. This similarity to the ecological argument does not, however, mean that it is on as firm a pragmatic footing as the latter. In fact, its central assumption is quite dubious. It is not and never has been the case that a goodly supply of material goods has spilled over into all quarters of society. In general, what has happened is this: The greater the supply of material wealth and goods, the greater the difference in life-style between those who have and those who have not. Extreme poverty and subhuman standards of living have always been found in societies possessing extreme wealth. And what is more, the producers of this wealth generally have had little share in it. It is those who administer or legally possess it—in a word, those who serve little or no practically useful function—who have enjoyed it. Therefore the basic assumption of the argument is false: It is not the case that those who are useful are participants in the life-style they engender. Consequently, if consistency is of any interest at all, this particular argument does not hold. It is not the case that those who can no longer produce ought to be removed. For those who do not produce are not presently removed, and the life-style of the society has not thereby become depressed. Furthermore, so it could be argued, on account of that lack of productivity that depression, if it obtains, is the result of entirely different sociodynamic factors.[1] Of course, one could always reply to this by saying that consistent application of the underlying principle would result in the removal of this

1. It should be noted that all this is premised on the assumption that consistency in treatment is a desirable thing. But then, this assumption is not peculiar to the present context. It governs my whole discussion in this book.

social injustice, and that the argument in fact was committed to such a course of action. That would indeed remove our objection. But it would still leave the underlying ethical assumption of the preceding argument. It would also leave untouched the thesis that the quality of life is a relevant consideration in the present context. That assumption, familiar as it is, still awaits proof.

The Psychological Argument

The third argument, the argument from psychology, is based on the medical fact that with increasing age, calcification of the brain and accompanying senility set in.

> Those who are old have lost much of their mental acumen, simply because of the physiological deterioration of their brains. This is a biological inevitability. While this does not necessarily entail that from a physiological point of view such individuals are incapable of survival or that they are in any overt way nonfunctional, it does have very definite psychological effects. These old people can no longer think or reason properly. They may even be so far gone that they regress to infancy. In such cases, no point is served in keeping them alive, neither for themselves nor for anyone else. Therefore they should be killed.

This argument has a two-pronged approach: one, directed toward the individual himself; another, directed toward the society. Because such a person is of diminished capacity, he should be killed: both for his own sake as well as for the sake of others. All this sounds reasonable on the surface; or at least in a certain context it does. But precisely why ought we to accept the underlying assumptions? Person x should be killed for his own sake; but person x, although senile, is happy. What more could he want? He is not aware of what to others may seem an undignified mode of existence. Therefore that avenue of argument is closed. As to the claim that he ought to be killed for the sake of society, does that not really amount to a claim of convenience? Because it is inconvenient and psychologically depressing to take care of the senile and old, therefore they ought to be killed. The logic of this is unclear. And if the general thesis underlying this claim were to be applied consistently, it would follow that *all* who are inconvenient, whose existence leads to psychological depression, and so on ought to be killed. And while such a position would have consistency on its side, very few of its proponents would be willing to go this far. As usual, we shall simply mention and not discuss the ethics of the matter. The argument assumes but does not prove a utilitarian theory of rights and obligations and merely assumes that there are no absolute values.[2]

The Moral Argument

With this, we have come once again to the crux of the whole problem: the question of ethics. Whatever the practical pros and cons of this particular suggestion—whatever the pragmatic merits or demerits of senicide—the point remains that without a solution to the moral issue, the question cannot be settled. However, there is a moral argument in favor of senicide. That is to say, there is an argument in favor of senicide which bases itself on truly moral premises. It is this:

> The welfare of the community as a whole is of greater moral significance than the welfare of any particular one of its members. Nor is the latter's happiness and contentment of overwhelming moral significance when compared to that of the whole. In the case of the old and senile, the welfare and happiness of the remainder of society are definitely infringed upon. Consequently, it is not merely morally permissible but downright obligatory to change this state of affairs. Lacking the means to achieve rejuvenation, the only thing left would be to remove old people from the

2. I also ignore the fact that frequently the old are not incapacitated, as the argument suggests. I ignore it because I have already provided for such a contingency in my definition of senicide.

scene. That, however, is merely a euphemism for killing. Therefore, from a strictly moral point of view, it is our duty to kill the senile and old.

It is precisely because this argument addresses itself to the underlying moral issue that it is so powerful. If the utilitarian premise is true, and if there is an infringement of welfare as stated, then the argument will not merely be valid but also sound. That is to say, not only will the conclusion follow from the premises, the conclusion will also be true. The questions of paramount importance, therefore, are whether or not this moral thesis is correct and whether such an infringement obtains. As to the latter, that may be the case. As to the former, we shall not attempt to give an answer at the present time. In the next chapter, we shall explore some of the ramifications of the theory and shall suggest that in at least one of its forms it involves a contradiction. For now, suffice it to point out that if the theory is correct, then it sanctions not merely senicide but also abortion, suicide, infanticide, and even certain types of murder.

EVALUATION

Is senicide morally permissible? Is it obligatory? Or does it amount to the crime of murder? The present section calls for an evaluation of the arguments pro and con and, if possible, for a solution. However, as should be obvious by now, a definitive solution to the problem will be impossible unless certain fundamental questions concerning the nature of ethics have been resolved. In particular, the question of utilitarianism requires an answer: Is the thesis of utilitarianism correct, or is it merely a principle of convenience? Are there absolute moral values and standards, or are these only of relative validity, applicable only within the social context in which they arose? Is there such a discipline as ethics at all—are there moral values—or does the whole amount to no more than a relative system of mores codifying the historical predilections of a particular person, group of persons, or society?

To attempt a solution lies beyond the scope of the present

chapter. But that does not mean that we cannot attempt to supply the schema for an answer. It is just that here, as before, this schema will be conditional, contingent on the truth of certain ethical premises.

Let us therefore return to the preceding discussion. The first thing that should be noted is that whereas we have presented the case for senicide as part of the position of the new morality, it is part of this position merely by implication, not by actual acceptance. That is to say, very few if any proponents of the new morality actually advance an argument in favor of senicide. It is just that the positions on abortion, suicide, and euthanasia defended by the new morality imply logically the position on senicide that we have ascribed to them. That this is so is quite easy to see. The new morality, when not rejecting ethics entirely or espousing a principle of ethical egoism, operates on the principle of utility: the "greatest happiness principle." All and only those acts are morally acceptable that produce the greatest amount of happiness for the greatest number of people. Difficulties of interpretation aside, it is this principle that is supposed to justify abortion, suicide, and euthanasia. However, as but a moment's reflection will show, the principle licenses more than merely these practices. In fact, it enjoins as morally obligatory every act which, all other things being equal, produces the greatest happiness for the greatest number. Therefore, consistent application of the principle demands that if we can show that infanticide, euthanasia, and so on are happiness producing in the requisite sense, and if we can show that senicide also shares this characteristic, then each of these acts will be morally acceptable and right. In fact, it will be our duty to engage in them.

As we said, this is the position to which the new morality is committed; and as we also said, the new moralist rarely if ever penetrates that far in his deliberations. As such, his failure to do so constitutes an interesting datum that may shed some light on the motives underlying the new morality. We shall not pursue this. Instead, let us note that whatever other shortcomings the traditionalist's position may have, at least it is not devoid of consistency. Furthermore, for the new morality, the issue of whether or not someone is a person is of little if any significance. In the face of the common good, a rock, baboon, or shoemaker count equally, or almost so. For the traditionalist, the issue of personhood is overwhelming: if someone is a person, then by that very token to kill him with deliberate intent and purpose is to commit an act of murder. Rocks and baboons—any non-persons—do not count at all.

So far in this book it has been our aim to show that at least on the issue of personhood, the conclusion (although not the argument) of the traditionalist is correct. Obviously, the final verdict will not be in until we have addressed ourselves to the fundamental questions mentioned above. But even without this, we can propose the following—always, of course, keeping in mind the conditional nature of our proposal: The fundamental question is whether or not an old person is in fact still a person. Here there is no hard and fast answer that can be quantified in terms of a certain number of years. That is to say, if our definition of personhood is correct, then it is not a matter of course that anyone who is a person at age seventeen will be a person at age eighty or age ninety-five. Personhood, after all, as we understand it, is defined in terms of potentiality for a certain type of awareness, where that awareness is said to be grounded in a particular type of nervous system or its analogue. Therefore, if, through age, the nervous system deteriorates so as to be incapable of properly human function without a radical constitutive change, then the individual in question will no longer be a person.

The first issue to be resolved, therefore, is whether or not the individual in question satisfies the criteria for personhood advanced in chapter 1.[3] Having answered that question for a particular case—and, presumably, having answered it in the affirmative—the solution to the problem follows as easily here as it did in all previous cases. To commit senicide is to commit murder, if the act is committed against the wishes of the person in

---

3. I should emphasize once more that this does not require actual awareness. The constitutive potential for awareness is sufficient.

question. However, the individual himself may request to be put to death. In which case, if he has substantial moral reasons as indicated in our previous discussion of suicide or euthanasia, then the action will be morally acceptable: an instance of allowable euthanasia.

The question now is what counts as a substantive moral reason? On the basis of our previous discussions of suicide and euthanasia, we can immediately rule out mere inclination, personal preference, boredom, tiredness, and the like. Following the guidelines laid down in the previous discussions, we can say that only those considerations will count as excusing which show that the quality of life faced by the individual, were he not to be killed, would be of an unalterably and unremittingly negative character. Anything else, while perhaps excusable and understandable from a psychological point of view, would carry no moral weight.

But if this is the case, then it develops that there is no such thing as a morally excusable senicide. Senicide, after all, was defined as the act of killing an aged person who has deteriorated past the age of social usefulness. The fact that such deterioration obtains does not necessarily reduce the individual from the status of a person to that of a nonperson. Nor does the fact that the individual has attained a certain age have a similar result. Mere age and/or deterioration and/or uselessness, therefore, are not excusing conditions. The quality of life may be. But where that is the determining factor, we are faced with a case of allowable suicide or allowable euthanasia. Consequently, acceptable senicide, in the proper sense of that term, falls under one of these rubrics and is not murder. However, if we should have a case of senicide as initially defined—as centering around social utility and function—then, the excusing conditions mentioned earlier being absent, we should always have a case of murder.

6

Morality and the Practice of Death

Suppose that I were to use an experimental drug on your child in the hope that by such a desperate and last-ditch effort I could save his life; and suppose further that your child died: Would I be guilty of murder? Suppose, on the other hand, that I administered this drug to your child when the situation was not so desperate; and suppose once again that your child died as a result of receiving the drug. Once more, would I be guilty of murder? Suppose, finally, that I were to administer the drug to your child solely in order to see what would happen; and suppose that the outcome of this was as we have said: Would I be guilty of murder then?

These three cases pinpoint a spectrum of possible actions. And, as is to be expected, the conclusion in each case mirrors the nature of the action. In the first case, we should want to say that all other things being equal—due care having been taken that no unnecessary or unreasonable risks obtain—I should not be guilty of murder. I should not even be culpable for negligent practice of medicine. We might, indeed would, deplore the outcome of the event; but I should be held blameless for it. As to the second sort of case, our assessment of the situation would be quite different. We should probably feel that since the state of affairs did not warrant such desperate expedients, the child was merely being used for experimental purposes or—what is more likely—that I, as a doctor, was guilty of negligence and malpractice. The accusation of murder, however, would not stand. Finally, in the third case the verdict of murder would be unequivocal and clear, at least as far as popuular opinion is concerned. Such experimentation with the lives of children is deemed morally indefensible and inexcusable.

Does this apply only to experimentation with the lives of children? Consider the following, analogous cases: Suppose that we performed medical experiments on human adults who had not volunteered for that service and who may or may not be aware that this experiment runs the very real danger of death. Suppose further that death ensued. Are we guilty of murder? And to complement the preceding situation, suppose further that we performed medical experiments on adults who had volunteered for such a service, in full knowledege of the possibility of death; and suppose also that death occurred. Again, are we now guilty of murder?

As to the first case, once more we are tempted to reply in the affirmative. In the second case, the answer would not be quite so clear. For, so we are tempted to argue, each individual has a right to his own body and existence and can dispose of it as he pleases—provided, of course, that the nature of this disposition does not (seriously) infringe upon the lives and rights of other members of the society. This, at least, would be the position of the new morality. The traditionalist, in all probability, would condemn all of these cases as instances of murder—all cases, that is, except those where a serious attempt is made to save the person's life by means of that drug. This intention of saving a life makes all the difference in the world.

The traditionalist's response requires little analysis. By its very nature—as its name indicates—it is traditional and has received detailed attention for quite some time. The interesting response is that of the proponent of the new morality: Why does voluntary participation in such a program make the situation all right? Is it not still true that the death of a person resulted from the deliberate participation in a sort of activity where death was known to be a possible outcome? Is this not playing with a human life? And is that not tantamount to murder?

To appreciate the position of the new morality we have to remember what was said in our discussion of suicide and euthanasia: this position assumes that any individual has the right to complete disposition of his life. Let us ignore the question of whether or not such a claim is defensible. Let us instead note the assumption on which it is based: Human life—the life of a person—has no intrinsic value. What value it has is the result of the value we place on it. If we decided to value it highly, then it will be valuable for us; if we decide that it has no value at all, then whatever status it may have in the eyes of anyone else, for us it is without moral significance.

And this brings us to the next point: Together with this relativistic theory of value, the position of the new morality assumes a certain theory of what is wrong and what is right. An act is wrong if and only if it infringes on the rights of others; it is right if it does not do that and, moreover, aims at producing a situation which is valued by someone either for the sake of something else or for its own sake. Doing one's own thing is all right, so long as you don't bother anyone, and so long as you are indeed doing something which is valuable or leads to a situation that you value or deem to be valuable at the present time.

Once more, let us disregard one-half of this analysis. That is to say, let us ignore that part of it that deals with the procuring of a situation, event, or thing that we value. That part is relativistic in nature—at least it seems to be so—and this we expected. The interesting part of the analysis is the first clause: So long as the rights of other people are not infringed upon, the action will be morally right. The interesting thing about this clause is not that it presupposes a definition of 'right' which must be given without reference to what it is right to do. Instead, it lies in the fact that whereas the whole position was allegedly relativistic in nature and supposedly involved a denial of all moral absolutes, this clause clearly shows that this is not the case. There is at least one more moral absolute: the duty not to interfere with the rights of your neighbor.

There are two possible ways in which this position could be maintained: (1) on the basis of the claim that there simply are absolute rights in the universe and that these rights have in-

dividual persons as their focus; or (2) on the basis of the claim
that there is only one absolute right-making characteristic and
hence duty: That the happiness of the greatest number of people possible should be the aim of all acts.

Both of these are advanced at different times by the proponents of the new morality. The first lies at the basis of the
claim that it is morally acceptable to commit suicide. Whether
this claim is successful or not is another matter. The point is
that ethical egoism and the absolute rights of persons are here
taken to carry the day. The second, on the other hand, is adduced as justifying abortion and euthanasia: At least, in some
arguments this is the case. For instance, it is maintained that
even if an as yet unborn child should already be a person—as
by the physiology of the matter it frequently is—its rights as a
person are superseded by the rights of the mother and of the
existing society. The happiness of the greatest number takes
precedence over that of the few. Or, in the case of euthanasia,
it is sometimes said that in the interests of the community it
would be better if the incurably ill or insane were killed. Once
more, the watchword is the happiness of the masses.

As we said, both types of justifications can be encountered
in the reasoning of the new morality. And this fact explains
the peculiar air of incoherence, coupled with reasonableness,
which pervades this position. By themselves, such positions are
quite coherent and do not necessarily involve a contradiction.
Together, however, they invariably do. For they stand at opposite poles of the moral spectrum. Ethical egoism, if it agrees
with moral utilitarianism at all, agrees with it only by accident:
While it may happen that the best way to advance the individual's interest is that of indulging in utilitarian practices, it
need not be so; and when it is not, utilitarianism goes by the
board.

But that is merely one aspect of the difficulty facing the position of the new morality. Another is that ethical egoism in the
form indicated above cannot actually be implemented. If everyone has essentially the same right to, let us call it, "self-fulfil-
ment," then sooner or later in their implementation, these rights

are bound to conflict. When both you and I want to exercise our right to do x, but only one of us can do so; or when your exercise of the right to do x interferes with my exercise of the right to do y, what are we to do? The position itself provides no criteria for the ranking of rights. And if it did, ultimately, by the nature of the case, it would have to be utilitarian in nature. It is unclear how this would work.

Utilitarianism

This brings us squarely to the issue of utilitarianism as a moral thesis underlying the position of the new morality.[1] As we just saw, the issue devolves ultimately to possibility (2): Which act results in the greatest amount of good for the greatest number of people? That act will be right and, most probably, obligatory.

At least so far as euthanasia and abortion are concerned, the new morality will feel very comfortable with this position. The theory, at least in general, provides all the answers that the new moralist himself wants to recognize. But—and this generally goes unrecognized by the proponents of the thesis—it gives more answers than those with which the new moralist can feel comfortable. It does not say that invariably abortion or euthanasia is the morally right course of action. In fact, in some cases it could demand the death of the mother or her unhappiness and unflagging misery for the rest of her life. In the case of euthanasia, an analogous reversal of conclusions could sometimes be forthcoming—to say nothing of suicide and all other practices of death.

To see how this is the case, and that it follows with inexorable logic, let us consider the thesis of utilitarianism in brief detail. As a moral theory, it is of respectable antiquity but gained prominence and even currency only through the work

1. For a good discussion of utilitarian and various other moral theories, see Richard B. Brandt, *Ethical Theory* (Englewood Cliffs, N.J.; Prentice-Hall, 1959), which includes bibliographies at the end of each chapter.

of individuals like Jeremy Bentham[2] and John Stuart Mill.[3] In a nutshell, the theory goes as follows: There are no absolute values in the universe; there are only absolute rights and obligations. These, especially the obligations, can best be summed up under the heading of "the greatest happiness principle": that act and only that act is morally right which produces the greatest amount of happiness for the greatest number of people.

The thesis has something comfortably scientific about it, for it comes equipped with a calculus: After all, to be capable of implementation it has to be able to tell us how much happiness an act is (likely) to produce. Indeed, we should also have to know what happiness is. To both, Mill gave a solution. He argued that happiness is identical with pleasure, and that pleasure can be ranked according to four parameters: kind, intensity, duration, and distribution. In other words, having defined happiness in terms of pleasure, Mill went on to suggest this schema of what he called a hedonestic calculus. Given any particular situation, we could in principle sit down and calculate which of the alternate actions open to us yields the highest proportion of pleasure over pain. The latter would be the morally proper act. Furthermore, since life is not always sufficiently leisurely to permit individual and particular calculation at all times, we could determine general rules beforehand, so that when an emergency requiring immediate action on our part arose, we would know the right sort of thing to do.

In essence the new morality proceeds along such utilitarian lines. But like so many utilitarian theories, it does so inconsistently. For, consider the outcome of the principle of utility: All and only those acts are morally right which produce the greatest amount of good for the greatest number of people.

2. Cf. *The Principles of Morals and Legislation* and, above all, his *Deontology* (published posthumously, 1834).

3. Cf. *On Liberty* and *Utilitarianism*. For a good historical exposition of traditional utilitarianism see Edward Albee, *A History of English Utilitarianism* (New York: Collier, 1962).

This principle means quite literally what it says: *Any* such act is morally right. Suppose, now, that we return to our case of medical experiments. In the light of this principle, our answers require reevaluation. In fact, some will be downright wrong. In the case of the child, if the outcome of the experiment is knowledge that benefits other children—if it saves their lives— then by the four criteria of utility, the amount of happiness produced by this experimentation will be greater than that resulting from a refusal to experiment. Therefore it is right that the child should be experimented upon. The happiness or life of the child itself matters not one whit. Or consider the case of the adult person used in medical experimentation. The same sort of reasoning applies. Nor does it matter whether the person in question gave his permission for such an experimentation or even knew about it. The principle of utility makes this sort of course of action morally correct and not a species of murder.

The point bears repetition: The principle of utility licenses *any* act that has the desired preponderance of happiness over misery. And since we are only human, the situation becomes even more liberal. We cannot know, with full and certain knowledge, what will be the outcome of our actions. We can only assume with reasonable certitude what it will be. If we were bound to act only in full knowledge, we should never be able to act at all; a knowledge of the whole universe would be required. Consequently, the principle of utility is actually much less stringent in character. It requires not that we know what the outcome of the action will be, but that we be certain, by all standards of reasonableness currently operative, what will obtain: That act is right which, upon due and reasonable deliberation based on reasonable review of the relevant facts, seems to be productive of the greatest amount of happiness for the greatest number of people.

The possibility of error, therefore, is admitted. But if we take due care in our deliberations, and taking such care, ascertain that all other things being equal the present state of our knowledge inclines to one act in particular as the right act, then if we accept the principle, it will be our duty to engage in that particular action, no matter what our feelings on the issue might be. In many cases, that might prove unpleasant. However, that is not the end of the matter. There is something very vicious about the principle. This is best brought out by considering the following question: The principle centers around the happiness of the majority. Precisely which majority—which "greatest number of people" is meant? The majority of people who are now alive? The majority of people within a given social context? Or the greatest number of people from now on into the future? If the first, then the following could very easily happen: 90 percent of the population at the present time would become exceedingly happy if, unbeknownst to them, the remaining 10 percent were to be killed and their wealth distributed among the survivors. Or, to take an example close to home, 65 percent of the population—the population of the underdeveloped Afro-Asian countries—would be happy if unbeknownst to them, the remaining 35 percent were to be killed and resources formerly possessed by the latter made available to them. Consequently, by the principle of utility, it would follow that such an act of mass murder would be morally right. In fact, it would be meritorious.[4] Thus, it would seem that the principle of utility would condone and even enjoin homicidal actions on a global scale so long as the result provided the required surplus of pleasure over pain for the majority of the existing population; or, more correctly, if it were reasonable to expect that this should eventuate. Very few proponents of the principle of utility have been or are willing to countenance such a state of affairs.

If "the greatest number of people" were interpreted in the second way, as invoking the happiness of the majority within a given society, global slaughter on the scale just suggested might be avoided. It would not be a certainty, but it might be the case. However, an analogue of the global situation could

---

4. It is here understood that the resources thus liberated are used to improve the quality and situation of the life of the remaining majority.

very easily develop. It would be perfectly within the limits of the principle that genocide within a given society could be practiced. Certainly, infanticide, senicide, and selective euthanasia could be morally justified and would not be murder.

This state of affairs might be avoided in the third interpretation. On this basis, let us recall, the shape of the future and the happiness of persons who do not yet exist will be deemed relevant. Thus, an action will be morally right if and only if, on due reflection, it seems that it would produce a greater amount of happiness, for people already existing as well as for those to come, than any other action. On this score, genocide of the sort indicated might turn out to be immoral—not, however, because genocide is mass murder, and murder of any sort is morally reprehensible, but because, of all things being considered, it could result in a state of affairs where people in the present as well as the future would fear for their lives and be utterly miserable. The intensity of the misery thus produced, as a function of the absolute total of people existing both now and in the society to come, might outweigh the happiness produced at the present time. Nor need this reasoning confine itself to genocide. On this third interpretation, all other things being equal, any act could run into a similar problem of justification.

The implications of these considerations, so far as the new morality is concerned, are no less unacceptable than are the consequences of the utilitarian position we have just developed. For instance, at its moral best, the new morality denies personhood to fetuses, and thence argues: The fetus, not yet being a person, has no rights. Therefore its happiness and/or welfare cannot enter our deliberations. Consequently, the happiness and/or welfare of the mother-to-be is all that really counts.

In and by itself, and within the parameters of discussion delimited by the premises, there is no faulting this argument. However, as indicated some time ago, the new morality sometimes appeals to utilitarianism as its ethical foundation. Let us, then, add the premise of utilitarianism to the preceding reasoning. In that context the argument may not even have to deny personhood to the fetus. The amount of happiness produced is all that counts. And on that score abortion might well be the answer. However, as emerged from our discussion a few paragraphs back, utilitarianism, when properly and consistently developed, cannot confine its calculations of happiness solely to those individuals who are already on the scene. As our third interpretation above indicates, the happiness of future generations must be taken into account as well. Only then does the concept of total happiness attain its full sense. However, precisely how such a calculation is to proceed may be unclear. In fact, clarity may be lacking on several points. This much, however, is clear: If the happiness of future generations is at all relevant—and the context has it that it is—then by that interpretation of the principle of utility future generations will have rights that extend into the present temporal context. Otherwise, as we said, their happiness could not now be of moment. This, however, implies two things: First, that if the new morality accepts this futuristic interpretation of the notion of "greatest number," fetuses who are as yet unborn will definitely have rights. That is to say, they will be potential persons, and as potential persons they will enjoy a moral status on a par with that of people already on the scene. Second—and this is really the important thing—it implies that the argument of the new moralist on abortion is inconsistent with the principle of utility: It is not a foregone conclusion that the greatest happiness for the greatest number of people will result if—in a given situation—the fetus is killed. On the contrary, it might obtain if the mother were killed. To ascertain which is the correct course of action, we should have to calculate. Nor could the outcome of our calculations be foregone, and the calculation a mere sham. For that would deprive the position of the new morality of its alleged utilitarian justification.

As we have seen, the sort of impasse in which the new morality finds itself if it assumes a utilitarian moral thesis is not confined to the issue of abortion. Its position on suicide, infanticide, senicide, or euthanasia would be faced with a similar threat of incoherence. Thus, in regard to suicide, the utilitarian thesis is sometimes adduced as justification in favor of such an action, since the amount of misery in the world would be reduced because of such an act, and there would be a corresponding rise in overall happiness. However, as should be only too obvious, the principle of utility—as we have shown —is not as such concerned with individual happiness, nor even, as such, with happiness here and now. Therefore, by a train of reasoning analogous to the one traced above, mutatis mutandis, it might develop that suicide is definitely immoral; that instead the morally correct thing for individuals of a suicidal bent to do is to become walking organ banks for those who require transplants or to become blood-manufacturing units for people in need of transfusions. The possibilities are boundless, and we have only begun to scratch the surface. As to candidates for euthanasia and senicide, here, too, a rigorously applied utilitarianism would—or at least might—yield conclusions other than those supported by proponents of the new morality. Likewise with the issue of infanticide. All sorts of unpleasant possibilities suggest themselves.

We need not go into any more detail or develop the alternatives any further; our point has been made. The principle of utility, when consistently and coherently developed and applied, is highly inimical to many conclusions advocated by the new morality. That is to say, only an inconsistent application of the principle will come anywhere near giving the new moralist what he wants. It is therefore surprising that the principle should be appealed to so frequently; or, that in the absence of an explicit appeal, the new morality tacitly bases itself on premises that have the principle as their foundation. Accordingly, let us abandon that principle. Instead, let us return to two theses which we touched upon above—that of ethical relativism and that of ethical naturalism in its extreme form—and let us see how the new morality fares with them.

Ethical Relativism

Ethical relativism, in its various versions, fits the requirements of the new morality quite well. It observes that there are no absolute moral standards common to all societies; much less that there are standards adhered to by all individuals. From this the new morality concludes that moral values have no universal validity but are relative to a given individual, society, or context. And from this, in turn, it is thought an easy matter to defend abortion, suicide, euthanasia—even infanticide and senicide—in a manner consonant with the position of the new morality: simply by appealing to individual differences and the principle of relativity. What we feel is right, goes.

But nothing in life is free, and certainly not this defense of the new morality. In this case, the price is rather high. The defense is bought at the price of logical inconsistency and of an invalid argument. As to the first, inconsistency resides in the fact that if the thesis of relativism is ethical, as it is understood here, it would follow that diametrically opposed value judgments would be both true and false together. In other words, the law of contradiction would be abrogated. This state of affairs could be avoided only by renouncing general validity and even interpersonal meaningfulness for value judgments—a prohibitive price to pay, since it implies the breakdown of communication and an abrogation of the universal validity of the new moralist's thesis.

The invalidity of the argument involved is best shown by recalling the initial premise of the old argument: Different people and different societies value different things, or attach different degrees of value to the same thing, or follow different codes of behavior. From this, the argument concludes that therefore there are no absolute moral codes nor intrinsic values, but that instead morality is relative, and value is attained only in and for a given context. However, to argue thus is to confuse having value with being valued; and following a code which is assumed to be morally correct, with an actually correct moral code. That is to say, in the case of value we have a confusion between being the object of the psychological attitude of valuing and having a certain intrinsic value. In the case of codes or mores we have a confusion between a code of behavior as espoused or followed and a system of absolute moral norms. It is only when these are confused that the argument for ethical relativism can go through, unless, of course, an independent argument is adduced to show that there are neither intrinsic values nor absolute moral codes. But such an argument cannot proceed as above. For, it is perfectly possible that there are intrinsic values but that most if not all people hitherto have been mistaken about them, that there are absolute moral codes but that most societies have not recognized them. Nor is this claim entirely fanciful; there are precedents for something very much like it: People used to believe in the existence of the ether and of phlogiston and used to maintain that the earth was flat.

Finally, over and above the preceding shortcomings, there is this difficulty with ethical relativism:[5] If accepted as true, it would result in an inability on our part to act. Or, failing that, the result would be chaotic. For consider: If there are no absolute moral standards and no intrinsic values, then if we wanted to engage in what we considered to be the right sort of behavior, we should have to ignore whatever anyone else might say about the matter. In other words, we should have to decide and act in an egoistic vacuum. Any communication of an evaluative sort by someone else would have to be ignored. Pragmatically speaking, this sort of situation would very quickly deteriorate to the point where we ourselves would become psychologically unstable. Or, barring that, we should have the chaos referred to above. For if each individual did what he thought was right, and if, as is only too possible, what was thought to be right differed, the fabric of social interaction would be torn asunder and we should be back to a primitive state of natural egoistic behavior patterns. In a word, society would not exist; chaos would result.[6]

5. Strictly speaking, what follows holds only for a personal ethical relativism.

6. In a somewhat different context, cf. Hobbes, *Leviathan,* part 1, chap. 13 and passim.

Ethical Naturalism

In the light of what was just argued, it seems only fair to conclude that the thesis of ethical relativism is so beset by logical and practical problems that its acceptance raises more problems than it solves. Let us, therefore, turn to the second expedient mentioned previously: the thesis of ethical naturalism. And here, let us be quite precise about what the meaning of the phrase is: For present purposes, ethical naturalism is construed as the thesis that there are no peculiarly moral unanalyzable and primitive ethical properties in the world; that the referents of moral terms are not nonnatural properties[7] that can only be intuited. Instead, so this theory has it, ethical discourse amounts to talk about or sophisticated expressions of feelings, inclinations, emotions, pleasure, pain, and the like.[8]

One advantage of such a theory is that it would immediately safeguard the position of the new moralist in regard to the shibboleth "Do your own thing!" Since moral evaluations will reduce to mere statements of preference, perhaps even to exclamations of pleasure or pain, such statements cannot lay claim to universal validity, nor will the possibility of moral conflict arise. After all, such statements will not be judgments having interpersonal validity, but merely autobiographical re-

---

7. On moral properties as basic and nonnatural, cf. G. E. Moore, *Principia Ethica,* chap. 1 and passim. For good introductory discussions of this and related moral issues, see W. K. Frankena, *Ethics* (Englewood Cliffs, N.J.: Prentice-Hall, 1963), and Mary Warnock, *Ethics Since 1900* (London: Oxford University Press, 1966).

8. Strictly speaking, this is not what is meant by ethical naturalism in a philosophical context. There, it is generally called "noncognitivism," and utilitarianism in its various forms is called a species of ethical naturalism because moral properties like good and evil are explained or defined in terms of ordinary, natural properties which do not require intuition for their apprehension. However, for our purpose, this label *naturalism* serves very well: it is *natural* to identify feelings with values, even though it may be wrong. For a classic exposition of ethical naturalism in our sense of the term, see C. L. Stevenson, *Ethics and Language* (New Haven: Yale University Press, 1944).

ports. Everyone may "do his own thing," at least from this moral point of view, because everyone is right. The thesis also has the advantage of evading the inconsistency and contradictions pointed out in our discussion of ethical relativity. Finally, it will license precisely those acts of killing which we ourselves find acceptable. In this sense, then, it appears to fill the bill.

However, ethical naturalism of the present sort is beset by grave difficulties. The theory as we have sketched it is based on the central contention that there are no absolute moral standards and values and that even the relativist, with his conventionalistic attitude, is mistaken. However, very little insight reveals that if this position really were to be adopted—quite aside from any question of its being true—what would result would be unacceptable to the moral naturalist himself. For if there really were no moral values and standards at all, and if ethical evaluations were mere autobiographical reports, it would follow with inexorable logic that anything was right—subject, of course, to the feasibility of the action as dictated by the laws of nature and the actual state of affairs. Thus, the killing and torturing—in fact, inhuman and inhumane treatment of any sort—of anyone would be perfectly acceptable in any ordinary sense. After all, judgments to the contrary, while perhaps designed to express the desire for cessation of such activities, would carry merely autobiographical force. The same holds for judgments of position evaluation: They would be merely autobiographical expressions of a favorable attitude, no more and no less. Nor would it be morally justified in any ordinary sense to interfere with any particular course of action solely on moral grounds. Interference would be possible only on the practical grounds of personal survival and with the possession of psychological skill or brute strength. In other words, this theory of value and obligation, since it would make all moral assessments mere autobiographical remarks, would deprive the new moralist of any support he had claimed for his contention that anyone —mother, father, or society—has any rights.

Such a state of affairs, although credible to some, certainly does not seem to reflect the position of the new morality. That position is very much premised on the assumption of certain rights. It is just that the new moralists differ from other people on the issue of who possesses these rights or whose rights take precedence. But there is more to the issue than this. The new morality also assumes—indeed, explicitly states—that some moral judgments are simply wrong. Whatever we may think about the correctness of this evaluation in particular cases, the fact is that in arguing thus the new morality countenances the possibility of conflict between morally evaluative statements. If ethical naturalism were the thesis of the new morality, this would not be possible. On that thesis such judgments would be autobiographical remarks; and autobiographical remarks cannot conflict. At least, not in this way.

Ethical naturalism,[9] therefore, cannot lend support to the ethics of the new morality, any more than did ethical relativism. In fact, the only theory that comes close to fulfilling that function is the theory of utilitarianism as we have discussed it above. That, however, leaves the new morality in an uncomfortable position. If it accepts the thesis of utilitarianism —and uses this as the foundation of its moral contentions— then the consequences pointed out above ensue: The limits of morally permissible killing may in part be drawn as the new morality wishes, but not invariably, and certainly not for the reasons generally advanced. Furthermore, consistent employment of the thesis of utility means, at least in some cases, that the new morality must deny mothers the universal right to abortion and deny other persons the right to suicide and euthanasia; in other words, it may prohibit precisely those sorts of acts which at present the new morality enjoins. On the other hand, if the new morality seeks support for its contentions in

9. As understood in this emotive sense. There are other versions, as for instance those who define *good* and *evil* in nonmoral rational terms. In the end, however, all such attempts reduce either to a variant of utilitarianism or to a variation on naturalism as we have defined the term. Consequently, since we have dealt with both of these positions, even if only briefly, we shall pass over the others. A similar line of reasoning, mutatis mutandis, applies in their case.

any other ethical theory, it either does not receive it—as in the case of moral absolutism—or the support it receives is simply evanescent. Our discussion of naturalism and relativism have made this abundantly clear.

THE TRADITIONAL POSITION

The preceding deliberations, both here and in the previous chapters, may have left the impression that when we get right down to it, the issues in question are really quite clear-cut: that all that is required is that we see the correctness of the traditionalist point of view and that a little reflection will result in our making the right judgment.

Nothing, however, could be further from the truth. The issues are not clear-cut. Nor is it at all obvious that the position of the traditionalist is in any better shape than that of his rivals. Indeed, if there is any substance to our previous analyses, the traditionalist will find himself in as a bad a situation as the new moralist: Both positions are riddled with inconsistencies and unargued assumptions. To mention but one—albeit one that is fundamental—the traditionalist's position is grounded on the thesis that there are absolute and intrinsic moral values. How is the existence and nature of these values ever ascertained? The traditionalist here frequently talks of intuition or appeals to the obviousness of certain judgments. But that is not proof. It is merely an attempt to persuade. In other words, it is an appeal to psychological convictions and attitudes. As we have pointed out many times before, while this may be effective in inducing conversion to an opinion, it is entirely without probative force. What is intuited and what is obvious are matters of conditioning and ought not to be confused with matters of fact. Nor does the appeal to revealed moral tenets fare any better. Belief is required for their acceptance. And that, surely, is not only not logical proof; it is also putting the cart before the horse.

CONCLUSION

The moral traditionalist, therefore, also has his work cut out for him, and the prognosis for his success is no greater than that for the new moralist. But what does that do to the practice of death, as we have been concerned with it? In a nutshell, it indicates once and for all, from a purely theoretical point of view, what we have been urging in particular detail in the preceding chapters: Current discussion on the practice of death in our society is fundamentally untenable and confused; it is completely devoid of that character of finality which the proponents of the diverse positions attribute to their respective solutions.

Obviously, the matter cannot be left here. To abandon the issue at this stage would be like diagnosing the illness of a patient without doing anything about it. We shall therefore attempt to indicate the direction in which a solution is to be found. The development of this solution and its critical defense must be left to an undertaking devoted wholly to that purpose.

To begin with, we must refrain from attempting to develop partial solutions which merely "feel right" or possess intuitive appeal for a given person in a particular context. Such work is piecemeal and devoid of all validity. Instead, we must resolve once and for all the two basic issues without which any attempt to settle any issue in ethics is just so much idle speculation: We must see whether or not there are absolute morals laws and intrinsic values and we must decide once and for all the issue of what counts as a person. If the first turns out to be decided in the affirmative—if the stance of the absolutist is correct—we can then proceed to the business of determining precisely what those values are and what the moral codes are like. If the investigation comes up with a negative conclusion, then we need go no further. It will establish the correctness of the conventionalist and naturalist thesis that moral evaluations are either context-dependent historical assertions or mere statements of preference. Anything, literally, will be right, and we should stop fooling ourselves that this is not the case. We may do what we like, even in the practice of death. The only restraint will be the pragmatics of the situation and our personal inclinations.

If the absolutist's position is correct, we must turn to the second issue: the concept of a person. For, if the absolutist is correct, it will be this concept that will do the greater part of the work. Moral duties and obligations will obtain primarily toward persons; and certainly, so far as the issues of homicide and murder are concerned, this notion will stand in the foreground. And here, we must keep in mind a very fundamental point: It cannot be a matter of definition that what counts as a person is identical with what counts as a human being. Consequently, we cannot proceed on the assumption that personhood and humanity are identical. We must look and see. It may transpire that our inclinations in this area are vindicated. However, it may also happen that they are not: that the class of beings which are persons is much more inclusive than the class of adult and normal human beings. In this context, we shall have to consider the nature of fetuses, of children, of the senile, and even of animals. To proceed otherwise would be to beg some very fundamental issues. In fact, it will probably turn out that personhood is identical with or closely related to the actual possession and/or potential for a certain type of awareness. If this is so, and I have argued repeatedly that it is, then we shall have to extend the ambit of our investigation even further: Anything which simulates an analogue of human awareness will have to be considered. "Human," because that must always be our starting point: It is that with which we are familiar. "Anything," because it might turn out that inanimate, even artificially constructed objects, possess an analogue of human awareness. Fanciful as this may sound, it might be so. We cannot afford to be mistaken. And in making this last claim, I have of course once more betrayed my bias: There are absolute values, they do attach to rational beings called persons and that class of persons is not exhausted by *homo sapiens*. But before greeting the nonhuman person whoever he might be, let us clear our own backyard: Let us determine the moral treatment of humanity.

Index